ESCAPE
from
Appalachia
Who Will Rescue Me?

MARY FRANCES BARRON

Escape from Appalachia
Who Will Rescue Me?
Mary Frances Barron

To contact the author: francie@franciebarron.com

Copyright © 2024 Frances Barron. All rights reserved. Except for brief quotations for review purposes, no part of this book may be reproduced in any form without prior written permission from Frances Barron.

Published by:

Mary Ethel

Mary Ethel Eckard
Frisco, Texas

Library of Congress Control Number: 2024910637
ISBN (Paperback): 979-8-9904576-3-8
ISBN (Hardcover): 979-8-9904576-5-2
ISBN (Ebook): 979-8-9904576-4-5

Disclaimer: While the stories written within the pages of this book make up the sum of the author's childhood, they were also seen and remembered through the eyes and sensibilities of a child. To maintain their anonymity, in some instances, the author has changed the names of individuals and places, as well as some identifying characteristics and details such as physical properties, occupations, and places of residence.

DEDICATION

To George
The best ever non-hound dog, a Democrat, and a loyal friend.
My constant companion inspiring me to be a
better self by simply staying by my side.

To Susie
You shared yourself and your family with me and I am forever grateful.

CONTENTS

Preface xi

1. Three-Time Loser 1
2. Family History 6
3. The Early Years 14
4. Dad 23
5. Aunt MaeMae 27
6. The Industry and People of Point Marion 32
7. My Best Friend, Susie 40
8. The B&O Railroad and Public Transportation 44
9. George M. Leader 46
10. Miss Berg's Kindergarten 53
11. Special Jobs 58
12. It's a Boy 66
13. New York City 71
14. Delaware 77
15. First Grade 82
16. Time Out 89
17. Poltergeists, Banshees and Apparitions 94
18. Paying Bills 101
19. Pollution, Contamination, Scorn 108
20. Stewartstown Road 114
21. The Patches 121

22. Davidson Patch 125
23. Churching 129
24. The Preaching Pulpit 135
25. The Church Ladies 143
26. Holy Rollers 148
27. Firehouse Shenanigans 152
28. Learning to Get My Way 155
29. Supper Time 159
30. The Wind in My Hair 162
31. The Hate 166
32. Talley Ho 170

Photo Gallery 175

33. Pure-Bred 191
34. Wife Beaters 199
35. Buddy and George 206
36. Families Survived 213
37. Exploring Free Spirits 218
38. Crazy People 224
39. Fourth Grade 230
40. The Eagle Flew 233
41. Mrs. Ratchet's Fifth Grade Class 236
42. Rants and Routines 240
43. The Coloreds 244
44. Mama, the Relief Woman 249
45. Pigtails and Freedom 255
46. Wonder of Wonders 260
47. Aretha and Greene County 268
48. White Walls 272
49. Point Marion Servicemen 276
50. Do I Need a Bra? 282

51. Growing Up	288
52. The Promise	292
53. The Earth Moves	297
54. Overwhelming Sadness	305
55. The Clouds Parted	308
56. Oh Happy, Happy Days	317
57. My Hearts Companion, George M Leader	325
58. Broken	327
59. Missing Jane	337
60. The End of an Era	340
61. The Escape	342
62. Return to the Hills	345
63. The Grip of Appalachia	352
Epilogue	359
Afterword	361
About the Author	377

PREFACE

The area of Point Marion, Pennsylvania, after running the Indians out, was originally settled by scrapping Indian traders and outcasts who preferred to live in the outpost areas of the growing nation. Then the occasional farmer, hill dweller, and townsfolk began to migrate into areas that would later become the river towns along the Monongahela River that winds itself through the bowels of this section of forgotten Appalachia. Because Point Marion was at the confluence of dual rivers and a natural spot for crossing, it became a stopping point for getting supplies before navigating the river north or taking a wagon further west.

The Two Rivers

The point of Point Marion is made up of two rivers flowing north: the Monongahela River and the Cheat River. The muddy, angry Monongahela River rushes north, screaming out of West Virginia. It floods. It is turbulent. It resembles the dark rebellious vengeance of a scorned lover. The water of the Monongahela is considered dead due to decades-long contamination from the raw sewage of the populace, coal mine run-off, and sludge from coal mines abandoned long ago.

The murky Monongahela meets the gentle blue-green waters of the Cheat River at my own despairing town of Point Marion. As the two rivers unite, they clash together in a swirling backwash, not unlike the eye of a tornado, swishing into each other, attempting to mix the green-black Monongahela River into the blue Cheat River. The result is a tumultuous confluence of mud and sand where the two reluctant rivers are forced into their challenging handshake. The shore on both sides of the now combined river is thick, deep, brown muck on both edges, going back to meet the sharp weeds for at least ten feet on both sides of the river.

The Monongahela has a long path before it reaches Point Marion. Its source is in the far-reaching bowels of the numerous craggy mountains of West Virginia. The ice melts in the mountains, and the water begins tumbling out of the hills and into the crevasses toward the valleys below. It is a slow trickling stream at first, then picks up speed. In a spring where there have been particularly heavy snow and ice in West Virginia, the results are an unpredictable rising river and sometimes torrential and uncontrolled floods in Point Marion.

The Army Corps of Engineers

The Army Corps of Engineers began building locks along the river in the mid-1800s, dividing the Monongahela River into manmade locks every six to eight miles, created to control the chaotic river. While the locking system was successful in keeping a steady depth of water for the movement of traffic on the river, still, it is turbulent and floods. The angry river refuses to be completely controlled by modern-day inventions.

The free flowing water between the locks are pools named after the little towns closest to the lock. The Point Marion pool runs from the West Virginia border to New Geneva, Pennsylvania.

The riverboats, moving near the little towns along the river, danced with the current going north and struggled against the current going south. Usually, empty boats moved southward, so the kick was not as great as the wrestling control needed to keep the heavy, coal-laden, northbound boats in the dredged channel from running into shore, each other, or a bridge piling.

The riverboats handled as many as nine huge barges at a time. When the boat reached a lock, the muscled riverboat handlers untied the barges from the pusher riverboat and sent the barges through the lock, in groups. Sometimes there were three or four boats with barges waiting to be separated and then tied into the lock in a pool.

The barge boats coming south would

WHOOCT. WHOOOT. WHOOooooT

their steam-powered whistles as they approached the point, ready to make the steep right turn to follow the Monongahela River south and pass under the Greene County bridge in front of my house. The three long whistles warned the boats moving north to Pittsburgh that the barge laden pusher was making the turn and needed half the channel to pass. They also notified the Lockmaster at Lock 8 of an approach.

One purpose of the locking system was to ensure that the huge coal-laden barges pushing north from the coalfields of West Virginia to the steel mills in Pittsburgh kept the coal industry alive. (In the end, nothing could keep the Appalachian coalfield industry and the steel mills to the north alive.)

Once combined with the waters of the Cheat River at Point Marion, the even stronger Monongahela River continued its march toward Pittsburgh, then on northwest to merge into the Ohio River, and finally, these waters that originated in the mud and ash of southern West Virginia tumbled into the mighty Mississippi.

The riverbanks were a muddy way of life.

The Complexity of Poverty and Isolation

Appalachia is known for dense pockets of population surrounded by stark isolation. I was born in and grew up in one of these isolated pockets in the Appalachian backcountry. The borough of Point Marion is a town of 1,330 people one mile north of the Mason Dixon line that separates West Virginia from Pennsylvania. The town is one more rusting relic of Appalachian despair.

With bleak surroundings and dried up industry, the air and water were contaminated beyond imagination, and the people were dirt poor. Life in the entire Appalachian region was a day-to-day desperate getting by. To understand the complexity of my childhood, one needs to grasp the history of the area, the mindset and brokenness of the people, and the hopelessness that comes from living in poverty. Just scraping by.

Once I escaped the culture and desperation of Appalachia and discovered my true self, I began putting together the puzzle pieces of my childhood, the complexities and secrets of my family, and how the reality I lived shaped me into a young woman who was determined to leave and never return.

Through my stories, I peel back the layers of my early life and highlight a resilient drive that rammed me forward, even when no one else boosted me. I share how I have been mocked, undervalued, disregarded, and betrayed, and I lay bare the horrible decisions I've made and the times I felt joy and despair. I painfully share my major stumbling blocks and expose the angst of my spirit on this tortuous path out of the Appalachian undergrowth.

As you walk through my early days of discovery, my hope is that you will amble along the path with me, learn from my many mistakes, and laugh with me at the absurd. Along the way, wonder at and then understand how one's surroundings and inherited DNA, dismal as they may be, can be deployed into becoming more than what was left behind.

From Broken to Brave

This book is a testament of how a resilient spirit amid abject adversity is sometimes showered with the quiet caring of the hidden angels surrounding us who light our path; the souls whose silent walk restored my heart, acting as beacons; quietly moving with me.

> The everyday saints among us.

Frances Barron

1

THREE-TIME LOSER

It was my third birthday. My older sisters and I sat politely at the dining room table. I smelled the sweet and snarky mixed-up odor of the caked jam and lard stuck to the oilcloth tablecloth from last summer's jelly and grease gumminess. I don't think Mama, in her privileged upbringing, ever learned to wipe down a pasty plastic tablecloth after a meal. Dad certainly never did any cleanups. That was a "woman's work."

The remnants of last summer's sticky crumbs melted into small blobs of goo from the heat of the coal fire glowing in the grate of the fireplace in the small room off the kitchen where we ate. A few of the hounds slept and yawned in a pile under the table. The room was warm; the air was close with smoke that was not moving up the congested chimney. The smell was ash and dog sweat. My favorite coon hound was licking my toes.

Our two-story clapboard house was 300 yards from the muddy banks of the wide brown Monongahela River. The winter shrilling wind would build up power as it gusted off the river and reached angry arms around the lath and flaking plaster walls of our house. Rushing air hit the cracks around the windows and the open eaves of the house. The odor near the cracking walls was that of drying leaves mixed with the pungent stench of mold from the flooded waters that would march into the house every spring along with the icy cold breath of Jack Frost. It was mid-October, the time that we began living in the rooms with fireplaces where a coal fire could be banked up.

I watched, through the musty streaked windows, the wind blowing the late falling October leaves in a wild dance around the yard. The loose branches of the unruly bushes and weeds scratched against the frosted windows of the crowded room. The sound of the scrape scuffling on the windows, combined with the wheezing winds through the cracks of the plasterboard, lulled us into a heavy-eyed daze.

Without a sound, I felt the grip of his boney hands grab me around the ribs and pick me up into the air.

WHOOSH!

In a split second, I was in a standing position on the fireplace mantle, which was twice the height of my body. There I was. I could not get down. I plastered myself with my arms stretched out, face first, against the sizzling searing plaster wall of the chimney above the fireplace. I knew I was going to fall flat down on the hot grate of the smoldering glow of the coal inferno underneath. I stood still. A panic cry started deep in my throat. It was the kind of wet cry with hiccups and drool that comes out of the nose. I was so scared I couldn't make a noise. I couldn't breathe. The deep orange smoke from the coal fire was burning my eyes.

Dad had noticed a tear in my worn-out dress. Being the third in line for anything I wore, this was the third go-around for the same tattered dress. Then Dad started ripping at the holes in my clothes and singing,

> "Oh, she's a sad, sad tomato - she's a sad, sad tomato… a comic valentine."

The singing grew louder as Dad threw the shreds of my dress into the fire below. My two older sisters laughed aloud as expected.

The room brightened as the smoldering coal in the grate caught the scraps of material from my dress and flamed up. The song went on for another verse. Finally, he lifted me and put me down,

> "You should know better than to wear torn clothes, Francie."

That was it.

Dad never noticed that we had no choice but to wear worn clothes. He lived in his memories. The rest of us lived in the real world. It was day-to-day desperate getting by.

> "I am a three-time loser, Francie."

On our birthday, we could ask for our favorite food to be cooked for supper. Granted, the repertoire was a large can of baked beans and lard fried crumbed hamburger, or spaghetti noodles and crumbled hamburger with a can of tomato sauce, or a can of Chung Wing Choy Chinese food, or a can of beans and a hard-round fried lump of hamburger.

That was it.

I always chose the spaghetti noodles and crumbled hamburger with the tomato sauce for my birthday dinner. The noodles were soft and chewy. I had cavities in all my back teeth, and it was hard to eat anything else.

Then everyone would sing,

> "Happy birthday to you, happy birthday to you, happy birthday, dear Francie, happy birthday to you!"

I was the center of the family for that one moment in time. Once a year. Mama would join us for supper time and the singing. She and Daddy looked at me, and I think they loved me right after the song. But it was clear to me, even from the earliest age, that us girls had little value in the eyes of Mama and Daddy. It seemed that in Dad's mind, having girls was a sideline, an unnecessary steppingstone to when a boy would arrive. Dad peppered his conversations with how useless girls were and how he was waiting for the anointed boy to arrive.

Then Dad would give his dialogue about the night I was born; it was his three-time loser story.

> *"I remember the day you were born, Francie. Yes, you were born right in this house. Doc Waystinger was drunk that night, still sitting up at Augie's, and did not show up, so I delivered you myself. Yup, when you were finally born, I was so sad. I said to your mother, 'Well, Charlotte: I am a three-time loser --- three girls in a row. I will never have anyone to leave the property to. Who will carry on the name? What do you want to name this one? It doesn't matter... I wanted to name my boy after me... and then I got... another girl...'"*

My birthday every year was punctuated by this story.

> Dad would keep telling it.
> > Three times in a row!
> > > Three girls.

In the early days, when Dad went through his three-time loser story, I thought Mama was ashamed she could not produce a boy to carry on the coveted Dillinger name.

She seemed to be in a mist.

    She was not emotionally present.

        But, little by little, I began to see that she was overwhelmed with her own gradual slide into the oblivion of the hills.

            She was slowly being buried in the oppressive hopelessness that living in the bewildering mountain environment can create.

                Later, I figured out that she was depressed.

                And finally, I accepted the fact that she had a strong anger festering in her.

                    Whatever it was, it was so overwhelming that she could not reach out to her three girl children.

In the background, she began her mantra to us,

    "One day, you kids will get out of here ..."

FAMILY HISTORY

Dad told us stories about how much money his family had when he was growing up. He entertained us with amazing descriptions of fancy cars in the 1930s, beaver coats that went down to the ankles, fraternity parties, and visits to New York.

When Dad was growing up, the family property on Penn Street in Point Marion consisted of three houses and a small apartment building with four units. His family had lived in the Greene/Fayette County, Pennsylvania area since before the French and Indian Wars.

> *"Yesseree, kids, my great-great-ever-so-great-grandfather was the first white male born west of the Monongahela River. George Dillinger was his name."*

Even then, girls were not counted.

Dad's family, the Dillinger's, initially settled around 1780 in Greene County, Pennsylvania, across the river from Fayette County and Point Marion. The town of Dilliner, on the west banks of the Monongahela River, is named after Dad's ancestors. The original Dillinger who settled the area walked across the

Appalachians from Virginia with a rifle and the workings of a grandfather clock strapped to his back. This was a woodsman who was not looking for religious or economic freedom; he wanted to be alone on his own land.

No doubt, a dutiful pioneer wife slogged along with him scrambling over the weeds, stones, and streams on craggy trails beaten down by wild animals. But of course, family lore does not mention her.

Even then, women were of no consequence and not mentioned in the oral history of our clan.

The only indication of this bedraggled pioneer woman was that the first-born child of the first Dillinger was a boy named George. She bore a son to claim her place in history. Any girl children were not mentioned.

My earliest ancestor was looking for a place to call his own where hunting game was plentiful and there was fertile soil to grow corn and vegetables. He discovered the verdant area along the river and staked it out as his own.

The family survived on tenuous terms with the migrating Indians who had a totally different relationship with the land than the white intrusive settlers. The Indians believed that the land was a spiritual giving resource that humans could not own.

The Native Americans revered the abundant land. They held it as a sacred honor that was to be cared for and, in turn, would care for those who had a connection to it. No one person could exclusively own the land. They were the original stewards of the land.

The settlers were determined not only to live on a staked-out piece of ground, but also prevented others from any connection to it.

This dichotomy of core values and beliefs could never be resolved. The deep thread of spiritual connection with the land is part of the very DNA of the Native Americans. In the end, most of the Indians were summarily murdered, and the rest were marched off in forced exile. Today no trace of Native Americans remain in Southwestern Pennsylvania.

Dad's great-great-grandfather, Ambrose, started a ferry in the early 1800s to move wagons, people, and goods across the Monongahela River between Greene and Fayette counties. The ferry was the only way to get across the river for 15 miles in both directions. We still have pictures of Dad's great grandfather, Old Len, who lived to be 101 years old, poling across the river after dropping off a load of wagons on the floating ferry.

In the mid-1800s, the family moved to the Fayette County side of the river where the town of Point Marion was being developed. In 1850, the family built two homes plus a pump house for the ferry operation. The primary house was built as a four-room upstairs, four-room downstairs saltbox. In this original house, there was a fireplace in three rooms for heat and two center chimneys. Due to the concern for fire and flames, the women cooked in a shed twenty feet away from the main house. I was raised in this house.

Around the turn of the century, the kitchen was added to the main house as a sort of lean-to. The shed was converted to a wash shed and was where the women of the family would do the washing in big iron washtubs over a fire. The well was right next to the washhouse in a sort of overhang contraption so buckets of water could be lifted on a pully in a block-and-tackle kind of affair from the well.

Before the First World War, it was possible to bring gas power into the house for cooking and lighting. Running water was brought to the house with the ingenuity of my great-grandfather, Old Len. He replaced the outhouse with an indoor toilet, sink, and bathtub that he added to an upstairs unheated room. He hand-dug a sewer that directly dumped into the river.

Old Len's son, Walter Leonard, had a small gas furnace put in the dugout crawl space of the basement around 1937. Prior to the furnace, the house was heated only with coal grate fireplaces in the three rooms upstairs and the three rooms downstairs. When Great Grandpa added the gas furnace, he closed off some of the coal grates. The gas lamps that supplied lighting were changed out for electricity, and he put a ten-gallon hot water heater in the dugout space under the house.

Unfortunately, in the late 1930s, a bridge was built, and the Dillinger ferry immediately became obsolete. Dad's grandfather, Walter Leonard, and his wife, Sara Moralee, retired. Their youngest daughter, the beautiful Mamie, died at 20 years old of typhoid fever in the early 1900s when the water of Point Marion was contaminated with the dreaded bacteria. Sara never recovered from the tragedy of Mamie's death.

Their second child was Walter Sumner Dillinger. From all accounts, Walter was a bit of a playboy who became an alcoholic in his later years. He became the town Burgess and married a girl who traveled from Ohio to work in the bustling town of Point Marion. Her name was Mabel Tallentire. Their other daughter, the oldest child, was Emma. Walter and Mabel had two children, a girl they named Eleanor Margaret and, three years later, a son named after his grandfather, Walter Leonard. My father.

Dad's Upbringing

When Dad was three, his mother was dispatched to a sanitarium: a place where people were sent who had tuberculosis. The sanitarium was a home in Ohio where the critically ill young mother died three years later. At her death, my dad, Walter Leonard, was six and his sister, Eleanor Margaret, was nine.

When his wife was sent away, according to family legend, Dad's father ran off with a "whore" and left his two children with his mother, his dad, and his maiden sister, Emma, who spent the prime of her life raising her drunken brother's two children. Emma stayed on the homestead and cared for her parents until their death. Emma is one of the saints who touched my life.

After his wife died, Dad's father married the "whore." The legend goes that dad's father had nothing to do with the children and was known as a town drunk. Dad was 13 when his father died, and, after Aunt Emma died, the "whore" got one-third of what was left of the family estate.

Years later, I discovered that the woman my grandfather married was from a well-known local family and was highly thought of by Aunt Emma. The two were even close friends. The "whore" status in the family folklore appears to be from anger developed by the next generation.

Grandpa Len arranged to send his grandson, Walter Leonard, and his granddaughter, Eleanor Margaret, in the grandest style, to the finest colleges that money could buy. Since Len and Sara Moralee were pillars of the United Methodist Church in Point Marion, Eleanor Margaret was sent to West Virginia Wesleyan College in Buckhannon, West Virginia. Old Len expected her to find an educated man, marry well, and be taken care of by a rich husband for the rest of her life.

Walter Leonard, after graduating from Point Marion High School, was sent to the prestigious Bucknell University in Lewisburg, Pennsylvania. He was given a brand-new Stutz Bearcat sports car, a full-length raccoon coat, and a handsome allowance.

Len, as my dad was known, joined a fraternity, met my mama, and graduated five years later. His major was something nebulous he called "business."

Mama's Upbringing

Dora Frances Breece, born in Seattle, Washington in 1888, married Dr. John Charles Rathbun, her college sweetheart. Before his marriage, my grandfather was a Professor of Civil Engineering in Amoy, China. He spoke fluent Mandarin. Mama was born in Seattle, Washington, and grew up in New York City in a ten-room apartment, complete with maids' quarters, on Riverside Drive, overlooking the George Washington Bridge and the Hudson River. She was raised in a privileged environment and had every advantage a society girl could have.

An only child, she traveled around the world with her college-educated parents. One such trip was on a tramp steamer, which included touring all of Europe and the Orient. She spoke conversational French and was adored by her father, a Ph.D. Professor of Civil Engineering at the City College of New York.

There's a picture of Mama standing tall next to her father, looking straight into the camera with a happy smile and penetrating confidence. She had aqua blue eyes, shapely legs, and stood five foot eight inches. In this picture, she wore a white silk dress with shell buttons from her neck to the hem. A matching white silk belt was eased around her thin waist, and she wore a wide brim, white, straw hat, cocked over her left forehead. She was a beautiful, black-haired svelte girl with creamy, clear white skin. Her father wore his signature brown suit and hat. They were standing in front of a train station.

The Enchantment

After Mama and her parents returned from a tour of Europe, her father decided to send her to Bucknell University because a dear friend, Dr. Orin Oliphant, was a tenured Professor of Engineering there. Mama wanted to become a civil engineer, like her father. "Uncle Orin," as Mama called him in the many stories of her enchanting period at Bucknell, was a successful writer, lecturer, and researcher, and he had an extensive library in his home.

Mama was easily admitted to Bucknell and, in 1933, took the train from New York City to Lewisburg, Pennsylvania. She lived in the school dormitory for girls. After her first semester, she became a sorority sister and lived in the Delta Delta Delta sorority house.

Mom and Dad met at Bucknell University. Mama said during that first semester, Dad started courting her in his Stutz Bearcat automobile. I imagine this privileged girl from Manhattan was swept into a dream when she met Dad with his amazing stories of his family's historical background. That and the Stutz Bearcat may have convinced her that he was real. She said,

> *"Your dad was a real sharp dresser, and he could go anywhere and do anything he wanted. He was tall and handsome and had unlimited money from his grandfather. He was a party-er. We could drink and smoke and spend time with friends all the time. There were so many parties. We would drive along the rivers around the university with the top down on his Stutz. We joined the polo team, we each had our very own polo pony, and your dad became a standout with his pony on the field. Everyone envied us in those days."*

According to Mama, she never got to take the civil engineering courses. The school abruptly moved those classes to the boys' dormitory, and in those days, girls were not allowed near the boys' dorms. Only boys were permitted to major in engineering. So, she switched her major and graduated in four years as a math major. Her parents were agreeable. After all, a girl does not need a career. Her mother had never worked outside the home, and, for goodness' sake, Mama was never expected to have a career. She was destined to marry a rich college boy.

On December 11, 1937, the year they graduated from Bucknell University, Mary Charlotte Rathbun and Walter Leonard Dillinger were married in New York City. The wedding picture shows a small wedding party with my mama and Dad seated side by side in the middle of a group of twelve smiling people. Grandma and Grandpa Rathbun, Dodo Dillinger, my dad's sister, and several unknown college-age people surrounded the happy couple. All were dressed in Gatsby garb. Very camp. Fancy hats, smooth sleek dresses on the ladies, and dark suits on the men. It is the one picture I have of my parents where neither had a cigarette in hand.

Mama thought she had married well.

She had scored a ringer...

3

THE EARLY YEARS

Right after my parents' wedding in 1937, Grandma and Grandpa Rathbun, my mama's parents, took off on a two-year trip around the world, mostly by steamer. My parents drove together to Point Marion, Pennsylvania, which is in the heart of the Appalachian backcountry. Mama had visited Appalachia with Dad before they married, but I think she believed in the romance of the mountains, and she and Dad thought the money they would have from their families would sustain them.

After returning to Point Marion, they set up housekeeping in the house my grandfather, Walter Sumner Dillinger, built in 1905 for his own bride, Mabel Tallentire. This house at 4 Penn Street was furnished and set up as it had been when Walter Sumner moved his two children to his parents' home in 1916, before taking off with the "whore." The house was musty and threadbare, but it was a place to live. The year was 1938.

Money-Making Ventures | The Coal Business

After my parents landed in Point Marion as newlyweds, fresh out of college, they soon realized they would need to create some means of making money.

Neither of them wanted to work for anyone else. As freshly minted college graduates, they figured they were smarter than anyone around and, in no time, they would own the town.

One of their more outlandish ideas to "make a buck" was to rent a small plot of land, purchase a used coal truck and an old, tired pony they named Bill, and create their own coal mine. Extracting a truck full of coal and selling it to others for heating and stove fuel was a simple, albeit dangerous, way to make some quick money in the late 1930s. The truck could hold 2 tons of coal and they could sell it for maybe $9.00 a ton. The rented land had a four-foot-high seam of semi-visible coal that could be accessed by chipping away large chunks of the black rock and digging into the side of the hill in the exposed cave. The landowner had already taken most of the easily available coal that was readily exposed.

Once my parents had grabbed large enough pieces of the black rock and tossed them into the truck, they would peddle their wares to the locals. As soon as they had gradually taken all the exposed coal, it was time to start the process of propping up the ceiling of the cavity, little by little, and crawling into the mine to pick the coal from the exposed seam. They built a rudimentary metal track for a small metal and wood cart to be pulled, by Bill the pony, in and out of the ever-deepening cave. Each day they would hook Bill to the cart, lead him into the face of the digging, scrape out as much coal as they could into the cart, reattach Bill to the other end of the cart, and march out with their treasure.

One fateful day an invisible hand gave them their comeuppance.

In their greedy zeal to keep getting the coal in the wagon they used to pull into the mine, they had not properly supported the ceiling. These two know-it-all college kids were taught a valuable lesson when the roof of the mine fell in on them. They managed to scramble out on their hands and knees by beating the poor pony, Bill, half to death as he dragged them toward daylight with the tethered rope they had lashed onto themselves. They left the wagon.

The venture lasted only a matter of months. They never went back to their mine. We kept Bill in the backyard until he died of old age. He was meaner than a snake, but Bill always had something to eat, and Dad gave him a respectful wide berth. He kicked and bit anyone who came near him. And no wonder.

The hulking coal truck rusted in the yard. A testimony.

The Minstrel Show

Both Mama and Dad had been in a theatre group while at Bucknell, so they decided they would make their fortune with a traveling minstrel show theatre production. Their operation would be more sophisticated than the minstrel shows that were so popular in the small towns of the day. After all, they were a rare breed in the Appalachians; they were college graduates. And, by golly, they were Thespians. Yesseree.

Having taken electives in theatre, they figured they were experts in making profitable shows. They were the producers and directors. Dad had some money for a grubstake from his granddad, who had died that same year. They gathered actors and stagehands and began traveling, with their little troupe, in a caravan of cars to towns along the rivers. They started in South Carolina. "Happy Birthday Diehl," my dad's loyal best friend, born in Point Marion on the same day as Dad, was their most able assistant. The traveling show venture lasted through six shows, but it was an item for discussion for many, many years.

Dad would say,

"Yes, we hired actors and lots of people and we had our very own production going on. We could have had a real profitable operation. Damn war came along and ruined everything."

Years later, Happy Birthday told me of the hilarious antics of how the police chased them out of the small towns on more than a few occasions due to some ill-defined activities of their troupe; and the fact that Dad never paid his bills. I witnessed throughout my life this marauding curse of not just ignoring debts, but abject refusal to be accountable for money.

The Newsstand

Besides the short-lived coal mine and the minstrel show, they used some of the money from Dad's grandpa to rent a storefront on Penn Street in Point Marion where they sold newspapers and ice cream. They hired a teenage girl named Theresa who walked to the store after classes at Point Marion High School. After working a few hours, she would walk home to Big Cat Hollow, an isolated wooded conclave several miles down winding dirt lanes outside Point Marion, where she lived with her family. Sometimes Dad would drive her home.

Years later, I would learn so much more about Theresa.

Dad said when the war came, he tried to enlist in the service, but they wouldn't take him because he was too near-sighted. Happy Birthday joined at the first mention of war in Europe and proudly served his country as a Private First Class in the US Marine Corps. Most of the boys and men between the ages of 17 and 30 in Point Marion were looking at each other and asking,

"*When you thinkin' 'bout goin?*"

Not *are* you going, just *when*.

Some finished high school first.
Most did not.

Dad's Three-Time-Loser-Status Begins

My oldest sister, Sara Charlen, was born in October 1941 while Mama and Dad were still operating the newsstand. The business was not profitable, and the hours were long. Not too many customers walked in for newspapers, candy, and ice cream. Most of the population walked directly to one of the many beer gardens that dotted the town. There wasn't much interest in reading the newspaper in Point Marion. The focus was on day-to-day survival.

Mama and Dad were desperate for money. They were accustomed to spending money, and their income did not match their lifestyle. Dad's inheritance from his grandpa had been spent on the almost catastrophic coal mine fiasco, the failed minstrel show, and the deserted newsstand and ice cream shop. Mama's parents made it clear when she married Dad and moved to Point Marion that her allowance was over. The affluence had not lasted, and the helplessness of the steep mountains began to underscore Mama's pervasive disappointment.

In 1943, news that the Manhattan Project was hiring at the Westinghouse factory in East Pittsburgh reached the Appalachian hills. The word was out. Anyone who wanted to help with the war effort— anyone not healthy enough or of the right age to be sent off to war— could get a job at the factory fabricating equipment for this mysterious mission. The local people called it the Stone and Webster job. Since Dad was a college graduate, it seemed reasonable that he could get a job.

They closed the newsstand and, in 1943, with Mama pregnant with their next family addition, Dad moved to Pittsburgh and rented an apartment on the east side. Mama stayed home with Sara Charlen. She was left with a child in arms, and a growing belly in the isolated town of Point Marion.

Dad would sometimes make the five hour drive home on the weekends, but the trip was tiresome because the road from Pittsburgh to Point Marion was narrow and poorly maintained. He would have to dodge deep potholes and avoid big lumps of stone and coal that had fallen off the coal trucks lumbering in and out of the hidden hollows on the mountain roads.

Dad's Aunt Emma lived next door to Mama. The two of them were close. She helped Mama with everything. Except for Emma, Mama was alone. Being deposited in the heart of Appalachia from New York City was a shock.

Mama never tried to adapt to the town and its people. She had inborn prejudices she carried with her as a sorority girl from the big city. She did not join the Methodist Church where Aunt Emma was an icon, and she tended to snub the other women in town. Early on, Mama made it clear that she was a card-carrying certified member of the Daughters of the American Revolution (DAR), and proud of it. The only other college graduates in the area were those who taught school and Mama would say,

> "Oh, a teachers' college. That's just a certificate.
> It's called a normal school. Not on my level."

Of course, her overt attitude resulted in further social isolation.

In March of 1944, Mama went into labor. There were two doctors who lived and practiced in town. One spent most of his time at a bar called the Brass Rail or at Augie's Beer Garden, blubbering over the good old days gone by. The other was in the township delivering someone else's baby. Dad had the family car in Pittsburgh, so Mama called a taxi to take her to the hospital in Morgantown. Of course, the taxi had to come from Morgantown to pick Mama up, so sister Eileen was born in the taxi. Mama was alone. Dear Aunt Emma, our ever-faithful solitary family member, was there for her.

Dad came home the following weekend and then went back to Pittsburgh, leaving Mama in Point Marion with the baby and two-year-old Sara Charlen.

My sister Charlen recalls days when Mama's parents would visit from New York City and spend hours in the garden with Mama and Daddy and Aunt Emma. Charlen says that Mama was happy and Daddy had some remaining means from his family during that early period. I saw pictures of Grandma and Grandpa Rathbun, Mama's parents, sitting on the lawn at 4 Penn Street, smiling and holding my sister, Sara Charlen. Something happened between them and my parents, because there were no pictures of them after Eileen was born in 1944.

Dad stayed in Pittsburgh until the bomb was dropped on Nagasaki in August 1945.

> *"As soon as that bomb was dropped, kids, they closed Westinghouse down and I came home. That day, it was over."*

Throughout his life, Dad kept a small, framed certificate on the wall above his desk from the War Department that affirmed he participated in the Manhattan Project.

> *"Yes, kids, says right here that I was essential to the production of the Atomic Bomb. August 6, 1945. Yup, indeed kids, I did my part ..."*

Many years later, I discovered that Dad did not make the journey to Pittsburgh alone. He took with him a local girl with whom he had a long intimate relationship. The two of them lived together, presenting themselves as a couple, as he pretended he was "helping in the war effort" and "doing his part" while living away from his family.

This local girl and my dad had a son in the spring of 1945.

Yes, Dad came home to his original family. But in doing so, he abandoned a young woman with his own child.

He left her. Alone.

A young unmarried woman from the entrails of Appalachia with a baby in her arms.

He masqueraded for the remainder of his life that this "dalliance" did not happen.

He was not the long-suffering, dutiful husband to my mama that he presented himself to be.

Who else knew this secret?

What kind of personality traits allow this kind of behavior?

Could I have inherited them?

Was I even his child?

Hello, Francie Girl

I was born in 1946. Dad said I was named after his best friend, Happy Birthday Diehl. He was Francis and I was Frances. For years as I was growing up, I would see Happy along the street in Point Marion. He never married. Happy was one of the many returned veterans from the war who served an ever-present vigil of days gone by.

I always knew where he lived in some rented small alcove in a back corner. He was a constant in my life, forever greeting me with a special smile and calling me by his name and my own name. He would shout out to me as I skipped along the sidewalk,

"Hi, Francie girl!"

My response was,

"Hey, Happy."

We were friends.

When I was born, I completed Dad's three-time-loser status. A station he would never let me forget. The boy child born out of wedlock with the local girl was not included in his loser status; just us three girls born to him and my mama.

My first clear memory is from my three-year-old birthday.

DAD

Dad was from the underbelly of the Appalachian valley. His ancestors had scratched their way through the underbrush and woods and weeds to settle the Point Marion area in the early 1700s. The mountains sucked him in, and, like an addictive drug, they called Dad's name every day. He would never leave.

Dad stood six feet three inches and was as skinny as a rail. He always had a cigarette in his hand or mouth with glowing hot ash at the end that could bump one of us and leave a small circular reddened mark with missing skin and ash. Dad never tried to burn us on purpose, he was careless, and, by suppertime, he had enough beers to forget he had a caustic burning cigarette in his mouth or between his orange-stained fingers.

In those days he smoked unfiltered Lucky Strike. He kept the pack of cigarettes in his front left shirt pocket and the refillable lighter in his pants pocket. All day, I could hear the click-snap of the lighter starting up a new smoke. They turned his front teeth the yellow straw color of the silver maple seed pods that helicoptered down from the massive trees in our yard.

CLICK-SNAP.

All year he wore the same dark pants with elastic suspenders clipped to the waist and flounced over his boney shoulders. In the summer he was shirtless. The mass of curly black hair on his chest would get caught in the stretch of his suspenders. In fact, there was so much space between Dad's trouser waist and his own belly, one had to be careful not to get an accidental peek at what was south of his waist. Dad was proud that he did not believe in underpants. In the winter, he would wear a flannel button-front shirt under the suspenders.

He had special socks he kept in a mysterious sock drawer we were never ever to look in. Dad had matching pairs of socks that he changed once a week. He kept Dr. Scholl's plaster pads pasted to his toes throughout his life. Every Saturday night, after supper, he had a stocking routine. He would sit on the sofa in the living room and change his socks. A ritual. None of us had matching socks or a sock drawer, but the routine of peeling off the crusted Dr. Scholl's pads, replacing them, and putting on a different set of socks was important to him. We never told him that his feet routine made the house smell like a rat crawled into the sofa and died there long ago. The permeating smell made the hounds perk up their ears and point their noses in a curious stance.

When Dad went to bed, he would hang his pants on the open door to his bedroom by the suspenders and walk around naked. He never got up until 1 p.m. The naked matter was just an upstairs issue, but that was where the only bathroom in the house was, which made it a bit awkward for all of us. But Dad made it clear he was the man of the house and we all tiptoed around him.

When he would walk uptown, a trip of 500 yards, he would put on a fedora hat and tip it to any female over the age of 30. He would touch the brim and say,

"How do"

and then walk on.

Dad had vivid memories of his past life. The reality of his today was crowded out with the mist of drink and dreams of what he thought he and his family were and had in the past.

> "Our family settled this area. Why your great-great-ever-so-great-granddad built the keelboats for the Lewis and Clark expedition. They set them off right here in the river in front of this very house. Yessir, that was something."

The stories of the people of Appalachia are told over and over again. A chant from generation to generation to somehow explain away the hardness that the heart of America has dealt to the people of the hills.

One night we were sitting at the supper table. It was dark outside. Dad started telling more stories about his old life when he had money. All three of us sisters tried hard to be as quiet and simple as we could with Dad. Especially at the supper table. Dad was reciting the story again about how he and his college roommate, Rousso, had

> "Caught a bunch of big black flies and attached the tiny tissue papers that you open Hershey chocolate kisses with and rammed them up their ass and then these flies were flying around like the Red Baron in his Sop-With-Camel. Kids, that was the most fun.
>
> "Yesseree, kids, we just sat in our college fraternity room and smoked and had so much fun that night. Those flies would buzz around the room. Then we would swat them with an ol' dish towel..."

I could only imagine what those Hershey chocolate kisses must have tasted like. Eating enough chocolate to have so many of the little white Hershey papers left over. Enough money to buy all the chocolate you wanted. Dad sure must have had some money in those days. The three of us girls never could figure out what was so funny about flies buzzing around with those Hershey papers attached to them. But of course, we laughed and laughed to keep Dad from reaching for the yardstick.

Mama was there in the shadows when Dad would go through his dialogues. By the time I came along, Mama had developed a deep disdain for the entire area where we lived.

By listening to Dad and seeing the strain in Mama's bearing, I resolved to learn from all the life lessons, no matter how outlandish, he was bent on describing to us, but to not let them define me or my future.

5

AUNT MAEMAE

My dad's aunt Emma was the first saint in my life. Aunt MaeMae, as we called her, smelled of sweet lavender and had the softest chest. Her hands were creamy white. She would hold me close and hum softly while we sat together on her porch swing. I am sure she loved me.

MaeMae was born in Point Marion in 1874. When I was born, she was 72 years old. She was a solid member of the Point Marion United Methodist Church, acting as the official keeper of the cradle roll until the day she died. MaeMae lived in the house she was born in. My mama, dad, sisters, and I lived in the house next door.

Before Aunt MaeMae died, she would take all three of us girls to Sunday school every week. We had shiny black patent leather Mary Jane shoes she bought for each of us. I remember so well how we would snap our feet as we were paraded by our loving aunt up the street in the matching paisley dresses she selected for us. She bought each of us our own white socks at Siegel's store. I felt so special and loved. The ladies at the church would say,

> *"Oh, there's Emma Dillinger's girls."*

I would sing *Jesus Loves Me* and *This Little Light of Mine, I'm gonna let it shine, shine all over Point Marion*. Aunt MaeMae would clap and say how good I was at singing her Bible songs.

On a cold day in the early spring of 1949, I was chasing my sisters around the car in the driveway,

> "You can't catch me, you can't catch me,"

they both were taunting. I ran faster than my three-year-old legs had ever run. All of a sudden, I saw that Mama and Dad were sitting in our old Packard car. My sisters jumped in the car, and they all sped away. I stood there alone. The wind off the river was brisk and sharp. It slapped on my face, and it stung the big salty tears that were running down my cheeks. How could this happen? They all left me without a word.

And there she was. Aunt MaeMae gathered me in her arms and swept me into her warm kitchen. She put two chairs in front of her little gas oven, lit it up with the

WHOOSH

of a lighted match, opened the door, and put her beautiful creamy white hands out in front of her.

> "Here Francie, you warm your hands with me, we are going to be just fine together."

And we were.

The rest of the family drove to New York City to see Mama's parents. They had decided that taking three children was more than they could cope with on those long tortuous country roads, so one was to be left with Aunt MaeMae.

Me. I loved spending that week with her and having her all to myself. I was sad they left me without a word.

It wasn't long after that Aunt MaeMae got cancer and, three months later, on March 8, 1950, she was gone. I was three years old. She died in the same house she was born in. She devoted her entire life to caring for others. Dad and Mama made sure she was all decked out in her best dress in her coffin in our front room for all her friends to visit.

She was a saint, hidden among us in Point Marion.

Aunt MaeMae's death was sad for all of us, but what happened after that was devastating for Dad. It seems that when her parents died, all the money and the land they had went to Aunt MaeMae, as their only surviving child. Of course, Aunt permitted Dad and Mom to live in the house next door at 4 Penn Street without charge. She had family savings to spend during those 15 years she outlived her parents. The problem was, with her death, the estate was to be divided among the survivors.

The survivors were Dad, his sister (Aunt Dodo), and, to everyone's surprise, the "whore" that Dad's father had married after Dad's mother had died. Seems that the "whore" was still living a healthy life somewhere in Ohio. Surprise!

It appeared that Dad, being one who negated the value of females, assumed he would be the sole inheritor since he stayed on the old homestead and, in his mind, had looked after his aunt. Dad believed that, as the surviving male, as his birthright, he would, of course, get everything.

He was wrong.

It was dear Aunt MaeMae who had so lovingly taken care of Dad and his sister when his mother died and his father left with the "whore." It was Aunt MaeMae who cared for her own parents in the family home until they died, and it was she who took care of our mama when she was alone, caring for babies, while Dad went off to Pittsburgh to work at the Westinghouse plant. Aunt MaeMae was the anchor of the family.

Not only would there be inheritance taxes and some debts to pay, but Dad would get only one-third of the remaining estate. (I have learned over the years that the successful arranging for inheritance is not a skill of my family. My own mother and father, as well as Aunt Dodo, left a tumultuous mess for me to sort out and clear upon their deaths.)

Aunt Dodo had, years before, after divorcing the college sweetheart she had married while still in college, run off to Pittsburgh with her lady friend partner and wanted to buy a new house in an upscale section of Pittsburgh -- Mount Lebanon, Pennsylvania.

She had escaped.

I thought she was embarrassed of us and wanted little to do with any impoverished relations. Of course, her rejection of us may have also been due to Mama's attitude toward Aunt Dodo's lifelong devotion to her female companion.

It was something no one ever talked about.

The Church Ladies would often ask,

> *"Is Dodo still with Miss Travis?"*
> *"Yes Ma'am, she is."*
> *"Tsk, tsk, tsk...."*

I certainly did not care about any relationship Mama or the Church Ladies would find unacceptable.

The "whore" wanted all the cash she could lay her hands on — immediately. So, Dad needed to come up with the money to buy out the other two portions of the inheritance. It was 1950 in the innards of Appalachia and Dad didn't have a job, but he was determined to keep the property. Dad hatched a plan to move our family into Aunt MaeMae's house at 2 Penn Street and turn 4 Penn Street, where we lived, into a duplex to rent to two families. He planned to continue to rent the third house, 1 Penn Street, where friends of the family had lived for three generations. (Sometimes, but mostly not, they paid a small rent charge.) Dad and Mama had to mortgage the property to raise the cash to do this and pay off Aunt Dode and the "whore."

I was four years old when we moved into Aunt MaeMae's house. With some of his inheritance money, Dad hired people to help him create the duplex.

I had hope that our family could somehow scratch our way out of the abyss of sadness and poverty.

THE INDUSTRY AND PEOPLE OF POINT MARION

The Coal Industry

The coal industry came to Appalachia in the early 1800s and remained the primary source of U.S. coal up through the 1970s. Depending upon the location of the coal in the ground, the coal owner did whatever was possible to extract the black gold as quickly as possible and then escape the man-made mess. The havoc created by these unforgiven capitalists on the environment and people of the once beautiful mountains and valleys of Appalachia will remain for lifetimes.

The major types of underground mining conducted in Pennsylvania's bituminous coalfields are room-and-pillar mining, room-and-pillar with retreat mining, and longwall mining. Room-and-pillar mining involves driving tunnel-like openings, oftentimes into the bank of a hillside, to divide the coal seam into rectangular or square blocks. Growing up, it was not unusual to see a cave-like structure in the curve of any hill, supported by wooden beams, near a house where anyone would simply dig out the coal needed for a household. The outcropping of a coal seam close to the surface can be anywhere from 18 inches to the height of a house.

The more sophisticated coal owner engineered the sites systematically and properly supported the roofs of the passageways and organized the withdrawal. The shaft mines have long been a popular method for retrieving coal that is deep in the earth. Masses of miners are sent underground in elevators to often travel long distances by trudging, or by a system of small jitneys that run along the haulage tracks to the face of the mine where the coal is being extracted. Working in coal mines is flat-out dangerous, but for many undereducated people living in the hills, it was a steady, well-paying job in a region where there were few opportunities for a person to make reasonable money and care for a family. Of course, only men could be coal miners.

The slow death of every breath a miner inhales of the small particles of coal dust, along with the possibility of exposure to toxic gases and the chance of long, painful debilitation from "Black Lung Disease," was typically ignored when measured against a paycheck that allowed food on the table most nights. The more immediate fear, and the torn soul of a miner's choice between the threat of being crushed, drowned, or injured from fires and explosions, when measured against the option of no work and little opportunity for caring for their family, made it a daily game of roulette with real time possibilities. The legacy of coal mining is crippled men, countless orphaned children, and coal miner widows facing a return to poverty.

The mountain top method or "strip mine" of extracting coal works well for a prompt "smash and grab." The full top of a mountain is removed, or if a smaller section is available, a simple dozer scrape-off is done for coal near the topsoil. This is popular for coal that can be accessed near the surface. The project consists of exposing the coal to the open air so the precious resource can be quickly extracted and moved out, usually on trucks, to the rivers or rails. This system entails first clear cutting the trees and growth from the surface of the land, (sometimes by a burn-off that further contaminates the air), or by cutting the trees and vegetation and hauling this mixture to the freshly twisted heap of debris that announces to the world "coal mine here."

The Slag Heap

This man-made soupy concoction typically begins with an initial layer of what would become a newly created mountain of muck and earthen waste. The coal operator, in the rush to expose the rich coal, often dumps the burned off trees and vegetation into a nearby crevasse in the earth. Then the remaining top dirt, rock, and rubble is scraped away, moved, and dumped on top of the base slice to expose the coal seam. The sections of the fill are a muddy, soft sandwich of dirt laced with sticks, stones, and boulders that have been crushed into smaller chunks. This overburden is squashed on top of the trees and scrub layer. The heaps of excess earth waste often create huge irregular dams that block natural streams in the once verdant valleys of the existing essential habitat. The resulting mountain is a slag heap.

With their natural stream flow disrupted, the water that organically would be winding through the creases in the mountain toward the mighty regional rivers has nowhere to go except to pool behind these fragile newly created earthen mountains. Eventually, this stagnant water would back up and become contaminated cesspool-like puddles or lakes held together in the receiving valleys by dangerously fragile soft, muddy, man-made earthen dams. A disaster waiting to happen. With one particularly wet spring, or a winter with extra snow melting into the mountain fold, the earth would begin to slip and slide.

And slide it did. Sometimes a slow trickle, then turning into a moderate waterfall, carrying slime and sludge haphazardly out of the noxious dam toward any gravitational path to the river valley.

Then, with the weight of the water and added rocks and debris, it gains speed and collects more dead tree snags, stones, and vegetation as it rushes toward the rivers that are laced in the creases of the valley floor. The river towns were regularly inundated with this turbulent, contaminated waste.

On the exposed area of the strip mine, once the coal seam is opened, the coal can then be extracted and hauled away. The new area looks like a barren moonscape and is treacherous for humans and animals. The resulting mixture of slag often catches fire and oozes its toxic chemicals into the surrounding land. Eventually, the effluent slag finds its way into the air and water, the rivers and ground water.

Coal companies have had a standard of operation: find the coal, mine the coal, exit from the community and the environment (leaving both in ruins), then go bankrupt, (legally disappearing) and start again somewhere else.

Driving through Appalachia, many of my friends have remarked on the beauty of the area. It is beautiful. (And from the roads it is incredulous.) However, one needs only to take a look at an aerial view to see the waste and destruction of what the original natives dubbed "the promised land." The damage to the ecosystem is not expected to ever recover.

The Glass Industry

In the early 1900s, Point Marion Glass Factory was built. The word was out to the hungry emigrants of Europe that there was an opportunity for specialized glass-making skills in this small town called Point Marion in the crease of a river. The glass industry was beginning to boom due to the easy availability of sand from the swishing of the river bottom at the confluence of the two rivers and the availability of natural gas needed for the heat to produce glass.

The People of Point Marion

In the late 1800s, as coal mines were being opened near Point Marion, many of the coal companies sent representatives to meet the unskilled laborers as they got off the boats at Ellis Island. Newcomers were encouraged to head to the Appalachian coal fields where there was housing and work. These unskilled folks from southern and eastern Europe came to America to escape hunger, oppression, and poverty. They were the strong backs, long arms, and hungry workers needed to support the coal industry.

The mixing of this new group of Europeans with the existing group of native Appalachians was chaotic. The Europeans, although anxious to be Americans, often settled in areas together and often did not speak or understand English. The existing population was not overly friendly and there was name-calling, outright discrimination, and a high wire intensity of constant stress.

The cultural mix of the population in Point Marion in the early 1900s included a hard-working mix of Italians, Belgians, some Slavs, various descendants of those who originally crossed the Appalachian foothills, and a mixture of others who found their way into the thriving community.

When Point Marion was being settled, those coming to town from the various European countries leaned toward sorting themselves into their own diverse ethnic groups in a specific area of town. Each group seemed to be relegated to their own general conclave.

It was refreshing to walk from one European-influenced area of town to another. The immigrants and their families began creating mini environments of their homeland with varying foods, cooking, gardening, housing structures and imbedded religious beliefs. Each group had their own grocery store, populated their own churches, had their own cultural holidays, and patronized their own beer gardens.

The Slavic people, who found their way to Point Marion to do hard labor on the riverboats and sand dredging cranes, congregated in an area surrounding the only Catholic church.

Immigrants from Italy came to build the furnaces and cut the stone needed for the glass ovens for the factory. Many of the first-generation Italians never learned a word of English, nor did they need to.

The Italians settled in Little Italy, a hillside of two streets east of the railroad tracks above the glass factory. The area had the aroma of roasting tomatoes and sweet peppers and the beauty of wholesome grapes grown from seeds brought from the old country. Each family had at least one grapevine and a cellar full of "dago red" that was heartily shared with a visitor. These houses along Grant Street and Jeanette Street were mostly two stories, many of them were brick and stone, some with wide stone verandahs; all handmade by the arriving Italian immigrants.

Little Italy was home to generations of families who would be living side by side in houses nearly right on top of one another: the Bruni's, the Turco's, the Jordan's, the Giannini's and so many other solid Italian American families. With their grape arbors and outside picnic areas, these loud and happy people were always singing and shouting at one another from their flower-laden windowsills.

The smell of baking bread and cookies in the area settled by the Belgians, with their neat lawns and freshly painted white picket fences, was indeed a fine walk through the diverse culture of these meticulous French speaking people.

The women were excellent at needlecraft and had homemade antimacassars on the arms and headrests of each piece of furniture. Known for their baking and French cooking skills, there was a wonderful smell emanating from the tidy rows of houses. The gardens were immaculate, and the houses were meticulously painted and tended.

The Belgians settled along the river in an area they called Harvey Town. The DuFour's, the Duliere's, the Firenze's, the Witteborts and DeGardyn's all chose the Point Marion area as their home. Most were from the area of Jumet, and French was their native language.

Many of these folks had come to work as the skilled artisans of the glass factory— glassblowers, glasscutters, chemists, and creative people of the highest order. They were Protestants and most were drawn into the Point Marion Methodist Episcopal Church.

Each of the ethnic groups seemed to tolerate the other reasonably well, calling each other dagos, micks, frogs, and hunkeys. The ever-present "crud" seemed the generic name for the catch-all group that was plain dirt poor. But there was outright discrimination in every way imaginable within the limits of the town.

Yet they all seemed to congregate together as a seamless amalgam when it came to looking after the children of the community, general safety, and common patriotic allegiances to the country they had adopted.

After a generation or two, people of the various ethnic groups were all intermarrying and, most days, having a loud, wonderful, raucous time. An accordion could be heard from the streets in Little Italy, a piano teacher could be heard instructing "doe re mi" in Harvey Town, and, of course, there was always the loud drunken shouting coming out of the beer gardens that laced every street.

The immigrants were generally gentle people who held strong religious beliefs and were forever grateful for the welcome they received as they took long boat passages across the Atlantic to their own promised land. Grandmas and grandpas who came from the old country as teenagers, who had worked in the factory, were esteemed and active parts of the family. Usually living in the same family complex, they shared their stories of struggle and salvation with the many generations of grandchildren and great-grandchildren who continuously gathered around them.

In the early 1900s, Point Marion was a thriving community with a successful factory that employed most of its inhabitants. It reflected a miniature version of the great migration. From the turn of the century through the 1930s, the Point Marion Glass Factory had a job for anyone who was willing to work. It was a one-employer town.

7

MY BEST FRIEND, SUSIE

Susie and her family lived at the end of Water Street, about a football field away from my house on the river, in a beautiful house her dad built all on his own. The house sat on the point of the two rivers and had a huge grassy yard with a split log fence around the sides. Susie's dad, Rudy, had a woodworking shop behind the garage where he had every kind of tool imaginable.

Susie was related to almost everyone in town. Her mama was from the Belgium people and her father was from the Italians. Her mama's sister married a son of the Jeanskin family from Big Cat Hollow. Her "Grandma TiPi" lived a stone's throw from Susie's house, and her other grandmothers were sprinkled all over town. Uncle Abe, the personification of a true gentleman who served in the Spanish American War, lived a few houses down from "Grandma TiPi."

Susie had so many grandmothers that, in order to differentiate them, we called the one who lived down the street from us "Grandma TiPi," named after her little papillon-looking dog who would tip toe after her. Grandma called him TiPi, so we called her "Grandma TiPi." She was Susie's mother's mother, and a wonderfully happy, white-haired, fireplug of a woman. She wore a baker's apron wrapped around her ample waist and bosom, and she was always in her well stocked kitchen making something with a smell that would waft out her screen door in a trail of a drooling, musky, whiff of baking yeast bread, cookies, or pie.

I was a pigtailed observer of the constant swirl of this large family as I had a ringside seat at the never-ending spin of the ever-moving parts of this eclectic group. I imagined myself watching this wonderful, magical movie of an ever-changing piece-meal drama, pressing my nose against the glass of the scenes and wishing I were part of the melee. They were all loud, gregarious, and bigger than life. The various members of the family had become an amalgam of the different cultures of folks who had arrived in Point Marion since the mid-1860s.

"Hey Uncle Nick, you going to Aunt Sofie's tonight?"

"Of course. I am taking Roseanne, Anthony, and Elaine. See you there. I am bringing the red."

A family so solid and glued together that the rest of the community gravitated to its side. A wonderful circus of people of all sizes and shapes, old and young, speaking Italian, Belgium, the southwestern Pennsylvania colloquial twang, along with the broken hillbilly-- youse (you all) and haints (ain'ts) and worsh (wash). Living all over town.

The original great grandmother and great grandfather of the Italian branch of the clan had come from southern Italy on a long sea voyage after 1900 to work in the glass factory. The early group of Belgians had come to Point Marion in the late 1800s to be glassblowers in the glass factory.

Susie's family was a huge raucous group that I longed to be part of. In my growing up years, I so enjoyed being included in their loud thumping lifestyle. I thought Susie and her brother Dominic had the ideal life, like Beaver Cleaver and Wally. I knew her mom was really June Cleaver, and of course, her dad, Mr. Bruni, was much like Ward.

One day, I was at one of Susie's many family gatherings when all the adults were drinking and laughing. I overheard her dad tell Uncle Nick,

> *"Francie is one of the prettiest girls in town. Look at her."*

I was shocked. I had never thought that, and no one had ever noticed my appearance. Susie was the gorgeous one. The straight black hair of her dad and the creamy white skin of her mom. She was two years younger than me and her brother, Dominic, was two years younger than her. Susie took piano lessons, had beautiful clothes, and had her own bedroom and a bed to herself. Her mom and dad adored her. Her dad called her "honey," and "sweetheart." He even built a playhouse for her in their yard.

Susie's parents were kind to me. Her mom was the best cook ever. She made a variety of different foods – not just hamburgers and beans – and sometimes she would invite me to stay for dinner. Susie's dad had been in World War II. When he came home from the war, he married his high school sweetheart, Mary Louise DeGardyn. Mr. Bruni was dark-haired Rudy Valentino handsome. Her mom had satiny light skin, soft light brown curly hair, and a smile that would light up any room. Susie's mom and dad ran DeGardyn's Café; a restaurant/beer garden up the street.

Susie's grandfather was not around during my lifetime. His story is an Appalachian legend. Susie and I never talked about him. Dad told us that Susie's grandfather got into the "liquor business" during prohibition.

> *"Old John DeGardyn was a real businessman in those days' kids. He knew how to make a buck. Boy, oh boy, he was quite the Dandy ... He would run the moonshine up the river from West Virginia on a riverboat in the dark and store it in those red garages just across the*

street from his house. He sold it all over the township. Good stuff, by God. Too bad those dam revenooers caught up with him and sent him to the pokey."

This amazing family had a love that filled the town. They survived every imaginable travail yet stood together and laughed about it.

I learned to love and laugh with them.

8

THE B&O RAILROAD AND PUBLIC TRANSPORTATION

The route for taking any work product out of West Virginia to Pittsburgh and points north ran through Point Marion. The B&O Railroad mainline ran directly through town, cutting it in half whenever one of the frequent long, long trains would pass. There were three railroad crossings in town. The farthest south was in Little Italy, the middle crossing was to the south of the railroad station parking lot, and the main crossing was at Penn Street.

In the mid-1950s, the trains abandoned the station in Point Marion and left the unpainted wooden building in the center of Penn Street to rot in the sun. A wide cement area was south of the station. Dad said that long ago, it was where people parked their cars when they were going to take the train. The cement was crumbling and unsteady. In the summer, huge clumps and tall wind-swept tufts of weeds would grow up through the cracked surface.

The old train station was one of the largest buildings in town, located on a rusted dog leg of the main B&O line. The roof was covered with moss from the mold growing in the blackened building. After the mid-1950s, no train ever stopped. Just a frantic dash out of the hills of West Virginia to the hungry metropolises to the north. The old rotting station and the ramp that led to it were a reminder of the decaying town.

Public transportation in and out of Point Marion was sparse and haphazard. Occasionally, a Greyhound bus would intermittently slow down for a quick stop near the town's only drugstore on its way north to the county seat of Uniontown or south to Morgantown, West Virginia. If one did not have a car, there was no way to get out. Public transportation was nearly nonexistent through the 1970s. Even then, the narrow and winding roads were outrageously pocked with huge stones and potholes. There was one main road to enter and exit Point Marion and, because of the difficulty of driving on that decaying, unkempt road, few people passed through town. This seemed to be one more way to remain isolated from the rest of the world.

By the time I came along, the business of the coal mines, railroad, and glass factory was long gone. The roads leading in and out of Point Marion were a forgotten obligation of the highway department, save a few crumbs of road ash here and there authorized by a politician hoping to gain a few extra votes.

The people were in day-to-day survival mode. They were trapped.

GEORGE M. LEADER

It was one of those hot, sweaty, simmering August days. The steam of the ninety-degree temperature was pushing the water-logged heat waves in the heavy air, trapped in the low-hanging clouds, onto the surface of the muddy stagnant rivers. We called this time of year the "dog days of summer." The heavy air was forcing a rise of the dripping humidity to reach its hot, musty wet arms out of the rivers and up to the low-hanging clouds, trapping the wet heat in the muggy valley that was Point Marion.

It was August of 1950, and my best friend, Susie, had gone with her mama to visit one of her many Italian cousins. I was nearly four years old, left to drift around town alone, so of course, no shoes. I had dirty feet from tramping along the muddy riverbank, checking out what may have washed up with the river tides since I was last there. Just a dead rat near our house sewer. Swollen and bald. Mouth open and smelling like decayed rotten meat. The blue-green flies were buzzing around its mouth as the reflection from the light of the sun caught their wings in a shiny yellow glare.

BZZZZ. BZZZZ.

The maggots had set in and would devour the carcass by this time tomorrow. The orb of the sun was directly overhead and surrounded by a wide halo of thick mist.

Mama and Dad were either so comfortable with Point Marion that there was never a problem with us wandering around town from the age where we could find our way back home, or it is possible they didn't care. I was not confined. I could go anywhere I wanted. Anytime.

The big exception to any of us wandering around town, and through the townships surrounding the town, was that we had to be home for supper at twenty minutes to six every afternoon. The rule was that we had to be sitting at the sticky stained oilcloth-covered table. No excuses. If we were not home at the magic twenty minutes to six on the dot, it was the yardstick until we cried big crocodile tears.

The 2-inch-wide yardstick had the engraved stamped name, "Klein's Department Store" printed along the one-inch numbers. It had a hole in the top of it and hung on a nail. Dad kept it on the wall at arm's reach from his place at the head of the supper table, when it was not in use on one of us kids. It was a feared object. The yardstick was thin enough to

SNAP

when he grabbed it off the headless nail. It was reserved for transgressions like being late to supper, saying a bad word, or forgetting to say "yes ma'am" or "yes sir" to a grownup.

Sadler's Variety Store

I decided to skip my way uptown where the stores and bars were, trying to avoid the tobacco spit on the sidewalk that would get stuck in my toes. There were only a few streets to cross with cars going both ways, and I was good at the stop, look, and listen drill. I crossed Main Street and headed up toward Sadler's Variety Store in the middle of the block.

Miss Mabel, who was Mr. Sadler's only helper and one of the many Cawley girls from Stewartstown Road, used to make a new arrangement in the window display every week. It was my business every week to stand in front of the big glass and look at all the amazing things she would lay out, in perfect order, on the material she would scrunch up on the floor of the window. They sold everything I could possibly think of at Sadler's. I loved to wander into the store and stand looking at the little bins separating each item.

Bolts of colorful material, thread, rubber gloves, and baby dolls, whose glass-made eyes blinked shut when they were laid flat down, were wrapped in cellophane. Brooms, a genuine electric vacuum cleaner that was guaranteed to lift the dirt right out of anything, and laundry baskets. Sadler's was a treasure trove of every type of new-fangled gizmo I did not even know existed. I would spend hours standing in the aisles, walking up and down, looking at all the things that were available. The plank wood floors were so clean I could see up my skirt.

Of course, I did not dare touch anything. Just looking was an honor. As I walked down the aisles of the neat bins, the floor would creak in all the same spots under my steps. The floor groaned in more spots for Miss Mabel, as Daddy said Miss Mabel was as "wide as a barn door."

Sadler's had everything except, Miss Mabel said, not hardware. Mr. Sadler had a "Christian agreement" with Mr. Carlier who owned the Point Marion Hardware Store two doors up the street. Sadler's would never sell hardware and not drugstore stuff, because Mr. Hunker, the druggist up the street, owned Hunker's Drug Store. Mr. Sadler would not sell drugstore stuff and Mr. Sadler would not sell newspaper stuff, as Mr. Packrone across the street sold newspaper stuff and ice cream. Miss Mabel said they were all "good Christian men" and they all agreed to stay out of one another's business interests. That way, nobody in town had to keep a lot of unnecessary stuff, and if someone came and asked for a nail or a ratchet,

"Why I just send them up to Mrs. Jenkins at Mr. Carlier's."

I wondered what would happen if someone wanted something no one had. Of course, it would have to be some rich person, like Mrs. Gowers, whose family owned the sand dredging company. The Dillinger's never bought anything at any of these stores. We looked around our home place and made do with what we had.

On this hot August day, Miss Mabel had finished the most interesting window display. In one area, she had toy airplanes hanging from individual fishing wire strings. There was a toy train on a box, and in the foreground, small metal cars of all different colors, lined up by size. She separated another area with a bolt of cotton dress material, a lineup of seven different dress patterns, and a grouping of colored thread in front, with some different sizes of scissors and a pincushion beside it. Behind all this were two cardboard boxes covered with wallpaper. On the boxes were some crafts made by the Girl Scouts and some pictures of Boy Scouts. I spent a lot of time taking all this in. Miss Mabel came out of the store when she saw me standing there so long.

"Hey, Francie."

"Oh, Miss Mabel, this is so pretty."

Miss Mabel had a beautiful smile with two of her front teeth crossed in the center of her mouth in a little hug. One tooth in front of the other. Mama said she had cross-eyed teeth. I told Mama it made her look special.

The Railroad Ramp

I skipped up past the railroad ramp where a lot of the country people who walk into town for the day sit until they catch their breath before walking back home. The ramp was right across the street from Augie's Bar, so it was also a good place for the country women and their children to wait for their "ol men" while they sat in the bar.

The ramp was a set of eight stairs, 10 feet wide—wide enough to sit on, going up to a platform, which was 10 feet wide and went back the length of a railroad car. The entire structure was made from thick, rough railroad ties that long ago were soaked in creosote and plugged with tar. When it was hot like it was that August dog day, the wood exuded a pungent tarry smell, and the blackened wood sweated a black melt that stuck to my toes if I stepped in a greasy spot.

There was a drop-off from the platform on one side that used to be where people could step onto a railroad car. Now it dropped down into a rusty weed-filled set of tracks with old rotting rail ties. On the other side of the platform was a deserted wooden shack whose center had burned out long ago. The smell of that old fire still permeated the air around the ramp on a muggy day like that day. No one really went up the platform. People who were tired sat on the steps until they stopped wheezing, coughing, and spitting. Or until their man swaggered across Penn Street from Augie's, ready for a walk home up a winding dirt road.

I pretty much knew all the town drunks and bums, as Mama called them, that hung out at the railroad ramp. But that day was different. Along with the other drunks and the country women and their barefoot children, there was an old skinny, wiry fellow with blackened teeth sitting next to a box filled with a moving mound of hair.

"Hey, little girl, you want a puppy?"

He held up this tiny, tiny multi-black and white squealing thing. The thing was so young it still had its eyes closed and fit into the palm of his stained, calloused hand.

It was love at first sight. This little puppy was sniffing and mewing like a kitten. It started to suckle on the old man's thumb. That puppy needed me.

"Well, I'll go ask my mama. Wait, mister............"

I ran home as fast as I could.

"Mama, Mama, an old man on the ramp wants to give me a puppy. Oh, Mama, I want a puppy of my very own."

"What kind of puppy is it?"

"Oh, Mama, I don't know what kind it is. It's little and white and black and its eyes are closed. Mama, I need to go and get it now before the man gives all of them away."

"But we only have hound dogs in this family."

"Oh, Mama, please, please. That dog needs me."

"Well, all right. But you get a boy one. I don't want any more bitches here."

I ran like the wind back to the ramp, and the old wiry man handed me the most precious bundle. My life changed. I named him George M. Leader after the Governor of Pennsylvania. A Democrat, of course.

Susie's brother, Dominic, had a dog, Topper, who became pals with George. They were together as often as Susie and I were in those days.

George and I were inseparable. He was my best friend and my companion even though Daddy constantly reminded me,

> "He is just a mutt dog; he can't even howl like a real hound dog. That dog can't hunt. No nose."

When I would proudly march through town with my George in tow, the folks would call out,

> "Hey Francie, what you got there?"

> "Best dog in the county."

> "Don't look like no coon hound to me. He a huntin' dog?"

> "No, he's a Democrat."

> "Francie, what you going to do with a dog that don't howl and don't hunt?"

> "Everything. He doesn't even care that I'm a girl!"

George changed the course of my life.

10

MISS BERG'S KINDERGARTEN

In September 1950, I went to kindergarten in Miss Berg's afternoon class. So many children were born in 1946, the beginning of the baby boomers, ours was the largest class in the history of Point Marion. Forty-six children were in the class. Twenty-three in the morning session and twenty-three in the afternoon session. We were the largest number of children to enter Point Marion School at one time.

I was so glad to get the afternoon session because Mama could not get up early in the morning. My sisters were getting themselves up and dressed and off to school, and I was afraid I would start kindergarten off by being late.

Miss Berg was the nicest, most wonderful woman I had ever met. A Saint. Right up there with my Aunt MaeMae. She never yelled at us and handled twenty-three four-year-olds with true aplomb. Alone No teachers' aides and no curriculum guides. Just one getting-worn-out-approaching-retirement maiden and a small room in the Methodist Church basement, packed with children who had never been in a group larger than a Sunday school class. (Years later, Mama told me that the "whore" who ran off with Dad's father and stole the money that Dad thought he should get when Aunt MaeMae died, was a sister of Miss Berg! Miss Berg was an angel! Could the "whore" be so bad?)

As the tallest of all the children, I was long and thin with pigtails in plain hand-me-down, worn clothes. Being taught to only speak to grownups when spoken to, and having it drilled into me that I was a worthless girl, I was afraid to say a word. I had been told that teachers spank children daily and use big wooden paddles with holes in them so the smacks sting harder. I looked carefully for Miss Berg's yardstick. None.

My New Best Friend

Cara Anset was my new best friend. She lived next door to us in the bottom floor of the 4 Penn Street duplex with her sister Laura who was one year younger than Cara and me. Her dad sold cars at the Ford dealership in town and her mama stayed home and cooked, sewed, and cleaned their house. Cara was pudgy. Her dad was a huge man, the size of a door frame. Cara took after him. She was shy and sad most of the time because the boys would tease her,

"Anset. Fanset. Big and fat."

Always to the two of us, the taunting,

"Skinny and Fat. Skinny and Fat. What da ya think of that?"

I was the skinny one.

Ben Jones and Lester Schmidt, two boys in our class, were thick as thieves. These two boys, who I supposed were dearly loved by their parents, taunted us constantly. Dad used to laugh and say,

"Little boys have a penis, there is more to them."

"Dad, I just don't get it, is that why they get to tease the girls? Are they more important?"

Cara was teased because she was big. Not tall and bone skinny like me, but big. Big muscles and plenty of flesh all the way around. She ate the same stuff I ate. She was shorter and stout.

The teasers were merciless.

Cara told me that her mama would take her to Sears and let her pick out chubbette clothes made especially for her. Wow, going to Sears and getting new clothes not one person had ever worn before and not sewn up by your mama from her own old dresses. She was the first girl in her family, so I guess if you are the first girl in the family, and your dad works, you get new stuff at Sears, and then it gets passed on to the next girl.

But Laura got new dresses from Sears too. Mrs. Anset would buy matching dresses for each of them. Imagine two dresses of the same material, only different sizes. The dresses were not even worn out when Cara and Laura grew out of them. Mrs. Anset would tear the used dresses into rags and wash the windows or make doll clothes. At Easter and at the beginning of school, Cara and Laura got new socks with lace around the top edge, too. I used to watch them walking up the sidewalk, side by side.

As we both grew up and moved from one grade to another, I got firsthand experience of the discrimination due to size and what Cara went through. Besides the bullying of Ben and Lester and Francis Carney, who commandeered a push car and a toy broom to chase and whack the girls with, Cara and I survived kindergarten, thanks to Miss Berg.

Playtime

Cara, Laura, and I would play doll babies at her house. Mrs. Anset made doll clothes for Cara and Laura's dolls that were so beautiful. Little tiny snaps and ribbons fit snuggly around her baby doll's shiny hair. Cara would lend me a doll that was made of rubber and had glassy eyes that sparkled in the sun and eyelids that would close tight when I laid the doll down in a soft blanket of leaves. Sometimes she would sing little soft songs to our babies who were snug in the leaves.

Under the huge sugar maple tree, with its gnarling exposed roots and powder-like dirt around the tubers, we'd pretend they were little houses for the dolls with the big flat maple leaves. The leaves turned every shade of the rainbow that autumn, so our houses were more colorful than any other year. The huge catalpa tree leaves were bigger than our faces and smelled of the sweet flowers we sneezed through. The catalpa leaves served as big flat roofs for the leaf houses and as masks over our faces when one of us would need to be the dad of our doll family. Or they would serve as lovely, lovely kerchiefs when one of us needed to act out being the weak maiden in distress.

We would turn on the hose and make rivers flow through our little leaf villages. One day Cara told me that her mother did not like me.

> *"My mother thinks you steal our dolls. I told her you don't, but she thinks you do."*

Maybe she didn't like me because I never had a doll of my own, and I didn't know how to play dolls. It seemed to be a stupid thing to do, dressing up pretend babies and making believe we were little mamas. I knew from looking at my mama that being a mama was no fun at all. Being a mama was sad, no matter what you did.

I liked to make the rivers and put the leaves on our faces and tuck them into our clothes and pretend we were Indians,

WHOOP. WHOOP. WHOOP.

Mrs. Anset maybe didn't like me because I made up games that got Cara and Laura all muddy with the water from the hose, and I could not bring any of my own dolls to her house and my mama never made any lacey doll clothes.

My mama was tired. And sad.

Mr. Anset didn't seem to mind having two girls in a row. He was always smiling and laughing. Sometimes I would walk over by the Ford dealership where he worked every day on Broadway Street, and I would see him out in the lot where all the new and nearly new cars were up for sale. Mr. Anset would be outside walking around wiping a fly off a windshield here and yelling loudly to me, a passerby,

"Hey, Francie girl."

11

SPECIAL JOBS

Dad was always figuring out special jobs for his girls. Early on, all three of us were game to whatever we could do to keep Dad placated and maybe prove to him that we were valuable. Yup.

The Monster

When I was three years old, before Aunt MaeMae died and we were still living in the big house, Dad called all three of us together and announced,

> "I need the bravest girl I have who is just the right size to do this job that is so very special. Girls, it will only happen once a year! There is only ONE chance every year for this. Now, who is going to be my special girl?"

I stood in front of him in my bare feet. It was fall time before the leaves started to drop. It wasn't cold yet. I must have hesitated too long because Dad said,

> "Francie, I am picking YOU!"

Charlen, five years older than me, and much wiser, simply backed away. Eileen seemed genuinely disappointed she was not chosen.

Dad said,

> "Okay, this is a basement project."

He herded me off toward the basement with Eileen trailing behind us. The basement could be entered from steps in the kitchen or from outside the house. We all entered through the outside steps into the dark, cool, and damp cave. It had a cement floor with some puddles of water, random chips of stone scattered around, cobwebs, broken-up tools, and a low ceiling. Dad ducked his head to keep from banging it on the wood beams holding up the first floor of the house.

In the middle of the low, musty-smelling basement was what we kids called "the monster." This was a huge coal furnace with big, round, arm-like pipes reaching up to each register in the floor of the rooms above. Next to the monster was a partitioned-off area where a coal truck could dump coal through an outside window into the partitioned bin in the basement. In the summertime, the bin was mostly empty, except for a rat or two. The monster was cold, dark, and had a small door that resembled an open mouth flapping open in the summer.

In the winter, Dad would shovel coal into the door of the monster and keep a fire going for heat. The coal burning in the monster and the smoke from the fire, rising up from the giant's many arms to individual fireplace grates in each room on the first floor, kept us warm in winter. It was smoky and the heat was uneven, but it was warm. Each grate was a hazard in the winter as the fire was white-hot and the metal grates burned many a blister on our bare feet.

> "Okay, Francie. You are just the right size to help me with this special job! You take this broom that I am going to hand you and you sweep

> the dust out of the bottom and arms of the furnace. No one is as good as you are at this kind of thing. You are my special girl today!"

SWOOP!

All of a sudden, Dad lifted me up under my armpits and placed my bare feet firmly in the deep dust inside the monster. A broom was pushed in after me. Dad poked his head into the open door he lifted me through. He lit an old carbide miner's lamp and held it near the mouth inside the monster so I could see.

> "Okay, just knock down those cinders and that dust and sweep it into this coal bucket. I'll stand here and hold the light for you."

At first, I was panicked at being shin-deep in rough cinders and coal dust and seeing the arms of the beast from the inside. The smell was a pungent leftover smoke odor combined with moldy stale grime. The carbide lamp Dad held emitted a familiar sulfur stench. But, as I kept working with my broom and then a small shovel, I was fascinated with how the system of coal and pipe heating worked. We spent all afternoon getting a lot of the dust and ashes out of the huge creature.

When I was finally pulled out, I was coated in fine gray droppings from top to bottom. Dad took me to the yard and squirted me down with the hose until I was pink again. My clothes went into the washtub, and I trotted inside to change into dry clothes. I coughed on and off for a few days after my monster job, but I survived. And I was not afraid of the monster anymore. I even started to go into the basement and search around to understand the insides of how an old house could work with the belching smoke, tangled wires, and dripping lead pipes. No wonder the rats were comfortable down there.

What I did learn, other than more details of how coal was used, was that I was never really going to get and hold Dad's attention and get him to value me. Eileen, on the other hand, tried in many ways to get Dad's attention and please him. I had figured out early on that, since I was never going to grow a penis, I was not going to make the grade. Eileen never gave up.

Sledgehammer and Tomatoes

In the springtime, before the chain-smoking cigarettes and the years of ten or more beers a day etched away at any bit of energy Dad could muster, he had a ritual of putting in the tomatoes along about the middle of March.

Tomatoes in Point Marion were a springtime sacrament like no other. People would suffer through the bone-chilling cold, cold, cold with the coal-fired smoky furnaces that polluted our lungs and kept us breathless, the slush and the mud and the broken-down cars, the pain of the biting cold wind off the river, trying to keep the mittens mended long enough to last one more week while the snow melted, to come to the first day of spring and the importance of planting the tomatoes. Planting at the precise time.

Conversations in Point Marion would begin and end around tomatoes.

> "Got yer tomatas in yet?"

> "Nope . . . frost is commin agin'."

> "Got any tomata buds yet?"

> "I hear Mizz Hungar went to Morgantown and bought them hot house starts at Ritchie's."

> "Ah'll have mine by June 15, sherrenough."

> "Take care o' them tomaters."

Not wanting to miss the action after his afternoon Pabst Blue Ribbon beers, Dad would go searching in the cobwebs, snakes, and dust under the washhouse and drag out his old splitting tomato stakes. His next step was to go searching for a kid to hold the stakes. Dad's system was to measure out the tomato garden with a line of string wrapped around various yardsticks and plant a few seeds with a stake in a pocket of dirt every ten inches apart in his makeshift grid. The way he would get the stakes in the winter hardened dirt was to whack them on the top with his trusty sledgehammer while one of his girls held the stake. No preliminary digging. Just a strong

>WHACK.

I was well aware of how little Dad valued girls. I knew what was coming when he started pacing around the back lot in the early springtime. I made myself scarce when he began wiping away the spider webs under the washhouse and looking for his tomato stakes.

> *"Okay, kids, who wants to help me with the tomatoes this year? It's going to be one special girl for sure!!"*

Poor Eileen chirped up,

> *"Oh, I do, I do, pick me, Dad. I want to help. I'll be your special girl."*

I tripped merrily off with George to find some mud puddles to jump in to break the thin spring ice. I heard the whack, whack in the distance. Then,

> *"Oh My God. I think I've killed her! GOD HELP ME!"*

Dad came rushing across the yard with Eileen in his arms. Her arms were dangling down, and her head was flopping back over his elbow. He took her to the back steps, sat down, and her head was gushing blood from a gash above her eye. Out cold.

Charlen and I ran to the steps. I was thinking, "Well, he's done it for sure this time." All of a sudden, she came to. Dad said,

>"Eileen, can I get you anything?"

She answered,

>"I need a cold beer."

After that Eileen could grab herself a beer whenever she wanted. And she did.

The bleeding finally stopped. The scar from the gouge on her forehead was there for a lifetime. Walking up to Doc Hungar's was only for real emergencies -- obviously broken bones and the like, but not for a gouge to the forehead on a girl.

Old Tar Brushes

The house was freezing in the winter and sweltering in the summer. Throughout the house there were all kinds of nooks and crannies for playing hide and seek, losing stuff, and hiding things.

The entire roof leaked all the time. When it snowed, the slush would, of course, melt on the roof and melt into the holes in the tar paper that covered the roof and trickle in little rivulets under the tar paper into the attic. The water would run along the rafters and seep into drip spots that were everywhere in the ceilings of every room. When it rained, there would be a faucet of dirty water running through the drip spots to the point where we put holes in the plasterboard of the ceiling for the gushing water so the ceiling would not fall in. Pans and buckets would be placed strategically all over the floors to catch the moldy water. The hounds would have a heyday lapping it up here and there.

In the spring, Dad and I would get the old wooden extension ladders out and set up a labyrinth of pulleys and clamps so we could hook the ladders to the sagging eaves of the roof and make the climb to the top of the second-story roof. We would take the old bucket full of tar we used for this project every year and melt it down over a fire in the yard so it was not quite boiling hot –just a spreadable sticky goo. Then we would get out the old tar brushes and loosen them up with the melting tar. Dad tried to get me to carry the hot buckets of tar up the ladder but I could not lift them, so I figured out how to work an old pully-up system to bucket the tar up to the roof.

> "Okay, okay, Francie, you can try your pully system, just be sure you don't dump that slimy stuff out on one of the hounds or that dumb mutt of yours."

Of course, my George was close by. But he was smart enough to stay away from hot tar. Some of the hounds were a bit too sleepy to move around.

I was Dad's helper in this job. I volunteered for this one every year because I could learn lots of stuff about roofs and water movement and study the bugs in the trees that lay across the top of our house ... not to mention perfecting my crude lift system.

Dad said he had to have a lightweight kid to do the tar spreading and tar mooshing because he was too heavy and he might fall through into the attic. I crawled around wiping the warm tar on the roof from early on. It was exciting being so high up and walking gently on the soft, squishy rooftop that had layer after layer of cracking tar. I could see the river winding through the valley from a different point of view.

George would sit patiently by the extension ladder base waiting for me to come back.

The tar job never seemed to do the trick though. The water seeping into the house and rank mold smells were part of our very being. The gooey black tar remains would be stuck to my toes throughout the summer, but it was usually worn off by the time school started in the fall and I needed to wear shoes.

Every year the roof and our existence seemed to shift toward oblivion. The house was always in a constant state of disrepair and deterioration.

Mama and Dad became indifferent.

12

IT'S A BOY

Mama had a brother for us in October of 1950. She was 34. They named him Walter Leonard Dillinger, Jr. We called him little Lenny. I got to see a penis firsthand. I asked Mama,

> *"What is the big deal with that penis? Did you and Dad want a boy so bad just because of that?"*

She answered,

> *"It is more complicated than that Francie, for one thing, boys are stronger..."*

I said,

> *"Mama, Dad is not stronger than you."*

Mom was happier than I had ever seen her. She would hold this chubby lump of drool at her breast and sing to him day and night, making up songs and bouncing him on her hip.

> "Cof-fee nerves, cof-fee nerves, what am I gonna do 'bout coffee nerves..."

He was a beautiful baby. Blond curls, giggles, and pudgy. We girls dressed him up in our old dresses and paraded him around town in the old perambulator our mama's mother and father sent from New York for the first child, Sara Charlen. Mama and Daddy convinced us, and we believed, that he was the anointed prince of our clan.

> "Well, Len Dillin'er finally got his boy, Yesseree, he finally did it."

The birth of little Lenny was most remarkable. It marked the beginning of some of our most difficult years. Aunt MaeMae and her financial support were gone. My parents had spent any extra money from Dad's share of the inheritance to buy a red Ford station wagon and in trying to make the duplex rental property a place to generate income. Mama and Dad had bills they never had before and, except for the sometimes rent on the duplex at 4 Penn Street that was yet to be completed, and the occasional rent that was supposed to be coming in from the ramshackle house next door at 1 Penn Street, there was no money coming into our house.

None. Zero.

Often, as an adult, I have had friends say to me,

> "We were really poor when I was growing up, but I never knew it then..."

I think to myself,

> "For GOSH SAKES. How does one 'not know' they are poor??"

I knew every waking moment that we were poor.

When Lenny was born, we got a mama goat, Nan, who had given birth to a kid. We called the kid Speedy. Mama and Dad wanted to be sure there was plenty of milk for their boy. I am sure we would not have gotten a goat if Mama had another girl. Speedy and little Lenny had plenty of milk, but Mama said,

> "Nan is just not a very good milk producer. The milk is not for the girls."

We girls didn't care. We never tasted goat milk. It didn't matter much, because we never had milk in the house anyway, other than some cans of milk Mama kept for her coffee.

We struggled through that winter in Aunt MaeMae's house. It was cold because Aunt MaeMae did not have a coal furnace. Just a small gas heater. But we got accustomed to it.

The Thunder

Mama and Dad argued, but they had a huge screaming match in the summer of 1951 when Lenny was 9 months old, yelling and shouting and huffing around. Both were bull-headed. The stress of never having enough money was a constant anvil on the chest of every member of the family. I was sick to my stomach thinking we would not have enough food.

At some point, after several ventures to make money, Dad gave up and started drinking beer and watching the river flow by as a full-time occupation. He refused to even try to find a job to bring money into the house, and Mama refused to work with four children in the family.

We were at a standstill.

Then the thunder rolled in. There was a dark cloud in the house from their constant snipping at one another. The tension was so tight I could feel it like an elastic band on my forehead. I looked at my older sister, Charlen, sitting quietly at the dining room table, staring at a stain on the wallpaper, swinging her long legs with her parakeet, Herbie, nestled in her pigtails. She caught my eye and slowly shook her head back and forth to me. She put her index finger up to her face quietly trying to tell me,

SHHHHHH.

We all knew not to make a sound when the thunder of Mama and Dad started rolling in the house. It would usually build up to this huge crescendo and

POW.

We would hear the sound of the big door slam, or something thrown, and then the long tight wire of silence.

We were fortunate that Mama and Dad never hit each other like some of the other families around. Of course, we kids were spanked hard, and the dogs got kicked, but they never broke bones or caused blood to run. I was grateful for that. I saw other kids walking around town with bruises and cuts that I knew did not come from a natural fall over a stone in the road.

Of course, the country women would be walking around town, absently staring into the bars or the VFW or the American Legion looking furtively for their ol' man. These women were always there . . . a sad undercurrent of Appalachian life. Missing teeth, bruises. Sometimes a limp. Always with a few barefoot children with running noses and matted hair in tow.

Our family lived with constant tension in the air. Every breath was a confirmation that life was tenuous and an angry snap was under the surface.

Mama lived in a bubble of her own and Dad lived in his. Usually, they were civil to one another, but one never knew what would be next.

This time it did not end.

13

NEW YORK CITY

That day, Mama got so mad she piled me, Eileen, and little Lenny into the station wagon and took off driving. She left Charlen at home with Dad. I think she packed some diapers for Lenny and two blankets, but nothing for the rest of us. We were frozen scared. Mama did not speak. She would mumble under her breath about every half hour or so,

"god-damn son-of-a-bitch..."

She had the front window down as she chain-smoked Lucky Strikes and blew the smoke out the window. Some of the smoke would circle back through the car and hit us smack in the face. The plastic seats of the car were sticky hot and stuck to my legs and arms. She had Eileen and me on each side next to the windows in the back seat with Lenny in the middle. When Lenny cried, she would pull over onto the berm of the road and nurse him until he fell asleep. She stopped a couple of times to get gasoline and buy a packet of peanuts and more Lucky's. She told us to pee in the weeds. We sat in silence and watched the telephone poles flip by the half-open windows. It was so hot I could feel the searing smoke from her cigarettes seeping into my skin as the ashes dropped onto the seat beside her.

After driving non-stop for a full day, we arrived without notice at Grandma and Grandpa's apartment. I had never been to New York City where my mother grew up. We drove across this huge bridge that day (I later found out it was the George Washington Bridge) and looking at the buildings touching the clouds on the other side of the river. Mama knew her way around New York City. Once we crossed the bridge, Grandma's apartment building was directly overlooking the Hudson River. Mama turned right onto Riverside Drive and parked our station wagon on the street.

"Come on OUT, you kids,"

she ordered.

I could see she was still fuming from her days' long shouting match with Dad. Out of the back seat, we tumbled onto the sidewalk. We had been in the same clothes for a day, and Lenny's diaper smelled like our sewer. I grabbed Lenny and carried him behind Mama. There was a man in a red coat standing on the sidewalk who opened the double doors to the massive building in front of us.

"Good afternoon, Miss Rathbun,"

he said.

Mama marched us through an ornate double entry with a ceiling higher than a coal tipple. We trailed after Mama across a shiny stone floor to a door. The floor was cool and slick - we were still in our bare feet. She pressed a button and there was this whirring sound. The door opened and another man dressed in a red suit opened the door from the other side,

"Oh, so nice to see you again, Miss Rathbun,"

Mama asked,

"Hello James, is my mother in?"

Mr. James answered,

"Oh yes, she just returned from one of her meetings."

We entered a cage that started up. My stomach took a turn. After we stopped on the tenth floor, we followed Mama out of the cage the man in the red suit was driving.

"That was your first elevator ride kids,"

Mama said over her shoulder. She changed Lenny's diaper on the slick floor when we got out of the elevator. Then she walked through the door at number ten, and announced in a loud voice,

"I am here."

Mama had come to New York unannounced.

My grandma was a gray-haired woman with a dress buttoned up from the hem to the neck with these tiny pearl buttons. She had on stockings and black shoes that were laced up to her ankles. As she came into the entry hall where the four of us were standing, she looked long and hard at Mama. Eileen and I stood behind Mama, who was holding Lenny in her arms, and he nuzzled against her chest wanting to suckle. It was our first meeting. I had never seen my mother's mother. Grandma did not even acknowledge me or my sister or brother. She did not seem to notice that Mama had brought three children with her.

"Well, come in. You'll have to wipe your feet."

Nodding toward the three of us, she said,

> "You take them into the maid's rooms and clean up."

After we wiped the travel grit from our faces and hands with a wet rag, Grandma sat us down at her kitchen table and gave Eileen and me an egg sandwich on toast and a big glass of lemonade. Delicious. She did not say anything to us as she stared at Eileen and me as we ate.

Then we followed Mama into a sitting room where her father was seated in a big brown chair with starched-stiff, white lace doilies on the arms and on the headrest. He had a head full of fluffy, cloud-like, white hair. A small trickle of drool was starting to make its way from the corner of his mouth to his chin.

Mama told us that her father had started having strokes the year before and could not see us well. She sat beside him and held his hand. He slept a lot during our visit, and he repeated over and over,

> "I am a firm believer in the fraternal system.
> I am a firm believer in the fraternal system.
> I am a firm believer in the fraternal system."

Mama would say to him in a soft kind voice,

> "Yes, I know, Papa."

I didn't know what that meant, but I figured it was something related to being in a sorority.

We stayed in that apartment for three days.

When Eileen and I would get up in the morning, Mama would give us a peanut butter spread on a white bread sandwich and send us to a park that was right across the big street from the building. We would press the button for the elevator and talk to Mr. James. He would say,

"You little girls going out all by yourselves?"

I would chirp up,

"Oh yes, Mr. James, we are always on our own."

Then he would say,

"You be careful crossing Riverside Drive."

The door attendant in the red coat would watch us cross the four-lane street they called Riverside Drive. The park was a patch of green grass running between the busy street and the river. There was a sandbox and some benches scattered around facing the river.

Mama and her mother screamed at each other all day and all night. Just constant screaming. In the middle of the third night, I heard my grandma say for the fourth time,

"You were the most wanted child in the world - no one wanted a child more than I did."

Mama,

"Mother, you just can't stop. You just keep it up and keep it up and keep it up, until I think I am going to…"

(This epitaph was something she often repeated to us kids or Dad when she got out-of-her-mind angry. None of us ever stuck around long enough to hear WHAT she thought she was going to…)

This was worse than listening to Mama and Dad scream at each other. Mama was not able to give up. Ever. She was stubborn and it seemed that her own mother was the same. Dad would walk away – but not Mama and NOT her mother.

It ended on Friday afternoon. During one of the drag-out screams, Mama said,

"That's it…"

14

DELAWARE

Mama gathered us up, threw us in the back seat of the car, and drove across the bridge to what I later found out was New Jersey. It was rush hour traffic in New York City. Hot, hot in that boiling car. Mama said we had no money. She drove a long way. We reached Delaware as the stars were starting to come out and she pulled up to an open beach, piled us out of the car and said,

"Okay kids, we are camping here."

I was only afraid because we had no money for anything. I was afraid we would starve for sure this time. She parked the car and we trekked with the two blankets she had thrown in the car as we left Point Marion to a spot between three small hills that Mama called sand dunes.

"Girls, go find some wood and I'll make a fire."

Mama always had matches to light her cigarettes. She had been a member of the Girl Guides in her youth, so she knew how to make a fire.

Delaware was big and sandy and hot and breezy. The sand was burning through our toes and the weeds poking out of the sand in tufts were sharp and thorny. Once we crawled up and over the sand dunes and into the hard-packed wet water sand, Eileen and I ran and danced and kicked up showers of sand. Unbelievable that people could walk freely on a huge open expanse without someone yelling at them - or broken glass strewn around to cut their feet into shreds - or dog poop and spit - or mud and water bugs to tiptoe around.

My first experience of the ocean was the noise. Roaring, roaring. There were outhouses scattered around and, every once in a while, there was a faucet with regular water available on a piece of cement.

The two blankets Mama had thrown into the car when we ran away from Dad were used for a tablecloth, for a beach towel, and for sitting. We were all alone on a starry night as the sand started to get cold, sitting on our blanket with our bare feet toward the fire, getting toasty.

Maybe because Mama told us to sing,

"*Bringing in the sheaves,*"

over the campfire she made, a minister and his family who had a tent on the other side of one of the dunes felt sorry for us and gave us some hot dogs. Mama was nursing little Lenny, so I supposed Lennie was okay. We never ate much anyway. The minister and his family sat around the campfire with us most nights. We would sing gospel songs that Aunt MaeMae had taught me, and the preachers wife taught us some other songs. I loved the singing. They shared their hot dogs and beans with us.

They had three children, three little girls.

Mama said,

"You just keep trying and you might get yourself a boy."

That minister said,

"Oh, we are so happy with our girls, we'd be blessed to have all girls!"

The minister's wife looked at me and smiled. This was some odd family. They were always smiling. The minister kept saying with this big teethy grin,

"This is the life!"

His wife wore a bathing suit with a skirt around it. She looked like a little round brown banty hen as she corralled her three little girls in a line here and there. Each of the little girls were dressed alike. They had blond curls over their ears and Mama said they had the

"Same stupid beam as that preacher."

I wanted to be around them. They were kind without reason.

We tucked ourselves into the sand at night around the campfire and Mama would pack sand around us so we would not get too cold. We swam in the ocean. One early morning while I was still in my sand-bed, a fancy lady wearing a dress, who was camping in a trailer on the other side of a dune, stepped hard on my head.

"Oh gracious, is that a child?"

Mama answered,

"Yes, by God damned, it is. Watch your step."

(She followed this up with *"stupid bitch"* under her breath.)

I don't think the fancy lady heard the last thing because she gave us some marshmallows and graham crackers. Maybe to make up for my smashed ear. We toasted them with sticks we found. They were the best thing I ever had. All gooey and sandy.

I liked the fancy lady. She even had this little white, fuzzy, yapper dog that chased after us in the waves of the ocean. The lady told me her name was Miss Elizabeth and she was camping with her husband, Mr. Bruce, in the trailer. I did not tell her that I didn't think she was really camping with the ice in a container box and the metal chairs they had.

After three weeks and a good deep tan, Mama piled us in the car and drove the 400 miles back to Point Marion. She and Dad never talked about the abrupt vacation we took. They were at a standoff after our trip to Delaware. Mama said she would not find a job until little Lenny was in first grade. Dad said he had a bad back and since he was nearing 40, no one would hire him. Besides, they gave all the good jobs to the men returning from the service.

> *"You know, Charlotte, I couldn't go to the service because of my bad eyes, it is not fair."*

One day after we returned from seeing Mama's mother and the trip to Delaware, it came to me that even a preacher's family had a good life when the dad worked. I was five and went to Dad,

> *"Dad, if you would just get a job, we would have food all the time and the house would be warm, and we could keep the car running. We could pay the water bill on time and Mr. Gladstone would not turn the water off. I could have a cancan slip to make my dresses stand out and swish when I walk. I could have a new pair of shoes to start school. We could go on vacations like the other kids. We could have presents at Christmas."*

Dad said,

> "No one will hire me."

Most of the time, my friends' dads worked. Point Marion was not a hotbed of employment opportunities, but most people scrounged for something. Meredith Stewart's dad worked at the power plant and sold vacuum cleaners and Watkin's products door to door. Cara Anset's dad sold cars at the local Ford dealership. Lester Schmidt's dad delivered furniture for Klein's Department Store. Mr. Packrone spent long, long hours at the newspaper store. Patsy Cino owned the beer distributorship. Mr. Carlier worked at the hardware store.

> "Dad?"

Gradually I realized that Dad would not ever work or provide for us.

I stopped expecting anything from him.

15

FIRST GRADE

The Point Marion Elementary School was at the top of the hill above the main town. My family lived next to the river down in the valley, so I had a long walk through town and up the hill to school. Mama slept late, so we three sisters would get ourselves up and dressed and begin the hurried trudge through town and up the hill to school. Charlen and I had been blessed with thick, strong hair. Mama braided our hair in the evening before bed. She would braid our thick hair as tight as she could so the stray hair would not shag out around our faces as we slept.

No chance of that.

> *"Mama, you are pulling my hair so hard, I can't see! I look like I am Chinese!"*

She would say with a laugh,

> *"Francie, you have to learn to suffer to be beautiful."*

I never felt beautiful.

Eileen's hair was a family problem. Her hair was thin and wispy and there was no way she could sustain a braid. The rubber bands would roll off the ends of her hair and disappear into the dirt. When she was in second grade, Mama decided that the only solution to Eileen's hair was to give her what we called "a poodle." Mr. Hunker at the drug store sold Mama a box called TONI. It had a picture of a happy woman with beautiful curly hair and two men smiling at her. Mr. Hunker said that would definitely do the job for the mystery of Eileen's hair.

A poodle was a tight home permanent that kinked up every strand of her hair into a big ball of fuzz. Long before afros were in vogue, Eileen set the pace with her own poodle. She sported a poodle for a long time. Years. We could smell Eileen coming with the pungent odor from the TONI box. We have pictures of the three of us, Charlen and me dutifully staring at the borrowed Brownie camera with a knife-straight part from the middle of our foreheads that defined our pigtails and Eileen in the center with her poodle. Always in various stages of kink.

Anyway, Mama said if we wanted to have something to hold us over until we walked home for lunch, we could make ourselves some toast and rub it with a stick of oleo. I never had much time for that. I would be tumbling out of our shared bed at the last minute and jumping into the clothes I had left on the floor.

Charlen was in the sixth grade, and she was a fast walker. She left the house after Eileen and me but passed both of us midway, along about Mr. Lockard's Service Station. Eileen would leave the house before me. She never wanted to have any of her friends see her with me, as she considered me a crud. After all, she was in third grade. I noticed that Eileen tried to walk differently from me and Sara when she was going to school. She and her friends had perfected a customized hip swagger that was impossible to imitate and reserved only for her clique.

"Now, Francie, don't hang around me. You go find your own friends."

Mrs. Wing, First Grade Teacher

After the wonderous Miss Berg in kindergarten, we were all looking forward to seeing each other again in the fall and enjoying another rollicking time learning our alphabet and maybe even learning to read. Cara was starting first grade, too, so we walked together in those early school days.

Point Marion School took up a full block on what we called School House Hill. There was a huge brick building with two floors for six classrooms each and a bottom floor for a gym, the high school library, and the principal's office. There were three separate wood buildings on the site for the band room, the boy's shop, the girl's home economics classes, and the cafeteria. There was also a blacktop playground with swings along a high stone wall. This was for recess.

Mrs. Wing was a strict mountain of a woman. We were to enter her classroom at a certain time, sit all day in our assigned seats, and never, ever talk to anyone. Talking was a huge offense for the forty-seven charges in her room. The only exception was after she would line us up for recess or lunch and march us outside. We were allowed to talk outside. (In hindsight, I can only think that the woman was simply overwhelmed by the crowd of children she was singularly assigned to teach. No teachers' aides, no PTA volunteers. Just her.)

Born at the start of the baby boom and being the largest class to enter Point Marion School at one time, we were the beginning of the elephant moving through the python that the world, and little Point Marion, would be forced to cope with. Almost every one of the daddies, (except mine of course), had been to war and come home in late 1945 or early 1946. Those who were healthy enough to father a child began families.

Our sled-like desks were lined up in five narrow rows of eight children per row facing Mrs. Wing's desk. The last row near the windows had seven desks. Our teacher had us sit in rows in alphabetical order starting with the As in the first desk on the left near the door. Cara Anset sat in that first seat. I was a few seats behind Cara, and Lelanda Franks sat behind me.

When she was not writing something on the slate blackboard and talking to the class, or sitting in a circle in a reading group, Mrs. Wing would say something like,

> "Now you first graders, open your readers to page eight and do the exercise."

Early in the year, most of us were pretty confused because we had only learned our alphabet and counting with Miss Berg. Some of the others had mamas or dads who read to them, but most of us had no idea what she was saying and were too afraid to ask. Then, she would troop up and down each row snapping her ruler, looking for one of us violating an edict.

Mrs. Wing did not smell like the spring flowers that wafted around Miss Berg. She stood tall with a gray bun of unruly hair clipped at her nape, and she wore navy blue or dark brown dresses buttoned so tightly around her huge bosom that the little shell buttons stretched open the buttonholes and a child sitting beneath that shelf could inadvertently see into her gray corset. Her long dress covered her knees. She kept her wire-rimmed glasses pinched to the middle of her nose. Her shoes had a medium heel laced up to her ankles so we could hear the

CLACK, CLACK, CLACK

of her steps on the wood floor as she patrolled us. When she stood next to me, I could see the long hairs on her legs all tangled under the nylon stockings she wore. She was like a dark shadow hulking over me. I figured she must have been warm and uncomfortable in the get-up she wore every day.

I was obedient because I was afraid of the crush of her ruler on the back of my hands. She demonstrated the use of the dreaded ruler on Donald Snider on the first day of school as a demonstration for the rest of us because his mind didn't make him pay attention to much of anything. I noticed this in kindergarten. Miss Berg had given Donald special time, ever so gently wiping the drool from his ever-draining lower lip with the ironed hanky she tucked into her pocket. But Mrs. Wing used this to her advantage.

She was watchful for any transgression. She had various punishments that would be doled out to us:

> A whack on the knuckles for not paying attention.
> Sitting in a chair in the hall outside the classroom for talking.
> Then there was the threat of going to the principal's office. No one was sure how that would work, but the way she said it was scary.
>
> *"And you, Freddie Lockard! You will end up in the principal's office if you don't start talking louder when I call on you!"*

We all perked up when we heard her scold Freddie, who was about the meekest kid in the class. He was quiet and kind. Poor Freddie, he stared at the nonexistent spots on his shoes.

I thought to myself,

> *"Egads, if she is going to pick on Freddie, NO ONE is safe."*

He was neatly dressed and had his hair slicked over with gooey shiny stuff. Freddie was an only child. He was naturally shy and never talked loudly. His mama dressed him in pastel blue colors and ironed creases in his shirts and pants. I would sometimes see him uptown in Point Marion, hand in hand with his mama on one side and his daddy on the other. The three of them walked together, carefully watching as they crossed the streets.

George and I would skip past them, and I would say,

> "Hello ma'am, hello Mr Lockard, hi Freddie."

Even though George was a mutt, he had a good nose. As he passed Mrs. Lockard, he would lift his nose in the air and take a deep breath of her sweet rosewater perfume that followed her everywhere like a parasol.

I once heard Mrs. Lockard say,

> "That child should not be out traipsing around town on her own, why she doesn't even have shoes on. Harrumph. I see. She's one of those Dillinger girls."

I heard Mr. Lockard say,

> "Now Elizabeth."

The Sunoco Gas Station

Freddie's dad owned the Sunoco gas station at the corner of Penn Street and Morgantown Street. Mr. Lockard kept that station neat as a pin. He wore a uniform every day with the words SUNOCO on the left shirt pocket. He was a happy, friendly person.

One Saturday, George and I spent the afternoon learning how he ran his gas station. We sat on the pile of Dunlop tires he had for sale behind his "Special This Month Only" sign. When he had a break in dealing with his customers, Mr. Lockard explained to me about the big trucks that came to his station and filled up the underground tanks below his pumps, the way he calculated how much gasoline he received in his underground tanks, how much he sold, and how he checked and double-checked the amounts in his underground tanks.

There was a black hose filled with air that ran across the ground at both entrances of his station. When a car pulled into Lockard's Sunoco, it automatically ran across this black hose. Mr. Lockard had the hose hooked up to a bell that was right near his desk and at the car lift on the side of his garage.

PING. PING. PING.

Rain or shine, Mr. Lockard (always smiling), would march out to his pumps and say,

"How do, Missus Engle, would you like a fill up?"

He would happily wash the windows, check the oil and radiator water, and check the tire pressure. There were no credit cards in those days, but all the store owners in Point Marion had a credit system for Point Marion people.

"Shall I put that on your account?"

"Oh, thank you, Mr. Lockard. Goodbye!"

At the end of every month, on their payday, people were supposed to settle up with each of the business owners. Of course, my family never had a payday or an account. Everyone knew Dad never paid off any bills.

16

TIME OUT

There was a dreaded day in October when Mrs. Wing said one of her,

"First graders, turn your readers to page..."

OH NOO, I didn't hear the page! I hurriedly turned around to Lelanda and said too loudly,

"Whaat page?"

Before I knew what was happening, I was grabbed by the scruff of my neck and pushed outside the classroom.

"Now you sit on that chair until recess!"

The hallway was empty and cool. I sat alone quietly on that hard chair for what seemed like an eternity. All the other six classes were in session or at recess. A bell rang and all the sixth graders marched past from recess. Someone said,

"Charlen, isn't that your sister?"

My sister walked by my chair and stared at me. Then I heard a teacher's voice say,

> "Oh, that's a Dillinger girl. She must be a problem."

I could feel the hot waves of flush starting in my stomach and quickly moving to a ringing in my ears. I put my hands on my face and felt the seeping tears and the slobber coming out my nose. My mouth made this high-pitched squeaky sound. I was in full-blown blubber-shudder. I put my face in my lap and wiped up the drip drool tears as best I could figure out. I didn't want to be there. But I was.

Pretty soon, another bell rang, and the first-grade door opened. My classmates began walking out in single file. No one looked at me. At the end of the line was Mrs. Wing,

> "Okay, Francie, you can go to recess."

I tumbled down the steps to the playground and found a bench to sit on. Alone. My classmates would not come up to me for fear of the watchful eye of Mrs. Wing thinking they were sympathetic to me.

At dinner that night, Charlen said,

> "Hey Francie, what were you doing sitting in the hall outside first grade?"

Before I could say a word, Eileen said,

> "Francie, YOU were put into the hall? How COULD you do that to me! Don't say hi to me if you see me at school ever again!"

I said,

> "But Mrs. Wing is just a mean person. She's not nice to anyone! She even scolded Freddie Lockard!"

I looked at Mama and Dad and said,

> "Can't you guys do something to make her be nicer?"

They both laughed. Dad said,

> "Get used to it Francie."

Mama said,

> "There's lots of people like that out there, you just have to deal with it…"

Charlen said,

> "Just wait till you get to Mrs. Ratchet's class. She paddles everyone."

I asked,

> "Mama, if this is how school is, with teachers making kids cry and spanking them all the time, I don't want to go."

Mama answered,

> "That's life. Just get used to it."

By wintertime, I was thinking Mrs. Wing was getting frazzled with her large group of charges. Her voice was shriller, and her stockings were bagging. The stocking seam in the back of her legs was crooked these days, and the bun of her hair was wispier than ever. Her face was flushed red in patches. Of late she had been threatening us with,

> "You will be sitting in the coatroom if you do not behave."

The word *behave* was fairly nebulous for a group of forty-seven five- and six-year-olds.

There was one incident that resonated with all of us. One day during the winter, Mrs. Wing easily sneaked up behind Kenny Murray who had whispered or snickered to Lester Schmidt. Suddenly, she grabbed him by the ear and dragged him with much aplomb into the coatroom that adjoined our classroom.

Once she had Kenny in the closet, she closed the door and left him in that dark musty space with galoshes, mittens, winter hats, and heavy snow-melted coats. The closet had accordion folding doors that could be completely opened for us to hang up our outside coats and boots and mittens and scarves. But it could also be solidly shut without a sliver of light and any circulation of air. Even I was afraid of being sealed into that closet.

We could hear Kenny sniffing inside. We were terrified. At recess, the coatroom door was opened and there was Kenny sitting on the floor in a puddle of urine. Mrs. Wing sent him home in a huff.

The next day Kenny Murray's dad came to see Mrs. Wing. We were all sitting dutifully at our individual desks with our hands folded in front of us. Mr. Murray marched into the classroom without a knock – he swung the door open. We were all shocked. I could hear the breath go in and out of Cara sitting in front of me. Mr. Murray slammed his hands on Mrs. Wing's desk. He had on combat boots and was looking stern.

> "Madam, you will see me out in the hallway. NOW!"

Mrs. Wing was shaking. She said,

> "Class, put your heads on your desk until I return."

We did.

Mrs. Wing was never mean to Kenny Murray again.

I told Dad what happened, and he said,

> "Well, Roger Murray jumped on Corregidor. No one should ever upset that man."

I liked Mr. Murray. I wished my dad had jumped on Corregidor.

The tyranny of Mrs. Wing went on with our class and every class until she finally retired. I did learn my numbers and reading. Most of all I learned to keep my head down and I survived first grade.

POLTERGEISTS, BANSHEES AND APPARITIONS

The entire area of Appalachia is layered smack dab on one of the oldest mountain ranges of the world. For thousands of years, it was inhabited by marauding groups of native people who treasured the verdant valleys and mountains and had a spiritual connection to the God-given earth. No human owned the earth or any chunk of it.

From time immemorial the land was considered a living, spiritual, evolving treasure that people could commune with and use for protection. It would sustain life. The native people believed their charge from the divine spirit was to repay the land with caring and to reverently secure it for future generations. Their souls are embedded in the earth that their bodies occupied for thousands of years. This reciprocal system worked well for the ancient people and the land.

Three hundred years after the white settlers arrived, through every means imaginable, the people of origin disappeared and, to a large extent, the settlers laid waste to much of the land.

Other than the Indian burial mounds in the craggy hills surrounding Point Marion, or the occasional find of a finely chiseled arrowhead stone on the banks of the river or caught between the stones in the scum of a stream rushing toward the river, there is no physical trace of the people who inhabited the region for millenniums.

But their sacred souls remain.

> In the soft summer breezes.
> In the sunlight shimmering on a crest of the river.
> Whistling through flaming leaves on an autumn day.
> In booming cracks of thunder and electric jags of sizzling lighting in the midst of a calm humid day.

Always present. Standing as an eternal sentinel. In the shadows.

Some believe the curse of the current residents of Appalachia is emanating from spirits of the cruelly displaced native Indian people who historically inhabited and nurtured the land. Reaching through the invisible shield of time and strangling the life and spirit of today's inhabitants. . .these are the entities that thrive in the shadows of darkness. At times, malicious phantoms that torment the living, or maybe (if you're lucky) the spirit of a loved one watching over you

Banshees and Apparitions

One legend of the mountains is that the more spiteful banshees and apparitions bring with them . . .

. . . The curse of addiction
> To alcohol, tobacco, drugs, and so many others of life's temptations.

... The curse of mental illness

> The diseases of despair that permeate the life blood of every community, often manifested by suicide, murder, beatings, and bullying.

... The curse of poverty

> The circular never ending "spiral toward the drain" that plagues the day to day existence of so many.

Family Poltergeists

Dad was always looking for recruits in the ranks of his girls to participate in one of his hair-brained schemes to do something he would never do.

The house was old and creaky, and there were plenty of ghosts. Dad said they were friendly family ghosts so not to worry. Sometimes I would hear them screaming in the wind off the river, trying to get inside the house. When I lay quietly waiting for sleep, I would hear them walking around the room or creaking the floorboards on the stairs as they went about patrolling the old homestead. The area around the washhouse was a favorite haunt, as the old well had poisoned (with typhus) several of our ancestors in the late 1890s. Sometimes they would bounce around the little shed with a mysterious light.

We would be in the living room, and I would hear a ghost at the front door.

SCREEEECH.

> *"Dad, what is that noise?"*

> *"Oh, it's just a Poltergeist."*

> *"A Poltergeist? I am afraid!"*

> "Oh, don't be, I think it's just your Great Grandpa trying to get warm."

> "But it isn't warm in here! We are all so cold."

When I was in second grade, Dad called all of us girls together.

> "I have a really big job for whoever wants to help me. This is really important for our whole family. I need one of you lighter girls to do this. And I am paying a quarter!"

That left Charlen out. She was thin and wiry, but she was 13. I started to slink back because he had called us into his bedroom, a place we rarely entered, and the closet door was opened leading to the attic above.

I knew the Poltergeists hung out up there.

Eileen said,

> "Oh, Dad. Let me. Pick me."

This was AFTER the sledgehammer incident.

Charlen and I stuck around to see what could possibly be worth a quarter. Seems Dad had dropped a jewelry box full of important things down an interior chimney that was inside the attic which was inside the roof.

He said he was hiding it . . .

The roof was a mystery of its own. The story goes that sometime around 1900, Dad's grandpa decided to fix the roof. Instead of tearing it apart and fixing it, he somehow had parts of a new roof built over parts of the old roof, and he vaulted over the old chimney. Tar paper covered the newer roof and gobs of tar was used each year to fill and flow over and into the cracks as best it could. The attic was a crawl space that could be accessed only from the tiny three-foot by three-foot opening in the ceiling of the one-pole closet in Mama and Dad's bedroom.

Dad was always hiding things. I never could figure it out. We never locked our doors and we sometimes put the hook on the screen doors when we went to bed. So, who was he hiding anything from?

> "Now, Eileen, I will have to hold you by your ankles, upside down, for just a while in the attic and inside that chimney. All you have to do is grab that jewelry box. Now, Francie, you get up there and shine the flashlight down the chimney."

Eileen had tears. I could read her eyes,

> "Is this what I need to do to have Dad love me?"

I was thinking, "Whaat? I did not volunteer for any job. I hate that attic. It is more than black. It is pitch. I have heard the poltergeists up there while I am in my bed at night. It is smelly, dank, and moldy, and there are huge spiders. I would have to hunch down on a rafter making myself as tiny, teeny as I could in this space between the roof and the joists while Eileen is held upside down by someone who whacked her with a sledgehammer last spring? And then she would have to reach for some box full of something?"

> "Okay, France, here's the flashlight, don't drop the flashlight, and when I tell you to turn it on and point it, do it! And don't move around once you get on that board up there, I don't want anything else dropping down that chimney."

I was thinking . . .

"WHAT ABOUT ONE OF YOUR GIRL CHILDREN?!"

He grabbed me and lifted me above his head and pushed me into the attic through that minuscule hole in the ceiling of his closet. I couldn't breathe. It was pitch dark and damp and creaking. I couldn't even see my bare feet. I held onto the flashlight. I felt something crawl across my toes.

> "Now don't turn the light on till I tell you. Don't you go wasting any of that juice that's left in the battery. Okay, Eileen, here you go."

Eileen was white. He pushed her up through the opening and she was in the attic with me. I was hunched down as far as I could, so I didn't take up any room. Dad folded up his long, thin frame and squeezed himself into the space to the left of me. He squatted down and grabbed Eileen's ankles.

> "Okay, Eileen, I got you, start head down the chimney. Francie, you turn on the flashlight and aim it at her head."

> "Do it now . . ."

Luckily, Eileen's poodle had recently been clipped so her hair was not too bushy and in the way. My hands were dripping sweat on the heavy metal flashlight, but I held onto it and pointed straight down. Eileen slithered her head down into the interior chimney. The old bricks were not even and the cement between them was sloping to the inside of the chimney. It was thick with black dust and old spider webs.

Eileen said,

> "I feel something, Dad."

> "Grab it."

> "Okay, pull my ankles up."

"*I am going to bring you up now.*"

She was shaking and black all over. The frizz of her hair was dripping old black spider webs, hanging in globs. She handed Dad a lidded box the size of a writing tablet and as deep as two pencil boxes. He grabbed the box and squeezed out of the opening and into his room. Eileen followed him and then me. Dad reached into his pocket and handed her a quarter. Without a word, Dad went downstairs with his box. Eileen went into the bathroom, and I went outside to take a run with George.

Later, Eileen said she was going up to Barney's Theatre and spending her quarter on *Godzilla* and popcorn. George and I walked her to Barney's.

"*You sure are brave Eileen.*"

"*I know.*"

The attic poltergeists went back to loudly moving things around in the night.

THUMP. BUMP. SCREECH. SCRATCH.

18

PAYING BILLS

I was nearly seven years old, walking uptown across the street from Doc Hungar's office. The sidewalk was uneven and the weeds growing up through the cracks would trip me if I was not careful. My baby brother, Lennie, was three and a handful for me. He refused to hold my hand. When something interested him, he would walk to it, no matter where he was. If he was in the middle of the street, he would flick my hand away and start rushing to whatever he wanted to see. It was not unusual for him to stop in the middle of the street and yell at the top of his lungs until I grabbed him up and carried him to the other side.

He wanted to go to Sadler's store and look at the little metal stamped cars that were lined up in the small toy car-sized cubby holes on the child-sized shelves. They had wheels that turned and were painted bright colors. Whenever Lennie wanted a little car for his collection, Mama found the ten cents needed. He kept a shoebox full of little metal cars under his bed.

Mama said,

> "Here Francie, take this dime up to Sadler's and let your brother pick out a car. Keep him busy for the afternoon, I have to sit for a while."

The gray smoke haze from the Camel she was puffing encircled her head. She was sitting, with her feet in the metal washtub, under the pungent blossoms of the magnolia tree in our yard, facing the river. The hose was looped over the edge of the tub, filling it with cool water. Mama was coughing and staring idly at the river 100 yards away, watching George take his afternoon swim in the muddy river below. Unlike the hounds who had sleek, naturally close-cropped hair, George was burdened with the heavy thick fur of a mongrel.

It was a sweltering hot mid-August day. The mist was rising off the river as the sun beat down on it. The moisture in the air made waves of vapor to the point that, no matter what direction I looked, my eyes were blurry from the thick steam in the air.

On this hot muggy afternoon, I was trying to get Lennie to hold my hand so I could cross the street with him toward Sadler's. We were standing at the curb, watching for cars.

> "Come on Lennie, Let's recite the STOP, LOOK and LISTEN, BEFORE WE CROSS the STREET..."

We never wore shoes in the summer and the sidewalk was burning our feet. Lennie and I walked in the cool grassy area between the sidewalk and the street curb. Our biggest fear was stepping on a bumblebee or one of the dreaded wasps that made their mud packed honeycombs in the wet rotting rafters of the craggy buildings. Of course, I was trying to avoid dog droppings in the grass and keep Lennie out of it. Cleaning his toes after a wayward step in the smelly dog mush was my job. I was navigating Lennie through the cool grass when Doc Hungar came up behind us, tapped me on the shoulder, and said,

> "You tell your daddy that he still owes me money for delivering your brother."

From then on, Doc would stop me whenever he saw me and say,

"Now Francie, I expect to be paid. Did you tell him?"

Dad was known for not paying his bills. I felt ashamed. I hung my head and nodded,

"Yessir."

I could not speak any further. My words got caught in my throat. I liked Doc Hungar. It was not right that Dad would not pay him.

The first time Doc Hungar stopped me, I told Dad that he wanted to be paid for delivering Lennie. I told Dad that Doc Hungar was waiting for me and I would run the other way whenever I saw him, but Dad would burp loud and say,

"That ol' Son-of-a-Bitch."

"But Dad, you have to pay him. Lennie is growing up and you owe him."

"Harummmph."

I never could understand why Dad seemed to feel entitled to not pay his way.

Doc Hungar

Doc Hungar lived in a big brick house on the corner of Main and Penn Streets. His office was in his house with an entry on the side. People could make an appointment or walk into the waiting room, sign their name on a list, and sit down. A bell was attached to the entry door and Doc would come out of an interior room when he was done with the patient he was seeing.

He would see the next person who had signed in on the list or whoever was screaming or bleeding the most. His office smelled of strong mercurochrome mixed with ammonia. He did not have an assistant or a nurse, and he told each patient how much to pay him when he was done. People paid with cash, but he accepted goods sometimes from the poorest people who had no cash. A couple bottles of homemade wine, a bottle or two of moonshine, a bushel of corn, or even some canned tomatoes would do. There was no insurance. Doc made sure people understood he expected to be paid.

He delivered babies in homes all over the town and the township. He sewed up gashes, set broken bones, and pronounced people dead. He mixed up his own remedy poultices for folks, dispensed pills, and mixed antibiotic injections of all kinds. I was fascinated to watch Doc Hungar work in his backroom. He used a Bunsen burner to test urine. He even had an old hand-crank centrifuge machine so he could spin down bodily fluids and smash them onto a piece of glass and look at it under his small microscope.

Mama only took us to see Doc Hungar if we were bleeding and she could not get the hemorrhage to stop. Otherwise, she figured we would get better on our own. We did. On the rare occasion one of us needed to be stitched up or needed a boil lanced that Mama could not manage herself, I would make it my business to tag along so I could watch Doc Hungar work.

Doc usually mixed up his own medicine powders with a hand pestle and ceramic bowl and filled his own little white paper packets with his remedy. Sometimes he sorted through his cabinet for some big fat white pills. Mr. Hunker, the town pharmacist who had a drug store on the corner of Penn and Railroad Streets, kept a stock of apothecaries to fill prescriptions that Doc himself could not concoct. If Doc wanted Mr. Hunker to dispense a special potion, he would scribble out some scratch marks on a small paper and direct his patient up the street to Mr. Hunker.

There was another doctor in town who had an office on Main Street. Doc Waystinger was known to be an excellent doctor, but he developed a problem with moonshine. He spent most of his waking hours teetering on a bar stool at Augie's Beer Garden telling loud long dissertations on the evils of the world. He eventually had to give up doctoring.

Mama said that Doc Waystinger was supposed to help deliver me. She had Charlen run to his house when she was in full labor, but Doc Waystinger never showed up. He was too drunk to walk the quarter mile down the street to our house. Mama said she decided to change to Doctor Hungar with the next baby anyway. She said Doc Waystinger could only deliver girls and she wanted a boy.

Doc Hungar delivered our brother Lennie four years after I was born. Dad was beside himself. He thanked Doc Hungar over and over again and claimed throughout town that to get a boy, Doc Hungar should do the delivery! Getting a boy did not seem to make any difference in whether Dad would pay. Dad and Mama had a problem paying bills.

Most of the people who lived in Point Marion had an account with the store owners, the gas stations, Doc Hungar, and the like. I would watch the store owners write what the Point Marion family member got, give the person a slip of paper with the cost and what the person received, and on payday, the dad would go to the business and settle up. Maybe because our family had no payday, we had no account with anyone.

The Water Bill and Christmas

The water bill was a huge problem for our family. Mr. Gladstone owned the water company that channeled water through a mishmash of old iron, lead, and clay pipes to every house in Point Marion. His wife, Mrs. Gladstone sent a water bill every month by US Mail to every house in Point Marion. Every person was to pay their bill each month or Mr. Gladstone would have their water turned off at the street.

Mid-December, when I was seven, Mr. Gladstone turned the water off to our house. He said we had not paid our water bill for a long, long time and he was not going to turn our water back on until Dad caught up on the payments. No water to drink, cook with, flush the toilet that drained into the river, or take a bath. The standoff went on with Dad and Mr. Gladstone until Christmas Eve. Dad somehow got the payment caught up in the nick of time and we had running water for Christmas day.

> *"There won't be any Christmas this year kids, that damned Gladstone took our money for his water bill."*

Christmas wasn't so bad. We made decorations with rings of paper glued together with homemade glue (flour and river water and old wallpaper paste). We made little figurines with flour and rainwater, let them dry on the windowsill, and then painted them with food coloring.

Dad and Mama used newspaper to wrap things they had owned in what they called their heyday and gave them to us for Christmas.

> Charlen got a typewriter that Dad had used in college.
> I got a microscope that Mama had in college.
> Eileen got Dad's genuine hand carved wooden polo mallets and polo balls.
> Mama and Dad bought some new toy trucks for Lennie.

Mama had two other treasures from her heyday that she said kept her from going crazy. She had a 2.5-carat diamond engagement ring she wore most of the time and a wedding ring that was encircled with small cut diamonds. Throughout our growing up years, when we were on the brink of despair, Mama would go to Morgantown to a pawn shop and hock her diamond.

These times were sad for her because she was worried that she would not be able to get her ring back out of hock. Somehow, she always did.

Living on the edge and running from creditors was a way of life. I was worried that we would not be able to survive from one day to another.

Doc Hungar never stopped asking to be paid and Dad never paid him for delivering Lennie.

19

POLLUTION, CONTAMINATION, SCORN

Air Pollution

The struggling and naive town of Point Marion lies in the belly of the Appalachian corridor, in the southernmost region of Fayette County, Pennsylvania bordering West Virginia.

As of 1930, over 942 million tons of coal were mined in Fayette County alone. That calculates to 414 million tons of waste sitting around one remote and forgotten Pennsylvania county. The coal industry has continued for decades without any regulation.

Daily survival is paramount when there is no personal security and family despair is the cloud that hangs over every breath. Taking care of the earth for future generations has never been more than a politician's "thump" word.

The town of Point Marion seemed to be more of a reluctant recipient of the resulting spoil of the coal industry and an observer of the coal commerce than a participant. People came looking for jobs and prosperity and were left scraping for food and living in poverty and pollution.

Slag Heaps

Coal refuse piles are scattered across the landscape next to communities, rivers, and streams. Sometimes filling entire valleys. The towering slag heaps were the waste from the coal that was left after the rich bituminous coal was pulled out of the ground and then hauled away by truck, riverboat, or rail car. The shale would sit in a pile as big as a small mountain.

These sky-high mounds of left-over debris from coal extraction sites, both historically and currently, may catch fire as smoldering, oxygen-starved combustion mountains. A by-product is the production of noxious gas from the generation of steam coming from the moisture in the coal refuse. Slowly, as the fire continues to develop, avenues for oxygen migration through the refuse pile expand. This results in flames. Combustion of coal refuse allows uncontrolled toxic air pollutants and caustic gases to be emitted into the atmosphere. The acrid smoke hangs over Point Marion and the surrounding townships and is accepted by the people as just another day in the cloudless sky.

The waste from the spoils left by all types of coal mining is everywhere. Red dog was the main ingredient for roads throughout the coalfields. This road material is a strong shiny red stone that is a byproduct of the huge slag heaps that surrounded every coal town. Once some of the slag had burned down, it would turn into red chips, called red dog, which could be shoveled onto a road to hold down the dust and mix with the road mud and grease.

Acid mine drainage forms when rain and groundwater absorb the metals. Compounds in the waste, disturbed by mining, flow out of the hills, trickling in and out of the nooks and crannies of the woods. The town was overrun with the coal dust dropped from three main sources:

1. The regular long train open coal cars that sped north through town several times a day.
2. The constant rumbling of open bed coal trucks hauling coal on the potted crumbling streets through town from the small mines in the hollows that winnowed into Route 119. This was the only direct north-south highway, and it ran directly through town without a stop sign. Point Marion had no stoplights.
3. The six to eight barges of coal being pushed up the river more than ten times a day in open heaps at a steady clip.

To add to the pollution, most people had a cigarette dangling from their crusty lips as a means to alleviate their own inherent depression.

The air in the creases of the mountains where the rivers, schools, towns, and roads were concentrated was caught in a labyrinth of circular flow: from the ground to the low-hanging clouds, then back to the ground. A yellowish gloom settled above the people and buildings, from the open coke ovens less than a few miles away near Nilan, at Smithfield crossing, and at nearby Outcrop and Martin. Additionally, in the fall and winter, the coal-fired furnaces in nearly every building spewed heavy smoke and coal particles on any object with angles or surfaces large enough to accommodate a piece of grime. A mist of black dust would hang between the hills and obscure the clouds and blue sky, then soak into the fiber of the town and its folk.

Water Contamination

To add to the ever-growing problem of the contaminated water supply, small towns often had town sewers that dumped into the rivers through the storm drains running on the side of roads on the natural decline from the hills to the riverbanks. This water ran green into the river, and one could see gobs of toilet paper and other waste at the water's edge. Flies and roaches swarmed at the mouth of every sewer. For those dwellings along the river, the sewage ran directly into the river; sometimes several houses would combine into a bigger sewer.

The slag heaps from the countless abandoned coal pits and stripped areas also seeped pungent debris into the shoreline. Sulfur creeks were full to the brim with the acid drainage from the hundreds of long-abandoned coal mines. The creeks emptied their toxins into the Monongahela as it marched north to Pittsburgh.

The Scorned Earth

Long before big coal arrived in the coal fields with massive operations that mechanized full-scale mountain-top removal, smaller "strip" mines operated throughout the region. This system of coal extraction was used for generations in the areas around Point Marion. Even at the present time, the overall coal industry is both the adored and often scorned mistress of the people who are trapped by their own culture in the nooks and crannies of the ancient mountains.

The 1,500-mile-long Appalachian mountain chain, birthed in Georgia and winnowing out in Canada, holds in its belly the richest seam of primeval coal in America. This craggy string of peaks and valleys is one of the oldest on the planet. Yet, over the years, the sellout to mining of the environment in the Appalachian corridor has literally changed the landscape, as well as the water and air. The ecosystem is permeated by the leaching effects of coal waste. For every ton (2,000 pounds) of coal, there are 881 pounds of waste left on the land. That is 44% of the mined coal.

By the time the 1950s rolled around, there were few factory jobs, and those that were available paid subsistence wages. The huge glass factory buildings along the river in Point Marion were decaying and in disrepair. Only a few areas of the factory were irregularly occupied. On the street leading to the factory near the Point Marion ball park, there was a spot where there were huge mounds of colored and clear glass pieces that had been dumped over the years. These blobs of once molten glass were the waste and ends from the factory discards. They were not sharp or splintered because long exposure to the elements had smoothed them. They were all sizes and shapes, ranging from the size of a marble to the size of a baseball. It was a colorful mass of fascinating light-catching glimmer that anyone could kick through.

Like so many other remnants of the once bustling Appalachian economy, the huge, abandoned factory buildings along the riverbank sit rusting and decaying in the boiling sun and dripping cold. They are ever so slowly eaten through and engulfed in the weeds and growth of the brush as the dirt reclaims them into the scorned earth.

It seems that every industry in the Appalachians has been given a "get out of jail free" card as they grabbed their profits and left their waste for the devastated and impoverished remaining people to deal with. The gasping hulk of the decaying Point Marion Glass Factory is one more testament to the accepted "grab and go" of the mountains.

A Rude Awakening

An aerial view of the region's polluted air of the region is a shocking display of pock-marked exposed rock, orange-tinted sludge ponds, and winnowing creeks of the yellowed water of acid mine drainage, and monstrous slag heaps of smoking rock. All are the result of coal waste.

Of course, the people in the valleys have not had the luxury of a bird's eye view. The families below in the deep valleys are too busy with the day-to-day, never-ending, soul-sapping job of survival to give much thought to the land. The coal companies made sure the true impact and enormous volume of the devastation to the environment was hidden behind a strategic remaining tree line or weedy patch near the roads most traveled. Now that satellite imagery is available, it is a rude awakening for those able to comprehend the impact of the decades-long trade-off.

The sad crush on the surroundings is only a shadow of the devastating monster on the horizon of the health consequences of life in the mountains. The water is polluted, the air is contaminated, and the earth is scorched. The work of those who depend upon the strength of their bodies to survive often leaves them old before their time. The people of the mountains "live sick."

Today there are 3,400 miles of polluted waterways in Pennsylvania alone. And no one much cares...

20

STEWARTSTOWN ROAD

Stewartstown Road was a winding dirt road circling south out of Point Marion toward West Virginia. It was dotted with shacks and weeds and a squalid, putrid, mine-runoff stream crisscrossing the rocky potted way. It sometimes flooded the road, but most times it meandered along the crevasse of the berm, staining the rocks and mud with orange sulfur slime.

Stewartstown was a grouping of ten or twelve ramshackle places where people mostly survived. The folks lived day-to-day on meager welfare if they had Aid to Dependent Children (ADC). Otherwise, no welfare, no money.

The Stewartstown Road people had everything that could not fit into their shacks strewn around the open thorny weeded yards, overgrown with knee-high weeds with rusted objects sticking out. A broken toy tricycle, an old rowboat with a big hole in it, a decaying bathtub with rainwater for the dogs, the 1945 motor from the last old Chevy that someone took out and replaced with a Ford engine, and even an old refrigerator on its side collecting rainwater and mosquitoes. Timeworn sofas and chairs were put outside when something better was found on the curb in town. There was so much trash and rust and weeds and bugs that it was hard to tell one dwelling from another. Dad said the folks there were all related to each other anyway.

And everywhere dogs. Coon hounds mostly. The bitches and young males would be chained up with a slip collar on a stray piece of rusting junk. The puppies and old dogs stayed around chomping at flies in the sun. The puppies, not wanting to leave their mama, tried to stay under any porch. And the old hounds were too tired to move.

The snow and wet and leftover salt that was laid on the road to melt the ice by the highway department was harsh on the cars. Every car owned by people who did not have fancy white-walled tire cars, like the rich folks, had rust holes eating away the metal all over the wheel wells, fenders, and doors. The rust holes were so sharp they could slice up someone's legs if they walked too close to any vehicle.

The men did odd jobs and picked up things around the county, drove beat-up pick-up trucks or cars without doors on them, and drank. To keep the welfare checks coming, the women stayed home and had babies.

Tempers would run wild with the men when the welfare check came and there was money for booze. A day or two after check day, we would see one or two women from Stewartstown sitting at the long-deserted railroad steps in Point Marion with a nosebleed, eyes black and blue, accompanied by her confused and dirty children. Just stunned. No words.

Mama would say,

> "Well, she made her bed, now she has to sleep in it."

I was afraid for the railroad ramp women who sat on those steps. Some of them were girls with one, two, and three grimy little children standing quietly beside them. The little children were barefoot, had runny noses, and played in the coal dust and coke cinders that settled around the railroad ties. Big blue watery eyes, flushed faces, and streaks of coal dust all over their bodies.

The Stewartstown Road folks had no inside running water, just outhouses. There were dirty clothes hanging on the many lines draped from trees, or old non-identifiable long, weathered objects strewn about the yards outside the shacks. Most of the houses had some sort of rigged-up attachment to the power lines that ran parallel to the pocked dirt road and looped through a window to energize a radio or old flickering television.

Every few years, the highway department would scatter some red dog stone chips so the school bus and the mail carrier could navigate the potted dirt road. After the red dog was scattered, it was risky to go more than three miles an hour due to the spattering of the stones. Sometimes, when a new Democrat Assemblyman was elected to the Pennsylvania State House, there would even be a fresh batch of black tar sprinkled on the road to keep the dust down.

The shacks were randomly dotted along the road. The Cawley family lived in a two-room shack a mile or so south of Point Marion up Stewartstown Road near the Mason Dixon Line. There were six girls and four boys in the Cawley family; the family was known all around as good, strong, God-fearing folks. No women were coming to town with bruises and blood from this clan. All the children had been married off by the time I was in grade school, except one old maid, Miss Twila (according to Mama).

Jacob Cawley, Twila's dad, was a self-taught and enlightened preacher. He said he was personally called by Jesus Christ to preach the Word. Mama called them Holy Rollers, but the proper word was Restoration Branch of Jesus Christ. I called him Reverend Mister Cawley; his wife, Mae, I called Missus Cawley. They were kind to everyone.

Whenever a car would come dancing and jolting up the potted dirt Stewartstown Road, or a stranger would dare to approach, a chorus would begin with the hounds,

WOOOO. Wooooo. Wo. WOOOOOOOOO.

"Now you come-on ol' Henry Lee, that thar is no stranger. No indeeed, that thar is Mis-ter Dill-in-er,"

Missus Cawley would say, as Dad and I would go down the road in our own red (now faded pink) 1950 station wagon.

Sometimes I would see the two of them sitting at the railroad ramp with the beaten women who were waiting for their men to come out of Augie's Beer Garden. They would be saying a word of prayer and wiping a runny nose or two on the little barefoot children.

Dad said we were to call anyone who was grown up by Mister or Missus. Dad tipped his hat to the ladies and, of course, to any preacher.

Reverend Mister and Mrs. Cawley would often come into town to gospel. They had to walk from their shack on Stewartstown Road. Both would wear their threadbare Sunday best clothes when they came into town. They were both always smiling. Reverend Mister Cawley was a big hulking man, genteel and humble. Missus Cawley was short and round and soft. She had no teeth, and a tiny spray of spittle would land on my chin when she talked to me. I never wiped the spit off my face in front of Missus Cawley for fear of causing her an embarrassment.

They raised TEN children. SIX girls.

Dad said,

"Poor Cawley—SIX girls. Well, at least he got some boys."

I believed that the Reverend Mister Cawley loved and valued his girls equally to his boys.

I don't know why I could not convince Dad, or even Mama, that girls had value.

Crashing the Pyramid

One day that hot, sweaty summer, Mama took me with her to the A&P to get groceries. I enjoyed going with her because Miss Twila worked there. She was thin and wore a simple homemade calico dress with a circular collar trimmed in white eyelet lace. Miss Twila was a Cawley. She was good Christian stock and lived with her mother and father up Stewartstown Road. Proper unmarried women lived their entire lives with their mama and daddy.

Sometimes if Miss Twila was not busy at the cash register, she would arrange the soup cans into big pyramids with maybe cans of green beans or peaches on top. She said it was to make it colorful. She lined up the cans and faced the big pictures of yellow-orange peaches and deep green beans outward. All in a row. Exactly the same way for every can.

I liked the Campbell's soup display best. There were happy children in those pictures on the soup can labels. The women in the pictures were smiling at the children and there were big lumps of noodles and broth and meat in a bowl in front of them. I noticed that the children were pretty little blond boys. Sometimes there was a little girl. The soup label little girl was fair, blonde, with perfect teeth and blue eyes smiling at the little boy who had a big spoon of Campbell's Scotch Broth Soup in his mouth. The little girl was happily gazing at the boy. She was not eating.

While Mama was waiting for Miss Twila at the checkout, I caught sight of a little black bug that somehow managed to get into the cellophane of a Twinkies package. It was munching away at the yellow cake and was starting to drill a hole into the bottom where the soft white filling spills out on the cellophane. I was backing up to get a better look when I backed into Miss Twila's pyramid of cans. They toppled over with a loud smashing sound that caused some of the Church Ladies in the store to stare and whisper, pointing to "that tattered Dillinger girl with bare feet."

"Tsk Tsk."

Some of the cans got dented.

Mr. Roussos, the A&P Store Manager, made sure he and Miss Twila turned the dented cans to one side so customers would not see the dent when they put the can in their cart. Mama said that eventually those dented cans would get black spots and bust open. Not at our house though. We ate everything up right away.

Mama sent me straight home after the can avalanche. I said to Miss Twila,

"I am so sorry, Miss Twila."

She had tears in her eyes, but said,

"No mind."

I knew Mr. Rousso would have Miss Twila stay after, at no extra pay, to reset the canned display. She would be walking home on that lonely Stewartstown Road after dark. Again.

Miss Twila could be seen dutifully trucking her way to and from the family compound in all kinds of weather. She was a real lady and a devoted family person who could be counted on by her family and her employer. Mr. Rousso could not have handled the A&P without her. Even as a young child, I recognized her steadfast loyalty and kindness.

With the inherent stoicism that is so characteristic of the women of the mountains, she marched through her life being the loyal rock of ages that was expected and taken for granted.

I can close my eyes now and see Miss Twila, slightly bowing her head and silently smiling, moving on through any family need, any community need. Not judging, just doing, and being present.

As a child, I learned from her the importance of kindness and being available when called upon.

A tender heart among us . . .

21

THE PATCHES

The Patches

Many newcomers immigrating from Slavic countries were deeply embedded in the Catholic religion, and devoted to Jesus, the Father, and the Holy Spirit. Once arriving in the promised land of America, and without a tangible skill, they found their way to the nooks and crannies of Appalachia to work for subsistence pay using the only tool they brought with them –their strength. They gave their utmost through their sweat and muscle in a back breaking routine of digging coal.

When coal ruled Appalachia, the owner of the mines would create housing near their mines for their employees and families to live. They called these areas "patches." In creating these patches, the owner-builders embraced and extolled the myth that they were a benevolent friend to all. The coal companies would build 10, 20, 30, or more, wooden houses on a dirt strip near the coal seam they wanted to work out. These matching row houses were built close together, side-by-side, and known as "company houses."

The houses were usually board on board walls with a layer of single horizontal boards over the studs. No insulation. When the wind blew through the little communities, it would seep between the layers of board and create a fine whistle that could sing the babies or grandmas to sleep. Floors were 2x4s laid on top of stone pilings spaced six feet apart in a crawl space under the shack. The roofs were made of tin pieced together from what was routinely used in the mines. Water was usually a shared pump over a well between two houses. Each house would sport an outhouse in the back lot behind the shack.

The towns of the larger coal companies had more substantial houses that would sometimes include a small porch, paint on the outside, roofs shingled with asbestos, and a pump installed for the water well inside each house. They even put red dog chips on the road between the houses to keep down the dust and mud.

These large companies were those that owned a promising vein of coal. They would build small Catholic churches in the company town as an ideal system of crowd control, and some of these patches even had a post office. But the plan of these larger companies was to stick around for a few years before going bankrupt and walking away from the mess of the landscape they had made.

After the men found work in a mine, the coal company would deduct rent for the use of the house, the water, and the outhouse from the miner's pay each week. There was usually a company store in each small patch where the miner's family could charge their groceries and home supplies. What was owed to the company store was also taken from the miner's pay each week. In the cold weather, the coal needed to warm their home was also charged to the miner's paycheck. The families began living hand to mouth in their newfound country of hope. Often, at the end of the week, the miner owed the coal company and there was no paycheck at all. If a miner was injured and unable to work, terminated or fired, there was no paycheck and he and his family were evicted from the house.

Slag heaps would announce the entrance to a company town patch with its huge shadow on the community, deep biting sulfur smell, glowing fires inside them, and dirty smoke circling toward the sky and burying the valleys in the dense gray dust.

These small communities are everywhere, hidden behind the long-abandoned rotted-out wood of coal tipples and slag heaps that dot the landscape of Appalachia. These days, many of the smaller patches are completely abandoned and stand as small ghost towns down an old overgrown red dog road in the weeds.

Economic Decline

Near the beginning of World War II, the town of Point Marion began a decline into an economic and emotional depression from which it would never recover. The factory began work for the war department and, at the same time, the technology and demand for creating glass changed. The factory began employing fewer and fewer people.

When a coal mine was worked out, the patch would eventually be forsaken by the coal company. In the late 1930s, 40s, and 50s, many mines were being worked out or abandoned. Some larger, deeper mines were still in production, but these mines were mechanized to the point that fewer workers were required and then only those workers with specific skills were retained. There was no work in the mines or elsewhere for the limited skill of a pick and shovel coal miner who often suffered from Black Lung Disease.

In the late 1940s, for people who could find work, Point Marion was a bedroom community with contaminated water from the sewers and old mine runoff emptying into the rivers. It was useless to toss a fishing line into any river. The river was considered dead. No one spent any time trying to catch fish along the Monongahela or Cheat Rivers. The air space above the town had the always present coal dust and smoke from the coke ovens and coal-fired furnaces. Combined with the water in the rivers, the cloud cover over the valley made the air repugnant.

As the smaller coal companies who owned the houses and company stores were leaving, they would sometimes sell the company houses to the renter or, more often, sell the houses in a patch to an investor. Sometimes the company store building would be sold to someone who wanted to have a bar or a general store. The bustling patch life was over.

The coal mines were no longer working. The people who worked the mines were stranded. This happened over a ten-to-fifteen-year period.

Many of the miners and their families stayed in the company houses. They knew no other way except the destitute leftovers of the scratch-by life. Their livelihood was gone. It was not unusual for a family to be in a company row house their family had rented generations earlier from a now defunct coal company.

Many of these patches around Point Marion were deep in the back woods. It would take a while to walk there from town. It was not unusual to discover a rat's nest of intertwined dirt roads sometimes leading to a small coal patch community. This presented a problem for the mail carrier, the school bus, and the firetrucks.

Those homes in the coal mine patches that were not near the river had their own outhouse for human waste a short walk down the path behind the home. Originally dug at least six feet deep, these outhouses were normally on the side of the house opposite the pump for the water well.

Of course, no one was concerned about contaminated water supply. People were focused on survival.

Quiet desperation . . .

22

DAVIDSON PATCH

Mine runoff contaminated much of the once beautiful freshwater creeks that flowed toward the rivers. Among the many larger free-flowing noxious tributaries around Point Marion, the unchecked contaminated water flowed freely into the pungent lifeless Monongahela River at Camp Run near the Point Marion ball park; at Dunkard Creek near Dilliner, Pennsylvania (across the river from Point Marion); and at the abandoned mine at Martin in the Point Marion lock system pool.

Camp Run Creek started at the old Davidson mine wash and meandered for several miles through the brush toward the Monongahela River. Long ago the Davidson Mine had contaminated Camp Run Creek, which still reeked a telltale sulfur odor. All the vegetation around the creek was dead, and the fish and crawdads that once inhabited the creek had died off. The rocks along the shoreline were for decades impregnated with the rusty mud brown stain of the sulfur that continuously seeped into the water.

Of course, the owners of Davidson Mine took off after depleting all the coal that was reachable in the entire seam. They left behind:

- a patch of small company houses in a community of 25 shacks off a dogleg dirt road,
- a mountainous slag heap that smoked year-round with the pungent smell of coke and, of course,
- the acid mine drainage that inflamed Camp Run Creek and meandered through the dead weeds toward the river.

The Davidson Mine had been a small operation of underground coal and, when I was in fourth grade, the coal had been gone for 25 years.

Exploring Davidson

It was about that time when Dad started collecting rent from the recipients living at Davidson Mines. He would forward the money to the out-of-state owner of the crumbling patch houses. We would go there on relief check day every month. Dad did this for about a year and, if he earned any money doing this, it did not change our lives. While Dad would go from house to house putting the few dollars of rent money in an envelope and giving out receipts, I would go exploring.

Davidson was a coal patch that started out with nearly 25 company houses, but only 12 houses remained. The patch of Davidson was a mile down an even narrower pocked dirt road after we would drive over the sulfur creek beyond the grouping of shacks on Stewartstown Road.

The road to Davidson Mine was just wide enough for our old station wagon. In some forlorn moment, it must have been a miner's wife who planted a mountain laurel in the spot in the weeds where those who had a car would make the left turn down the lumpy road that led to Davidson.

The houses were in two rows facing one another. The dirt road where we entered the patch ran down the center and continued beyond the houses, ending in the weeds at a one-story roofless and doorless cinderblock hut.

Beyond the hut was a hill with an opening braced by rotting timber on the top and more rotting timber framing the entry sides. The cave-like opening was shorter than Dad. There were rusty railroad tracks coming out of the opening, and there was an old rusty mine cart rotting in the sun. The minecart had thick tar-black pieces of wood wrapped with orange rusted straps of metal that were sprung loose from years of sitting in the sun and rain and snow. A mama dog was nursing her puppies in the shade under the cart. To the right of the opening was the slag heap for the mine. A mountain of black, gray shale tamped solid from years of neglect and still smoking. The smoke, wafting in random lazy circles toward the gray sky, was pungent and burned my eyes.

The Davidson patch had one-story, three-room houses with a porch that was the width of the house. There was a well between every second house, and each house had its own outhouse in the backyard.

Seven of the houses were occupied, and the remaining ones stood empty. The locals in the patch used the vacant houses for their dogs or as a place for the kids to play. There was electricity delivered through the tall, tarred-black telephone poles that brought the power south to Stewartstown through Point Marion. A tangle of black wire had been hooked on the telephone poles long ago. The wires circled from pole to pole and were held on the top of the pole by a colored piece of green glass. Then the black wire wrapped around the glass before looping onto the next pole. When the electricity reached the collection of shanties, each house had a frayed black rubber-covered wire loosely draped toward its chimney and then wired through a window.

Camp Run Creek ran bright orange near the road, and I could smell the pungent sulfur ten feet away. The noxious smell at the shoreline on a hot day took my breath away. In many areas of the creek, there was steam rising. There was no vegetation around the water anywhere. Dad said it was those,

> "Dammed coal companies that caused this. Yup. They came in, stripped the coal and left. Paid off a couple of dirty politicians. Then they took their money back to wherever they came from. And started again. YUP."

I would skip through the dirt of the town center, check out the puppies, and look for some kids to play with. Most of the people who lived there were older folks. The ol' man of the family had worked there and had never stopped renting the little company house. Some of the old folks were raising the children of their children who had years earlier succumbed to the call of moonshine. They had watched the patch deteriorate and seen themselves become even more isolated in the woods. The school bus stopped at the rhododendron on Stewartstown Road for the few children who went to school.

> "Dad, why don't these people move to town? Why do they stay here? It's so smelly and it takes a long time to walk to town."

> "It's in their blood, Francie. They don't know and don't want to know any better."

I decided this overwhelming sadness could not be what defined me.

I had to get out or I would be swallowed into the abyss.

23

CHURCHING

The mountain people of Appalachia live so close to the heartbeat of life that they seem to pulsate with the pain of living and less often with the joy of life. Their beliefs are often distinguished by the unique foot-stomping, chest-beating, tongue-talking fervor of

> *"Glory, glory, glory, to the highest,*
> *HALLELUJAH! TO AN EVERLASTING GOD,"*

tempered by characterizations of the depths of despair,

> *"Hell will burn your wicked soul,"*

sometimes all by the same person on the same day.

Aunt MaeMae started taking me to the United Methodist Church in Point Marion as early as I could walk. The church was beautiful and, like a good Methodist, the walk with the Lord was subdued.

Mama said,

> "Look kids, the only way you can tell a wedding from a funeral at the Methodist Church is when someone is wearing a big fluffy white gown. Everybody has their own way of finding out things. The Methodists have their own notions."

Methodists don't talk about anything specific. They don't talk about death. They don't talk about sex. For heaven's sake, they don't dance. They sang *Jesus Loves Me* and *This Little Light of Mine*, and then, after a covered dish casserole sharing in the basement, they would go home.

Sunday School

In grade school, I would get up on my own on Sunday morning, trying to find a clean matching set of white Sunday gloves that Aunt MaeMae had bought for us like all the other little Methodist girls wore. I would march myself off to Sunday school. Mama and Dad slept in so they weren't aware that I was going off to hear the Bible stories that Mrs. Bennie would tell our Sunday school class.

Mrs. Bennie was a pale, blond woman who smelled like the lilies of the valley perfume that Mr. Hunker sold in the back area of Hunker's Drug Store. Always in a freshly ironed pastel dress with a big full skirt, she would pull the small chairs of our little group around her in a circle and read to us.

The other kids were:

> Barry Gelton in his high suspenders that pulled his pants up his crack so tight that I could see his penis in front, with his Brylcream parted and slicked-back hair.

Harry Cutson with his freshly spiked crew cut and shaved slick sidewalls.

Meredith Stewart with her ruby-rimmed glasses, plaid skirt, and matching white gloves.

Patty Sue Chesley with her long blond tendrils and cancan skirt, white patent leather Mary Jane shoes with a gold buckle, dainty socks with lace crinkled around the edges, and white, white gloves.

And me in my third go-around paisley dress and white gloves that Aunt MaeMae bought for my sister, Charlen, so many years ago, then worn by Eileen, and now threadbare with me.

I would pull my chair up right across from Mrs. Bennie so I could watch how the pink lipstick on her lips moved as she read us the story. The books were printed each week by the Methodists somewhere far away in a beautiful Methodist pastel colored factory. She would give us little colored folded papers with pictures of happy, skipping children, with their mouths open and glassy eyes looking at the same picture of this middle-aged fellow with long hair and a beard and a white robe. The guy had two fingers pointed to the sky like a brownie scout salute.

Mrs. Bennie said this was Jesus and Jesus loved all children the same. He did not love boys more than girls. She taught us a song that went,

> "Yellow, brown, or black, or white, they are all so precious in his sight, Jesus loves all the little children of the world."

In the classroom, taped on the wall above where we sat, she had a picture of the white-robed bearded Jesus. He was surrounded by children who had bright yellow, chalky brown, deep black, and white, white skin. The only children that ever came to the Methodist Church were white, white. The pictures had smiling boys and smiling girls.

> *Where were all these children that Jesus loves who have such colorful skin?*

She would end her story with,

> *"And Jesus loves you and everyone."*

I wondered where this guy was who loved everyone the same.

After the story, we would sing a rhyming song together. Mrs. Bennie would open a thermos bottle she brought from home and poor a cup full of red Kool-Aid into little paper cups and give us each three vanilla wafers.

Mrs. Bennie was nice. She had one child, a boy, Howard. But she said she liked little girls and wished she had a little girl. Her Bible stories were magical, and I liked it when someone would read to me.

Vacation Bible School was even better. It was a two-week period during the summer when we would go every day to the church basement and do crafts with nice ladies like Mrs. Bennie and Mrs. Berwl. We would cut things out and paste them in the dotted lines in a paper book created by those same Methodists far, far away. There were brand new scissors and paste and crayons. And we got a glass of cold milk and two cookies just for coming.

Mrs. Bennie touched my soul.

Stained Glass Windows

Every Sunday, after the preacher told one of his sad stories about some mean person who was forgiven by Jesus, and after the preacher's wife hit a couple of profound chords on the piano, Mr. Stewart and Mr. Gapin would walk from the back of the church down the center aisle to the preacher. The preacher would hand each man a gold bowl with green felt glued to the bottom. They would each solemnly take the dish and march side by side down the center aisle handing the bowl to the people sitting in the pews. All the regular church dads would put a little white envelope in the bowl. I did not have any white envelopes.

When I was in fourth grade, Mr. Stewart came to see Dad who was sitting in the yard drinking a beer. He had his shirt off because it was a hot day. Dad always wore suspenders, so the elastic from the suspenders was catching the hair on his chest as he smoked his cigarette. I hung around to listen because Mr. Stewart's daughter was in my class and her mama was my Brownie Scout leader. He said,

"Hello, Leonard."

"Hmmmm."

"Nice warm day, Leonard.

SILENCE FROM DAD . . .

"I'm representing the Methodist Church. Your daughter, Francie, has been coming to Sunday school for quite a while now. We think your family should start tithing for the church."

"Not going to do that, Bob."

"But all the church families tithe, Leonard."

> "Take a look at those stained-glass windows on the west wall of that church Bob, most all of them say Dillinger. Our family paid our dues. We practically BUILT that damn church."

"Okay, Leonard."

Dad and Mama never told me not to go to the United Methodist Church or any church. They never talked about church or God or Jesus. They never went. I liked the singing and the stories.

I never did figure out why the Methodists were always talking about Jesus, but the stories were interesting, and I felt better about myself when I heard them. Some of the Church Ladies were kind to me even though I never had the white envelope that Mr. Stewart thought was so important.

To this day, I can still feel my Aunt MaeMae wrapping her love around me as I walked beside her in my shiny patent Mary Jane shoes into that church.

I hope I honored her.

24

THE PREACHING PULPIT

Sunday school started at 9:30 a.m. At 10:30 a.m. sharp, Mr. Hamrick would pull the cords to the church bell to announce that Sunday school was over, and church was about to start. Methodists fill up the back pews of the United Methodist Church. No one ever sits in front. It is part of the Methodist way of dealing with God. We never talked specifically about how we felt. We talked about general stories and songs written at least one hundred years ago.

And of course, the Church Ladies would whisper about the length of Mrs. Brandywine's skirt.

Each regular family had a special pew where they sat. I found out early on that if I sat in one of the pews that were for the regular families, I would be glared at by the Church Ladies and bumped hard in the back of the head when it was time to stand up and sing *The Old Rugged Cross*. Anyone who came in near the 10:30 a.m. Sunday bell had to sit nearer the middle of the church in the center pews and feel the scorn of the ever-present Church Ladies.

Mrs. Bennie was happy to keep the babies in the nursery during the one-hour church service. Some of the new moms would come to church so they could spend one hour away from their screaming babies. No man would ever hold a baby or change a diaper in Point Marion, so all new moms were exhausted. Once in a while, we would hear a baby crying and crying and crying, way into when the preacher would start the sermon. When that happened, Mr. Bennie would gently come into the church and motion for the exhausted mom to come and soothe her baby.

Mr. Bennie helped Mrs. Bennie in everything she did. He would stand beside her and hold her hand after the church service. He wore light blue sans-a-belt pants that were perfectly ironed with a tie.

The Methodist minister, Reverend Wardle, would enter the front from a hiding place behind the organ. We would all sit quietly looking at the ceiling and listening to Miss Neiman slide through the organ keys in the unique Methodist way that makes all the notes melt into the other so that no one can figure out what song is being attempted --- and suddenly, he would appear at the high preaching pulpit. Way above everyone else. I figured it was so he could look like he was descending from heaven on us. All of a sudden, his head would pop up,

> POOF.

He was dressed in flowing black robes buttoned up to his chin and loose to his ankles. Sometimes he wore a white, red, or black sash that was flapped around his neck and over his shoulders and flowed freely to his knees. Tiny spectacles perched midway down his big flat nose. He would start off with a long, soft, single syllable ramble, lightly mentioning some long ago, faraway place where people were a lot meaner to each other than they were in Point Marion.

The minister would talk quietly about Jesus and God for a while and, sometimes, if Mr. Cleavinger was snoring louder than usual, he would say something loud that bounced off the ceiling like,

"THE PHARISEES SCORNED HIM!!"

Usually, he'd end with,

"Let us all bow our heads in prayer."

This was one of my favorite times, because then I would look around and see who did have their eyes closed, who was praying, and who was looking at the ceiling or looking at the Church Ladies' dresses and hats. We knew the prayer was over when the mumbling by the minister would pause and he would boom

"AMEN!!"

One heartbeat after the amen, Miss Neiman would hit a long uneven chord on the organ.

WAAAAAAAAAAANNNNnnnnnnnnnnng…

Then came the endlessly boring part. Reverend Wardle would open the huge Bible that was on a high lectern in front of him and say,

"We will read from Luke chapter 23 verse 27."

This was the signal that everyone was supposed to scramble for one of the Methodist Bibles tucked into the seat pockets in front of the benches and furiously turn to the correct section of the Bible so they could read silently along while the minister thundered.

After he read from his Bible, the minister would start a long, single-tone monologue that would last fifteen minutes. He would talk about some ancient person who had seen a burning bush, a ninety-year-old woman who wanted to have a baby, or a man who had to kill his son because God told him to and he needed to prove his love for God. It was a sad story and told in whispers.

Fifteen minutes into it, there was a buildup to a loud scream by the preacher. I think it was to wake up Mr. Cleavinger who was snoring again by that time.

> *"JEES---SSUS loved Abraham so much that he told him to take his only son to the mountain and kill him with a knife! Now, friends, THAT is the LOVE of GOD."*

Miss Neiman would pounce a chord of the organ and hold it until the minister's wife began the notes to *Amazing Grace* or *How Great Thou Art*. We would stand, find the dog-eared sections of the Methodist hymnal that marked the place for those two songs, and sing the first and last verse.

> *"Please be seated."*

The minister then moved into his run-on, flat monotone dialogue.

> *"We have a few announcements,*

> *"There will be a covered dish dinner in the basement hall next Sunday at 6:30 p.m. All church families are to bring a covered casserole for sharing.*

> *"Mr. Louis James Frerer, Mrs. Joseph Handleman, Jr., and Miss Olivia June Reames are in the hospital. Mrs. Joseph Handleman, Jr., is not expected to live.*

> *"Mr. Howard Frederick Barnes passed last Saturday. Services will be Monday at 2 p.m. at Herod's with interment at Evergreen Memorial Park.*

> "Miss Julia Susan Frazee, the daughter of Mr. and Mrs. James Lee Frazee, Jr., will wed Mr. William Raymond Forrest, the son of Mrs. William Raymond Forrest, Sr., and the late William Raymond Forrest, Sr., next Saturday at 10 a.m. at the church. A cutting of the cake will follow in the basement."

Since my family was not one of the church families, we never went to the covered dish dinners in the church basement.

> "Mama, what's a casserole?"

>> "Oh, some damn thing the Methodists make up with a can of tuna fish, a can of mushroom soup, and smashed up potato chips on top."

> "Oh."

The only time we ever heard about any personal news in the Methodist Church was at announcement time. The Methodists did not talk about sickness, death, marriage, or births. All this happened, but no one ever, ever talked about it. Life events seemed to be an inconvenient and embarrassing current that ran under the surface of life.

Of course, Methodists never talked about divorce either. If anyone would dare to get divorced, they would never come to church again. Mrs. Buswell Larger got divorced. I heard Mama say that Mrs. Larger found out Mr. Larger was dating a man in Morgantown.

> "Mama, what does that mean, dating a man?"

>> "Never mind. You can't play with the Larger boys anymore and SHE is not invited to bridge club anymore. Ever."

I liked Mrs. Larger, she was a nice lady and her boys were kind to me.

I thought Mama should divorce Dad. Or maybe Dad should divorce Mama.

The aisles on either side of the pews were wood-covered and polished to a high sheen by Mr. Hamrick. As soon as the minister finished his monotone reading of the announcements, he would look up and down the center aisle to the back of the church to Mr. Hamrick, who would be watching for his signal to pull the long rope that was tied to the bell that teetered in the high church tower.

BONG. BONG. BONG.

Reverend Wardle would then sweep down the steps of the high pulpit, robes flowing in the flurry. With eyes downcast but chin raised toward some mysterious cloud, he would solemnly float down the wide center aisle, pausing halfway down the plush carpeted middle walkway. Then his longsuffering, dutiful, fluffy wife could slide off the upright piano bench at the far wall and maneuver between the center pews to catch up with him, huffing and puffing due to her excess weight and yearly pregnancy.

The preacher's wife held the unenviable position of piano accompanist and preschool Sunday school teacher. She was a short brown wren of a woman who never smiled and wore her white woven cracking plastic Sunday hat with white veil netting over her unevenly cut, mouse-brown bangs. A pink calico dress and a white plastic belt would finish off her Sunday attire.

Reverend Wardle's wife, the daughter of a Methodist minister from the Greensburg District of the United Methodist Church, had submissively gone off to the local Robbinsville Methodist College after high school. She was instructed to find a man studying to be a seminary student and marry him. She did this at the age of 19 and promptly began creating little Methodist pew sitters. She knew her life would be one of poverty and sacrifice, but that is all she knew. She assumed that was all she deserved. Her life had been that of a preacher's kid. Her mother was a piano playing, dutiful wife, and that is all she hoped to be too. She was a girl--of course she could not be a preacher herself.

Each Sunday, as Reverend Wardle paused at mid-aisle, she would reach for his highly held elbow, hook his arm, and the two of them would prance side by side to the back of the church. I was sad for the minister's wife, and I smiled to see this one moment of true glory each week when she would get to hold her head high and be noticed by people on both sides of the aisle. She indeed believed she was the person who was holding the church together.

As I watched her, I thought of the little muted hen Mama kept at the back door one spring and summer. This brown hen was afraid to be petted and would run whenever we came near. We didn't even name her, but she dutifully laid an egg every day for us.

PECK. PECK. PECK,

at the ground all day every day. Day after day. Our rooster, James, was a beautiful specimen. James was loud, profound, and unapologetic for his proud squawking at the crack of dawn. James pranced around the dooryard, scratching and crowing. He did not have to be bothered laying an egg every day for recognition of his worth and to ensure his survival. James had spurs on his claws.

Winter came early that year and the hen disappeared. Soon after that, Dad picked up James, handed him to me, and we drove to Len Hennigan's farm. Dad said as we tumbled over the potted dirt road to the Hennigan farm,

> "Let someone else be driven nuts with that damn morning racket."

I think the Hennigan's ate James the next Sunday. Dad had too many beers to swing a rooster by the neck.

Reverend and Mrs. Wardle, side by side, the round little chicken and the taller proud peacock in his flowing robes, would then turn toward the door and walk through the rear foyer out the door and down the stone steps. There, the Vicar and his wife would stand waiting to shake hands with the members of the flock as they emptied out the church. One by one. All the important families would march down the center aisle after them.

I enjoyed the pomp and circumstance of the Sunday church services. It seemed that, for one moment in time, some of the people in Point Marion could forget their circumstances and be calm. Of course, I was not important enough to participate in the formal closing processional of glad handing. Since I was alone and sticking around after Mrs. Bennie's Sunday school class, I would swoop behind the line of hand shakers and skip on home to the riverbank.

Even today, I sometimes find myself humming the refrains of *"How Great Thou Art"* and *"Amazing Grace."*

25

THE CHURCH LADIES

The Church Ladies each had their own Methodist Bible they carried in their purses, wrapped in a linen handkerchief with a crocheted border. Little white or black, soft leather-covered books, with gold along the edge of the pages so that, when it was closed, it looked like gold. On the front was their own name stamped in gold. I got a look at a couple of them,

> Mrs. William Paul Strosnider
> Mrs. Harold F. Thompkins
> Mrs. Franklin Joseph Bucky, Jr.

Church Ladies never had a name like Theresa Strosnider, or Margie Thompkins, or Helen Bucky. They were Mrs. (man's name) Something. Even the church bulletin would say,

> Mrs. William Paul Strosnider and Mrs. Franklin Joseph Bucky, Jr. motored to Morgantown for an afternoon of shopping on Tuesday.

The Church Ladies even created a cookbook they had printed and sold to one another. Each of the recipe entries had the recipe owner's name as Mrs. (man's name) Something.

> "Mama, why don't the Church Ladies use their own names? I don't get it. I can't figure out who is who."
>
> "Oh, who knows, Francie, these people don't have much sense. Maybe they don't think much of themselves."

Watch Out!

Mrs. UnCluck was the wife of the owner of the UnCluck Sand Company. Several of the church windows were inscribed with,

> In Honor of Mr. and Mrs. Alfonsino UnCluck, Jr.
> In Remembrance of Mr. and Mrs. Alfonsino UnCluck, Sr.

Mrs. UnCluck sat four rows from the back on the right side of the church with her grown daughter, Josephine, and her daughter's husband, Clearance. Mrs. UnCluck had only produced a single daughter, but Josephine and Clearance had produced enough children to have a namesake for nearly every character in the *Gone with the Wind* book. If Mrs. UnCluck decided there was something about the minister or the minister's wife she thought was amiss, she would inform Mrs. Walters, and then the entire "church family" would be talking about "the Minister problem."

After the procession down the thick, carpeted center passage, and my routine slithering to the side aisle and slinking outside, I could then duck behind the minister and his wife who were genuinely occupied clasping with both hands the Church Ladies' white gloves. I would hear:

> "Oh, don't you look grand this fine morning, Mrs. UnCluck."
>
> "Well, thank you Mrs. Thompkins, yes, I really hoped my sermon was meaningful."

> "Yes, indeed it is a shame about Mr. Williams, he was such a young man."

Methodist ministers would last no more than three years in Point Marion and then the district would move them on to another river town in the constituency. Depending on how the gossip was for the preacher and his family, they would be moved to another town either the same size as Point Marion or, if the Church Ladies had a decent report on the preacher's wife, they could move to a larger town and a larger church with a bigger stipend for the preacher.

Preacher's Kids

Around town, children of ministers were referred to as preacher kids. The preacher's kids were required to sit in the third pew to the left of the altar in stairstep order. The oldest sat nearest the center aisle, then the next oldest, and right down to the youngest. They would sit quietly, looking at their hands the entire church service.

The preacher kids were scrutinized by the ever-present Church Ladies. The preacher and his family were relegated to life above the poverty level. They lived in a well-maintained but sparse and simple house owned by the church, and they drove a basic car purchased by the church that was new every three years. They were under constant surveillance by the "church family" and their frightening informal leaders, the self-anointed Church Ladies. The minister and his family spent as much time as possible trying to stay in the good graces of the Church Ladies. Particularly, Mrs. UnCluck, and anyone who had the ear of Mrs. UnCluck.

I figured Mrs. UnCluck was a major player in the White Envelope Brigade. Thus, the power and pretense.

Although they were safe from hunger and had the assurance of subsistence level medical and dental care, the preachers' kids never had any luxuries. No cute dresses like the coal miner's kids and never, ever a new outfit for Easter like the Church Ladies' children.

They did have one nice thing going for them. The Methodist district would underwrite a basic education for them beyond high school. They were protected from the constant fear of being dumped into the state welfare rolls when they graduated from high school, like the rest of us. The preacher's kids knew nothing more than the life of servitude to the church and its written and unwritten rules and customs. A free ride to seminary school and then an assignment to a district church was the safety net every good preacher's kid seemed to fall into.

Of course, all this was the grand Methodist plan, as Mama would say. As long as a preacher's kid:

"did not get knocked up or knock someone else up" in high school.

When a girl in Point Marion would get unexpectedly pregnant, Mama would say,

"Well, her life is over,"

and it seemed to be. She had to drop out of school and marry whoever knocked her up. She had to go live with his family and get pregnant again and again. Mama told all her girls from the earliest age that getting impregnated was a death knell.

When a boy would knock up a girl, he was sent off to the US Army right away. GONE. The people of Appalachia are known to be the hardest core of fighting men, and the war department would aggressively recruit and dispatch our strong menfolk to the front of any war.

Mama would say,

> "Well, at least he got out of this crappy place."

The boy would most often be a Private in some branch of the service, usually the US Army, because the Service sniffed around the mountains for good fighting stock. Then he would be sent off to South Carolina or Mississippi and we would see him maybe once a year. The pay for a Private was not even enough to allow his wife and children to escape welfare. And with the subsistence wages of the US Army, there was no possible way for the pregnant new wife to move to an Army base in some foreign state.

The budding family without a daddy around would most often remain in the mountains, easily qualifying for Aid to Dependent Children and continue the never-ending circle.

> "Mama, these Church Ladies seem to just be hanging onto what their husbands are, they don't even use their own name."

> "Well Francie, maybe that's a way to muddle through living here."

> "Mama, how are these girls getting knocked up?"

> "Stop with the questions. Just don't ever let that happen."

It came to me that whatever I did, I did not want to get knocked up. I needed to find my own way out.

26

HOLY ROLLERS

One lazy Sunday, I went over to the Holy Roller church. I heard this loud music from a piano pounding away as I was wandering by,

        THUMP. THUMP. THUMP.

The sidewalk was
     vibrating,
          pulsing,
              resonating.

        WHOOP, WHOOP, WHOOP

was coming out the open doors of an old peeling paint, one-story white house on Water Street Extension, which ran parallel to the Monongalia River.

Water Street was cut in half when the bridge crossing the Monongalia was built in the 1930s. Before the bridge was built, the street started at the point of Point Marion and extended south along the river. When the bridge was built, the remaining road extended under the pilasters of the bridge. The dirt road under the bridge and extending south was aptly called Water Street Extension.

Lots of welfare recipients lived along Water Street Extension. Old sofas and stuffed chairs were on the porches. A hound would pant in the heat. Here and there on a collapsing porch was a wooden porch swing facing the road.

The houses were lined up on the dirt street, one close to another, facing the river. Each had two concrete block steps up from a gravel or red dog sidewalk to the entrance. Every spring when the river would flood, Water Street Extension was impassible. This made it more exciting because we would wade down the sidewalk or jump from porch to porch.

The people were friendly, sitting on their swing, usually with a bottle of homemade moonshine and a hand rolled cigarette draped from a lower lip.

Among the houses of Water Street there was a sign on the roof of the porch in the single-story whitewashed house with flaking paint and homemade letters:

POINT MARION APOSTOLIC CHURCH

Right under the writing, a big fat black cross was centered on the bare wood. That's it. No stained-glass windows with important people's names. No polished floors and no thick carpet.

I walked in the front door, and it led right up to the front where all these people were shouting. I sat down on the edge of a bench. They didn't have pews like the Methodists, they had smooth benches without backs. That made it easy to jump up and down and wave our hands above our heads. All the country people would go there. It was loud and happy. It was stamping with noise and thumping with what the preacher said was,

"Evah-lastin' love."

On that sweaty hot Sunday morning, the Holy Roller church was packed with people, and lots of people were sitting way up front in the first row. The preacher seemed happy to be there, shouting and kind of dancing in the front. He waved his hands then stopped, then STRUTTED from one wall of the front to the other. After a while, a few of the people sitting on the benches started incoherently blabbering loudly with their heads turned up to the ceiling.

The people were energetic and effusive.

They taught me some new songs,

"Thank God for the Blood," and *"Do Lord,"* and *"Wade in the Water."*

After that amazing morning, I would regularly sneak into this church when they were having services. These people were fun and happy, and they were nice to everyone. No matter what they looked like. Best of all, I never had to try to find a matching pair of clean white gloves before showing up. And they had a penny march. That meant all they thought you needed to give the preacher was pennies you might find in the cracks of the sidewalk. He was happy with that.

Most of the church ladies at this rollicking den didn't have many teeth. I saw some of the railroad ramp women there. There didn't seem to be any church ladies who looked at the other members with pinched lips and waving crocheted hankies.

The preacher walked around hugging people. Pretty soon we were all hugging each other.

I eventually told Mama about finding the Holy Roller church on Water Street Extension.

"Mama these people are so interesting. They are not so stiff like the Methodists. They LIKE each other and are NICE to each other."

"Look, Francie, these people are cruds. You can't go there. You might get bitten by a god dammed snake. Bad enough that you hang out with those snotty Methodists!"

We called the country kids *cruds*. Most were poor.

Point Marion had lots of churches. There was the Catholic Church, the First Christian Church, the Apostolic Church, the United Methodist Church, the Trinity Methodist Church, the Baptist Church, and the First Presbyterian Church.

On Sunday mornings, the bells from most of the churches would ring through the town,

GONG. GONG. GONG.

I was beginning to find that, somewhere buried deep within me, there was this undying ember of curiosity. My best advantage was that I could wander around anywhere with George at my side and discover even the minutest crumb of life.

Even though Mama had absurd opinions, I could choose how I would feel and react.

27

FIREHOUSE SHENANIGANS

All the bars in town were closed on Sunday and even Patsy Cino had to close his beer distributorship. The Pennsylvania Blue Laws prohibited selling any liquor on the Lord's Day.

Drinking liquor was not the same as closing the bars, of course. A lot of the die-hard drunks would sit on the black steps of the railroad ramp with a paper bag around their bottle of hooch, passing the time, smoking, and spitting. Of course, the VFW and American Legion were always open, and a slug of proper liquor could easily be obtained by our town's beloved veterans while they rehashed the various wars they were packed off to in their youth.

The biggest draw on Sunday afternoon was the Point Marion Volunteer Fire Department. This elite group of "inner-selected men only" had the ever-present Fire House. Indeed. Every single Sunday afternoon, at 2 p.m. SHARP, the ominous-sounding fire alarm would blare,

WHERRRRRRRRRRRRIEEEEEEEEEEEETTTTT.
WHERRRRRRRRRRRRIEEEEEEEEEEEETTTTT.
WHERRRRRRRRRRRRIEEEEEEEEEEEETTTTT.
WHOOP. WHOOP. WHOOP.

All the hound dogs in town would join in. All the dogs everywhere.

> WOOOOOOooooooo.
> WOOOOOOooooooo.
> WOOOOOOooooooo.

Then the cars and pick-up trucks of our devoted volunteer firemen (there were many, many) all over town would be tooled up and race at breakneck speed through town to get to the Fire Hall.

> ZOOOOMM. SCREECH. RACE. RACE.
> TOOT TOOT, HONK HONK
> Screech...

Of course, fires are a way of life in small-town America. A sad reminder of ancient buildings with frayed wiring, or some careless person who still used an oil lamp, or the dumb cluck who carelessly set a cigarette down. Fires were a popular way to gain revenge on a neighbor or raise cash through an insurance payout in the dark corners of Appalachia. The Point Marion Volunteer Fire Department was steeped in the tradition of devotedly trying to fruitlessly control fires.

At any other time of the week, the fire whistle was an urgent call to arms for those who signed on. But the Sunday afternoon fire siren was timed right after church and Sunday dinner to alert the many men in the fire brigade. The firefighters would rush madly to the Fire Hall, leaving families behind for the rest of the day. The only difference with the Sunday fire whistle was that the firetrucks never went out.

At first, I found this strange because I would check to see the direction of the trucks when they pulled out of the fire station. George and I would race to canvas the hills to see if we could spot the tell-tale looping toward the sky of white, gray smoke indicating the location of the fire. Then we would watch to see if the trucks went in that direction and how the volunteers did in getting the fire under control.

Early on, I asked,

> "Mama, I don't get it. The firetruck does not go out on Sunday afternoon when all the men race to the fire station. All their cars and pick-ups are still there."

>> "Francie, these men are just running away from their families so they can sit around all afternoon playing poker and drinking booze. They've been doing this for years."

George and I made it our business to go down to the Fire Hall and peek through the windows. The front door of the firehouse opened into an entry room. There was a big backroom that was closed off. All the men would go in through the front and disappear to the backroom.

Long after dark on Sunday nights, the men would stagger home to their families.

> "Mama, surely these women know that there is no fire every Sunday afternoon!"

>> "Of course, they do. The wives probably say good riddance, anyway."

The tradition was absurd, but like so many other of life's engrained habits, the families accepted it as normal.

Men had this escape, but women did not.

28

LEARNING TO GET MY WAY

The parades in Point Marion were amazing. This was a time when we were all reminded how important it is, if you happen to be a girl in Appalachia, to be attractive. If you were not pretty, at least you were expected to be flirtatious and comely at all times, to all men.

Boys, of course, did not have much substance if they were not playing sports and were not good at them. Football and basketball, for a boy, might even get them a ticket out of the clutching arms of the hills.

The marching cavalcades consisted of bands from every local high school. The bands were led by each high school's selected girls who were required to wear tight-fitting tops that dipped down on their breasts and pushed on the bottom of their developing bosoms. If one of the girls had more than a handful of flesh over her nipple, (which is often the case with the amount of larded corn pone available in the diet in the hills of Appalachia), the material was stressed to the point of revealing even more flesh. And, best of all, for the local gentry, there was a hint of pink at the top for viewing. The skirts the girls were required to wear barely covered their panties, (which were usually in a stark contrasting color).

The sniveling band director, Mr. Lastkey, insisted that the strutting girls do a hand flip at the back of their skirts to expose their behinds as they took each step. The topping on the outfit was white calf-high boots with swinging tassels and a baton each girl must carry in the exact same alignment as the rest of the girls. It was a Radio City Music Hall line-up in our own fair city, marching in a waving straight line right down Penn Street in front of Augie's Bar.

Mr. Lastkey chose a head majorette to lead the lineup of small town, would-be showgirls. This was the delighted chosen one who must wear an even more revealing costume, likened to a high-cut bathing suit under a feather hemmed miniskirt, and stand in front of the group of the panty flipping strutters.

Mr. Lastkey wore a pure white music man suit and marched beside the highest stepping schoolgirl.

"Bring on the dancing girls,"

I often heard him slur at the trumpet players as they sneered into their horns. Our music man was known for taking a few nips of hooch between band practice and before parades.

To top off the entire lineup of scantily clad high schoolers, there was a special girl titled the drum majorette, who wore the briefest costume of all. Something like a skintight bathing suit with sequins. No tiny skirts skimming the panties for her. This girl was required to strut out in front of the entire mass of the band and town folk and lift her legs so high that the crotch of her bright red panties pulsated for all the small town population to see. If this were not enough of a spectacle, the drum majorette was then required to perform a cartwheel (upside down, legs skyward) at every turn in the street. The crowd roared.

This performance was repeated at every river town in the area. The Mapleton Band and Carmichaels Band from Greene County, the Uniontown Bands, Point Marion Bands, and Masontown Bands from Fayette County, and so many others. Each had its own set of specially chosen, skimpily clad, high school girls leading the way.

The parades had a queen of the parade and her honor court. The queen was selected by the faculty at the local high school and was the daughter of a rich family who most likely donated money for replacing the lights on the football field. The queen and each of her court maidens sat on top of the backseat trunk of a convertible owned by a local. Bobby Crust, who owned the sand company, donated a convertible or two and, therefore, had the honor of escorting the nubile young queen around town.

There were big poster signs on the side of these cars that read: Queen Sara Sue Lashitsky, First Honor Maid Bonnie Mae Brewer, Second Honor Maid Lettie Sue Mayorinowski, and on and on. The queen and her honor maids wore gowns with deep plunging cleavage and slits up the sides of their gowns that would shame a Las Vegas hooker. Each member of the anointed town royalty waved gently in space like they were icing a cake with one gloved hand.

Next came the Boy Scouts, the Girl Scouts, the Little League teams, the Veterans of Foreign Wars, the American Legion, the firefighters, the fire trucks, and anyone else in town who had an idea of marching. This category, of course, included politicians from every conceivable office that could be elected, including the Local United Mine Workers of America (UMWA) representatives, and others.

There were speeches after the parades and sometimes a five-cent supper held by the local grange ladies. This after-parade milling around lasted all afternoon and into the evening. Of course, the skimpily clad band girls and the queen and her court were expected to circulate and mingle in their costumes.

The obsession with beauty queens and sports heroes is the standard in the Mountain creases. A means of defining one's existence and a platform for self-worth.

One moment of glory to be forever cherished.

29

SUPPER TIME

When I was eight, I found an old farm bell in the attic of the washhouse. All us kids made an agreement that when any one of us saw the grandfather clock hands move to the small hand on the five and the long hand on the six, we would start ringing that bell and screaming,

"SUP_PER TIME! SUP_PER TIME,"

at the top of our lungs. We would not stop screaming up and down the street until each kid was seated at the oilcloth table. Otherwise, there was hell to pay. I hated it when someone was late. It was the worst time to think one of us would be spanked so hard until we cried. I worried most about little Lennie. Us girls were used to scampering in as the bell was ringing. But little Lennie would go into the woods and make weed forts with Susie's brother, Dominique. I would call and call him and usually, sure enough, he would slide into a seat just in time. Usually.

It was a wonderful early fall day, when the oppressive, sweat dripping, summer heat was finishing up with its vise-like, humid pressure toward the river bottom valley. We had two silver maple trees and a giant sugar maple tree, planted in the early 1900s, right smack up to the house. The wind was blowing little breezes through the leaves that were starting to rustle with a chatter that only big, gnarly, fifty-year-old trees with thousands of unruly branches and millions of fat, fresh, every shade of green, leaves could muster.

CHATTER. WHOOSH.

Little Lennie was not at the table. We were all sitting there. Quietly. Dad was sitting down. All of a sudden, Lennie rushed in. He was only five years old. He was already crying,

"I'm sorry, Dad. Please don't spank me."

Too late. Dad grabbed the yardstick and whacked Len on his bottom and his legs until he howled and could not stop. I cried too. It was so frightening. Afterward, Lennie had to sit in his chair at the table and, as Mama called it, "make pleasant conversation" with us through that awful snorting sound and dripping nose stuff that runs in your mouth and comes after you have an uncontrollable cry. We couldn't talk much. Dad acted like nothing had happened.

"Mama, why does Dad have to spank us so hard all the time? It makes no sense."

"The man of the house gets to do that."

I felt so bewildered by Mama's attitude regarding the "man of the house" issue. It made no sense to me. She would stand by and allow her children to be mercilessly spanked for a minor infraction. She tolerated her husband spending his days in a drunken smoke-filled stupor while the family suffered, and as I learned much later, having an affair during their marriage that produced an illegitimate child whom he abandoned.

Mama was a well-educated woman. Had she been so emotionally abused throughout her own life that she believed his behavior was okay? Because he was a man? Maybe she loved him despite her disappointments.

Dad was like a skillet of hot grease simmering just before it spits an angry spoiling pop in your face.

I was afraid that I was learning to see this absurd behavior as normal and decided that I needed to stay on high alert not to be consumed.

30

THE WIND IN MY HAIR

I wanted a bicycle so I could go faster than the oppressive heat and feel the wind in my face blowing my pigtails behind me. I taught myself how to ride. Sometimes Susie would let me ride her bike, it was so wonderful. Shiny blue and white with black handlebar grippers and tassels steaming from a little hole where the heel of my hand would grab onto them. I had to hold on tight because that bike was fast. The big, fat, black wheels had white walls. Yep. White walls on a bicycle!

Susie's bike was so refreshing. I could feel the cool wind blowing in my eyes and through the gap in my front teeth, closing my eyes while I zoomed over bumps and splashed through mud puddles. I believed I was flying. Her blue bike had a black button on the center-dipping pole that had a real battery hooked up to a buzzer. Whenever I came up to someone walking on the sidewalk, I would press that buzzer so I would not run over him or her. Step aside, a fast bike is coming past you. My pigtails blowing behind me.

It was the sweatiest hot August we ever had. The clouds that hugged the river valley were a mixture of ash from the coke ovens. The smoke from the glass factory hung like a piece of dripping rusty tin over the crease in the earth that the Monongahela River created. Like I said before, Point Marion, our little town below, was nestled in the floodwaters of the muddy Monongahela River where the Cheat River emptied into it. I would look up where the sky was and see the musty, dripping, seeping, cover of silt smoke and the close water-sopped clouds. Not a breeze. The cicadas, thinking it was dusk, would come out earlier and earlier every day. Calling. Plaintively screaming. Chirping so loud I could not decipher the 4 p.m. train whistle from their mad frenzy of calls to one another. The sun was blotted out by the smoke and smog caught in the sandwich of a downward push of clouds to the rivers. Another muggy breathless day.

Mama came home with the news that August day,

> "Ethel Stout says she has an old bicycle in her garage, and I can have it. I will lash it to the bumper of the car and bring it home. You girls will have to share it, but she said she thinks it will work."

A bike! Susie and I can ride together!

It did come home tied to the rusty bumper of our 1950 Ford station wagon. It was dark green and black. The fender on the bike chain was smashed into the chain so it made the most interesting gurdy, gurdy sound as I pumped the metal rods that used to hold the rubber pedals that had long ago dried up and dropped off in the mold of Missus Stout's cluttered garage. Most of the time I had to stand up and pump the pedals to get up any hill when Susie and I went riding. It was old and the rust on the fenders would scratch my calves and leave long jagged marks if I was not careful. There was no kickstand, but I could lay it down in the grass whenever we stopped to slosh into a sulfur creek. Mama said it was tired.

I didn't mind taking it up to Burbage's gas station to fill up the tires with the free air pump Mr. Burbage had on the curb of Main Street for anybody who needed a pump up. I would walk Gurdy up to the air pump before Susie and

I would go out. The tubes in the tires were cracked in places but could hold air for a good afternoon ride. The wind was in my hair. I had wheels. Yup. Susie and I would spend hours searching out the town, going on hikes and riding bikes.

Sometimes after we were flat out of breath and Topper and George were panting, we would stop under the big old sugar maple in Aunt Maggie's yard and sneak around behind her peony bush and turn on her hose. The wet cool soak was a tickle on our bare toes. Topper and George would lap up the little trickles circling in the roots of the tree. Then we would rinse off our bikes and give the muddy rubber wheels a wipe down. Susie and I believed we were wiping down our own ol' horses. Just like Gene Autrey.

Sewer Gas

In the heat of summer, with the blazing simmering sun beating down on the mud banks of the two rivers, my dog, George, and I could walk all the way to the edge of the rivers stepping between the deep open cracks in the mud that made a crazy quilt of designs in the dried and caked deep muck. On these hot days, the black spiny water bugs, the size of my fist, would scurry into the cracks as we tiptoed through the weeds between the crevices where the fat glistening black bugs bred.

In the spring and fall, as the mud began to melt into a soupy sludge, no one could get near the river as even a stone thrown at the shoreline would sink deep into the brown, then sink deeper, into the black tarry grime. A man walking toward the river would sink up to his knees and George would sink up to his hind legs in the light brown, then black silt.

The riverbanks were so contaminated, Dad showed me how to push a stick into the mud and then pull it out and light the hole. The flame would continue until I counted to 100.

"Sewer gas,"

Dad said.

"Yup, that's just the sludge left over from the sewers."

The surroundings were bleak, and the people were dirt poor. People in the entire Appalachian region were too busy trying to survive day to day to worry about what was happening in their surroundings.

31

THE HATE

Mama would describe her life before marrying and moving to small-town Appalachia to me and my sisters.

"It's not like this in the rest of the world. People wear nice clothes; no one spits on the sidewalk; the air is clean; there are museums with beautiful art and statues.

The food – oh the food…

There is something called an automat.

Yes, Francie, you can walk to this big store where every food you can imagine is displayed behind these small individual glass windows. Each food item is on a separate plate. All you have to do is put some quarters in the slot next to a piece of fresh-baked cherry pie and the door opens to the pie. Then you just take it to a table and eat it. Eat the whole piece yourself. Then you just walk away. Someone comes and cleans the table after you.

You kids need to get out of here as soon as you can."

"But, Mama, where do people get the money to put in the slot for the pie?"

"Everyone has money in their pockets."

"Can't we go there now, Mama?"

"There is no money. Someday, you find yourself a rich man and get out."

"Mama, I have never seen a rich man here."

Mama made it clear to us that she hated Dad. I thought it was because he refused to work while we were hungry and desperate for warm clothing or heat in the house. I later learned there was another reason that ran like an unspoken thread through our lives. And through Point Marion.

Mama and Dad became smokers when they were in college. Chain-smokers. They each had a cigarette in hand and our house reeked of cigarette smoke. They both started out with Camels, moved on to Lucky Strikes, Mama migrated to filtered Winston Salem's and Dad finished his life with Kool's. There were ashtrays full of cigarette butts, three or four containers briming with dead cigarette butts in every room. They would have cigarettes going while they ate, till the last second before they fell asleep, and while they drove.

Dad drank beer. Lots of beer. A can of Pabst Blue Ribbon or Duquesne Pilsner was near his hand during waking hours. On Saturday afternoon we would drive the car up to the alley between the Quartemont Building and the Methodist Church, pull into Patsy Cino's Point Marion Beer Distributor, and have Patsy put three cases in the trunk. The beer would be stored in the washhouse and the empty bottles returned the next Saturday. There was cold beer in the icebox. I could not understand how we had money to buy beer and cigarettes. Mama had a lot of toothaches, so every day, she had to drink 90 proof Old Crow whiskey for the toothache.

We could not get welfare because we owned our property. Even though the bank owned it, and we were supposed to be making payments (because of Aunt Dodo and the "whore"). Dad said,

> "We're land-poor, kids."

Starting in 1950, we simply had no money. Mama and Dad were in their stand-off period. Neither were working, and money was scarce. Mama would say,

> "Leonard, I am not going to go to work until little Lennie is in first grade. He needs me to be with him."

Dad said that all the jobs were going to the returned soldiers, and he had a bad back and, therefore, could not work.

We did have a garden in the back lot and the corn, beans, and tomatoes from our garden kept us alive in those early years. Four times a year there was a distribution of surplus food done by the Pennsylvania Department of Agriculture. I would go with Mama to the Borough Building and stand in a long line with welfare recipients. Waiting. Waiting. When we got to the front, the clerk would ask for the number of children in the family and income.

I don't know what Mama said, but this was the most wonderful food we ever had. More than we ever had. Two big blocks of real cheese, yellow and soft in a carton that you could put on bread and fry in an iron pan with lard on both sides. Big cans of real cooked meat with gravy. We would get four cans, open them with a can opener, dump the meat in a skillet, and eat the meat and gravy. We also got real powdered milk. Since our mama goat, Nanny, went dry a few years after she had Speedy, we never had milk, so having powder to make milk anytime was amazing.

Dad hated for us to stand in the town surplus food line,

> "Charlotte, we are not cruds. We do not beg for food. How can you go stand with those welfare people and ask for food? My family is above that. I can't show my face at Augie's."

> "Sure, fine Leonard, we have no food. We are just as entitled to get that damn stuff as those cruds from Springhill Township."

We could count on a big yelling match when surplus food was distributed, but the yelling was so worth the food we got.

Mama never got over the hate she had for Dad. I could hear her mumble under her breath cursing him. Her anger was like a pervasive tight rope strung through my soul, the unspoken thread through our lives. Her distain for her circumstances was near the surface. I could feel the tension in the air like the electric zap of lightning waiting above the graying clouds in a sudden spring storm. Waiting. The family tiptoed around her seething.

I asked her why she didn't leave him and take all of us away. She knew there were other places in the world. She was born in Seattle, Washington and she grew up in New York City. Her parents had taken her around the world.

> "You make your bed, and you have to sleep in it. Where would we go?"

I had no answer. I had never been out of the hills.

What I did resolve was that I would find joy within myself, and I would guard it like a sacred prayer.

32

TALLEY HO

Evelyn Thompson (Evie), who owned Friendship Hill Farm, would stop by often to visit Mom. They had both traveled around the world and gone to exclusive schools. The two of them would sit in our parlor drinking Old Crow, laughing, and telling stories of polo matches and books. When Mama talked about her college days, her eyes would light up, and she would leave our dismal surroundings for the moment to describe an enchanted time of hope, excitement, and entitlement. Our parlor was the one room in our house that was off limits to everyone except Mama and her special friends.

Early on in her marriage to Dad, before her own father became ill, he sent her a baby grand piano from New York. She kept this one treasured piece of furniture in the parlor. Sometimes she would go alone into her own off-limits room and play old songs on the piano, like *"Whispering Hope"* and *"Aura Lee."*

Mama made slipcovers for the furniture in the parlor out of an old roll of monk's cloth that Aunt MaeMae had saved. She kept the lace curtains on the four windows starched and stretched. This room was her sanctuary. She even had an old wind-up turntable with an assortment of black vinyl records.

Mama and Miss Thompson would sit listening and tittering to a record of Victor Borge, playing the piano and making silly jokes. Laughing and swigging away at their bottomless crystal glasses filled with Old Crow, they would say,

"Talley ho,"

give a snicker, then toss down a gulp.

Miss Thompson was a hard worker and one of the kindest people I ever met while growing up in Point Marion. She ran the farm with her devoted husband, Chris Martin, who Mama said was from the Main Line in Philadelphia. They had three children who were usually off at boarding school. I thought she and Mama pined to have some intelligent female company.

George could tell when Miss Thompson was approaching. He would perk up his ears and lift his nose in the stagnant air and give a little cough. She smelled like the inside of her horse barns. She wore tattered clothes and high riding boots smeared with manure.

Although she was born in southwestern Pennsylvania, she was the granddaughter of J.V. Thompson, a native son of Fayette County, who in the early 1900s was estimated to be one of the richest men in America. Although Evie Thompson was raised at the Oak Hill Estate, built by her grandfather in Uniontown, she did not have the southwestern Pennsylvania colloquial twang in her voice like the rest of us from the valley. Her speech was clearly a New England accent landing with an *ahhh* on her vowels rather than an *AAA* like us. She and her siblings spent their growing up years at exclusive East Coast boarding schools.

It was obvious that running the Friendship Hill Farm was a huge responsibility and an enormous expense to Evie and Chris. They had horses, cows, servants, Irish wolfhounds, foxhounds, lots of workers, and an ancient mansion to maintain.

Mama would say,

> "Evie and I have the same problems, hers just have more zeros behind them."

Friendship Hill Farm was five miles outside of town, overlooking the Monongahela River north. It was founded by Albert Gallatin in the 1790s as he explored the wilderness of America. One of the most beautiful farms in America, Friendship Hill Farm has always been a proud reminder of the history of southwestern Pennsylvania.

Eileen and the Horses

Not unlike other little girls, Eileen went through a "horse period." It seems to happen when girls are seven or eight and disappears on its own when they are fourteen or so. Dad said,

> "Girls start looking like ponies along about seven or eight and then, in their mid-teens, they get rounder."

I have seen girls who have a "horse period" that lasts their entire life!

Eileen succumbed to little girl "horse period" when she was 9 years old, and it went on and on. She talked about horses, and she pretended she was a horse. She wanted a horse so badly that she begged Mama to drop her off at Evie Thompson's farm every day in the summer so she could help in the horse barns. If Mama could not drop Eileen off, she would walk three miles along the road to the farm. She would do every kind of scutwork imaginable at the horse barn. Mostly, she would shovel horse manure from one place to another for hours and hours. The stuff had huge swarms of flies all over it and smelled worse than our sewer. She LOVED it.

When she would come home from shoveling at that barn, she would walk around saying,

> "Tally Ho, Tally Ho,"

whatever that meant.

Eileen still trusted Dad. She believed he was living in our real world.

> "Dad, please buy me a horse, I will take care of it and ride it and brush it. We have room for a horse. I need one."

Dad would say,

> "Gosh, Eileen, we don't have a barn for a horse. We need a barn if you have a horse."

"Dad, if we had a barn, I could have a horse??"

Somehow, Eileen convinced herself that if she built a barn in our back lot, Dad would get her a horse of her own! She spent day after day in our back lot one summer sweating and digging the footings for a barn. She measured it out, tied strings to sticks and began a serious excavation project.

I would go out to her job area,

> "Eileen, why do you believe him? He will never get you a horse, he is just pretending. Why do you believe him?"

> "I have to believe him, France."

"Why? Don't enter his made-up world."

Dad was no help. Every once in a while, he would take off in the car. We would ask him where he was going.

"Oh, I have to go see a man about a horse."

Eileen would eye me with that "I told you so" look. Of course, there was never a horse. Eileen eventually stopped digging in the back lot. But she never grew out of her "horse period."

I never had a "horse period." Long ago I convinced myself that Dad was an imposter and, gradually, I began developing one of my strongest self-taught life lessons. I call it TNO: *"Trust No One."* Although I have had a few remarkable dalliances with this core self-value throughout my life, I remain a true disciple of the TNO theory.

PHOTO GALLERY

Figure 1 Point Marion

Figure 2 Two Rivers

Figure 3 Len Dillinger, Dillinger Ferry, 1912

Figure 4 Aunt MaeMae in the Flood, 1910

Figure 5 Mom and Dad, College Days, 1936

Figure 6 Wedding Picture of Mom and Dad, 1937

Figure 7 Aunt MaeMae and me, 1948

Figure 8 Me with my siblings, on the front porch, 1951

Figure 9 Summer Heat, 1951

Figure 10 William Moser, Point Marion Chief of Police, 1950s

Figure 11 Our Family Home, 1960

Figure 12 Amber, our "Genuine Blood Hound "

Figure 13 Baby boomers in the sixth grade

Figure 14 Before the Pigtail Rebellion ... My hair grew long, longer, longest

Figure 15 George M. Leader, The Best Non-Hound Dog

Figure 16 Me and Albert, High School Prom, 1962

Figure 17 Me and Albert, in the weeds, 1962

Figure 18 Woodville State Mental Hospital

Figure 19 Woodville State Mental Hospital

Figure 20 Tugboat taking coal to Power Plant, 2019

Figure 21 Coal Barge Pushers in Front of the House

Figure 22 Slag Heap in Appalachia

Figure 23 Company Patch

Figure 24 Company Patch

Figure 25 Company Patch

Figure 26 Mountaintop Removal Mining in Appalachia

Figure 27 Mountaintop Removal Mining in Appalachia

33

PURE-BRED

Dad refused to get a job working for someone else, which would give our family a regular paycheck. So, he tried to figure out how to create some wildly unheard-of way to make spending money.

I liked being his helper on these sidelines. My ever-curious mind saw a chance for learning the intricacies of some off-beat diversion. He tried collecting rents from the few straggling people left in the Davidson Mine patch and sending it to the owner who lived somewhere in the bowels of West Virginia. He got a few dollars for that to add to the beer coffer, until the stragglers eventually moved out of Davidson. We even did some rent collecting for the absent owner of the shacks left in the patch of Adah Bottom. There were receipts and tallies of debt and reports to owners that I learned to write up.

Miss Evelyn Thompson would drop off pieces of dilapidated furniture for Dad to repair. He routinely had an interesting-looking old wood-carved settee or table or sofa sitting in our washhouse in various stages of disassembly. Miss Thompson would say,

> "Now Leonard, this is a piece from the early 1800s."

> "Evie, this piece can only be wired together – it's falling apart."

> "Just do the best you can. I won't let anyone touch it once I put it back in the mansion at the farm. I just want to set it in the corner."

He would take the scratchy, ancient, horsehair fabric and try to reweave it. Or he would use putty to create a replacement repair on an ornate piece of wood. Then he would try to create a matching color of stain by mixing old paint. We would rewire old rusty springs together in the soft furniture and try to piece together some of the decaying fabric. I learned a lot about upholstery and woodworking during that phase of Dad's diversions. Dad never finished most of the dozens of repairs to the precious estate furniture Miss Thompson brought to him from Friendship Hill Farm. I think she came by to talk to Mama anyway.

After a year or two of the furniture sitting in our washhouse and getting caked with more dust, Miss Thompson would quietly take the furniture item back after spending the afternoon with Mama. She learned to have low expectations. Just like me.

Pure-Bred Bloodhounds

Another of Dad's money-making schemes was to get a pure-bred bloodhound.

One spring he started making a wire pen behind the washhouse. Mama raised chickens and ducks for eggs, but Dad suddenly decided to give all the chickens and ducks to the Buncic family who lived way back in Buncic Hollow.

Mama said,

> "Look Leonard, we need these chicks for eggs. How are we going to manage without the chickens?"

> "Charlotte, I can't have chickens disturbing my prized bloodhound. You'll see, this bloodhound will be a real money maker."

> "Oh, for God's sake, Leonard."

I was glad to get rid of the chickens because they ran loose at our back door and pooped all over the grass. It made a sticky mess on our bare toes. The ducks were much worse. They were big and mean. They would chase me and George and bite our bare heels whenever we walked near them. They would stand watch at the screen door and when we walked outside,

> SQUAWK. SQUAWK. SQUACK.

They would chase us and nip, nip, nip at our heels with their wings flapping. George and I would run like banshees. The times they would catch me, my heels would bleed like a stuck pig.

I asked Dad how a bloodhound was going to make money for us.

> "Well, Francie, bloodhounds are really important as dogs go. You see, they have the BEST noses. If someone robs a bank or if someone is kidnapped, or even if someone gets lost, our bloodhound will find that person, and I will get paid for using my very own bloodhound."

I looked at Dad. This was an incredulous notion.

> "But Dad, no one has ever robbed a bank in Point Marion. No one has ever been kidnapped. Except for Theresa Scaramella who ran away with the Baptist minister from Fairchance, who everyone thought for a day or two was kidnapped, no one has ever even gotten lost."

> "Once I have this bloodhound, I will get a lot of calls. And, I will make a lot of money, yes indeed!"

I could not figure out how Dad managed it, but he ordered a pure-bred bloodhound to arrive on the train all the way from Atlanta, Georgia. The trains stopped in Point Marion in those days ONLY for special deliveries. He said he was not going to have his dog tied up when she was outside, so he finished his wire pen for when she needed to be outside. Of course, the rest of our dogs wandered in and out of the house and wandered around town like any old dog. But Dad said this dog was exceptional and she would never be set loose like a

> "Common coon hound or a mutt like George."

The big day came when Dad's prized bloodhound bitch arrived on the train. Her exclusive papers had been sent by genuine certified mail, with a return receipt requested. Dad, Eileen, Charlen, and I marched up to the train station and waited a good long time for the 2 p.m. train. Of course, George was with me. Dad's prized possession was in a wooden crate with straw on the bottom. The train assistant handed the medium crate down to Dad. The thing reeked like dog crap. George started to back off. Dad opened the lid and lifted out his new puppy.

She was a beautiful golden-brown color with ten times the amount of skin hanging on her frame needed to cover her small body. She had long drooping ears and slurpy spit coming out her mouth. Dad said,

> "Oh, she is beautiful."

Dad named her Amber and everyone in the family fell in love with her. George hung out with her, but she was not allowed to wander. She had to stay in her cage near the washhouse whenever she was outside. She lived in the house with the rest of the dogs. She was the only dog allowed to sleep on the sofa in the living room.

Of course, our family had lots of dogs. Each person in the family had a dog. We never worried about what they would eat or drink. They were allowed to run loose and could find something to eat around town, on the riverbank, or in the backwoods.

Dad gave Amber special food and was careful to worm her. He spent lots of time having her practice finding one of us. This consisted of taking my shoe off and giving it to Dad. Then I would go into our backyard and hide behind a tree or go down to the riverbank and hide in the weeds. Dad would have Amber sniff the shoe and tell her,

"Go find."

Sometimes Amber would find us. Dad thought this was amazing.

"By god, that dog is really smart!"

As she grew older, Dad would have us hide in various parts of town. He would take a piece of our clothes and set her out searching. Sometimes she would come sniffing after us with Dad close behind. Sometimes they would go home, and Amber would sit on the sofa beside Dad while he drank a beer. I knew if they didn't find me and George in a couple of hours, they were not coming.

Amber grew into a beautiful dog. She still had too much skin for her body, and George and I thought the drool was disgusting, but when she barked, it was not the routine WOOO WOO WOO we heard from the coon hounds, or the ARRF ARRF George made. Her sound was deep and resonant and melodious,

HOWUULLL. HOWULLLLL

After a year of working with Amber with no Point Marion bank robberies, kidnappings, or missing persons, Dad said to all of us,

> "Well kids, the best way to make money off this bloodhound is to breed her to another full-blooded bloodhound. One that is registered like Amber. Yes indeed, I will make money on every single puppy she has."

Mama said,

> "Oh, for god's sake Leonard, we have enough god-dammed dogs now. Who wants a full-blooded bloodhound in Appalachia? These people want only hunting dogs!"

A month later, a big male bloodhound came from North Carolina on the train. I have no idea how Dad scraped up more money to have a big ol' dog sent on a train. We had never been on a train.

Dad called him Traxi. He was huge and loud. Mama put her foot down and said he was not an inside dog, so Traxi had to live in the backdoor yard, tied up by the neck. The only problem was that Amber took an immediate disdain to Traxi. She made it clear that this male bloodhound from North Carolina was not up to her Georgia standards. She ignored him.

Dad said,

> "Don't worry, when she comes into HEAT, she will change her mind."

I asked,

> "Dad, what's HEAT?"

> "You tell her, Charlotte."

> "That's when a mama dog wants to have puppies."

I asked,

> "Well, if Amber doesn't like Traxi when she doesn't want puppies, why would she change her mind when she does want to have puppies?"

Mama said,

> "Francie, just STOP it! You'll figure it out!"

It turned out that Amber did come into heat and, before Dad could put Traxi in her wire pen, she got out of her cage and ran off to Harvey Town. She fell in love with the police dog that Mr. Cappelli owned. Two months later, Amber had ten puppies. The puppies were black and brown. A lot of them looked like Mr. Cappelli's police dog, except they had big, long, floppy ears and too much skin on their bodies. They were cute and yipped and yipped all the time. Amber was constantly nursing them.

Three months later, Traxi died. Dad said he died of a broken heart because Amber couldn't fall in love with him. We kept Amber's puppies. They would go racing up and down the street in a pack. They loved to chase neighborhood dogs as a unit and sleep together in a heap of soft dog flesh. Amber only lived six years.

Dad said,

> "Those pure breeds just don't last that long, too shallow a gene pool."

After the bloodhound fiasco, Dad took a break from his wild chases toward free-flowing money without getting a job. These were difficult years of struggle with the constant decaying rage of Mama just beneath the surface, ready to raise through an opening of any situation.

As a child, I was accustomed to the lack of joy in our family. Mama was angry and sarcastic in most situations. She seemed unable to appreciate even the smallest ray of sunshine. Dad continued to dream.

I was finding that, deep within me, I could muster my own points of light.

34

WIFE BEATERS

We did have some frightening characters around. There was always a broken country woman from the townships sitting on the railroad ramp steps, staring at the lumps of shale between the rusty old rails and weathered ties. The trains had not pulled up on that rail dogleg section since 1930. Little children with runny noses dressed in dirty rags stood near their mama, waiting for the ol' man to walk across the street from Augie's Beer Garden. Then they all took the long walk back up the hollow, following their daddy.

"Mama, why don't these railroad ramp women go to their own mama's?"

"Can't ever do that. Their mama's won't have them. They made their bed and now they have to sleep in it."

"Why, Mama? These women are being beaten."

"They made their bed..."

Violence was all around. The scary nature and sudden outbursts of people was simply accepted. The area was so inaccessible, the locals would create their own system of disciplining their lifestyle. Just like the longing thread that spins through the soul of the people to cling to the mountains and their culture, the same thirsty appetite for aggression lies deep within these same people, or so it seemed.

In Point Marion, there was an aura of mentally deranged people who were either actively living in the town, leaving, or coming home from one of the state-run mental hospitals. To say there was an awareness by the populace of the "nut" down the street or the lunatic next door was an understatement.

This was the era before psychiatric drugs could moderate the response to mental illness. For many people, the only option for treatment was electroshock and confinement. Most of the men of the town had served in World War I or World War II, and most had served in the Korean War.

The early arrivals to Point Marion were descended from the hearty stock of settlers who scratched and fought their way across the Appalachian foothills from Virginia. Then came the immigrants with strong backs and long arms to work in the underground coal pits, or the immigrants escaping the tyranny in Europe of the mid and late 1800s. During and after World War I, another wave of hardy people came looking for a better life.

Scrapping and scratching and clawing at life is in their DNA. The people of Appalachia are fighters and hunters. Some of them have an affinity for killing and inflicting physical hurt on others.

The men of Point Marion are proud of their war service. Going into the service was what the boys did for their one chance to get out of the oppressive call of the river valley. These were fighting people. They were sent to war. Of those that came back, many of them were broken. These were before the days of sympathy for and understanding of Post-Traumatic Stress Disorder and before successful drug therapies.

The Veterans Hospitals were so far away that they were virtually inaccessible to our region's returned soldiers, who were all over town. All the time. The Veterans of Foreign Wars Post 447 and the American Legion were packed all day, every day. Sad, angry men who had given their best to a fighting nation stood bellied up to the bars and sat at the poker tables and drank, and drank, and drank, every day, all day. Each with a chew or a dangling cigarette.

Walking by the American Legion in the Harvey Town section of Point Marion, I heard shouts and the smell of sour beer and whiskey wafting from the swinging door. I heard men yelling angry epitaphs at one another, their spit on the sidewalk and chewed tobacco wads leaking into the gutter.

The VFW was on Main Street where route 119 went north toward the county seat of Uniontown, right around the corner from Susie's house. Cars would be parked in the mud around the building, scattered in all directions, with no mind to how the next fellow would squeeze his jalopy out when he staggered through the door.

George and I walked by the VFW as we routinely explored the town. Always the same bunch of rusted-out Fords, Chevys, and Buicks. Sometimes there were a few raggedy country kids waiting quietly in the back seat. Ratted clothing, runny noses, waiting for daddy to finish his business inside. The kids in the cars were always quiet. Just sitting. They knew if they made a disturbance there would be a beating. In the summer, the cars looked hot and steamy. In the winter, there was ice on the windshields. Sometimes I raised my hand in a shy wave, but otherwise, I watched my feet to miss the puddles.

Violence sometimes erupted in the street or at home with a mean drunk. When this happened, Bill Moser, the Police Chief, was called. He had been the Police Chief in Point Marion for as long as I could remember. He crossed the kids walking to school and he made sure there was no speeding of those young punks driving into Pennsylvania from West Virginia to buy stronger beer from Patsy Cino at his Point Marion Beer Distributorship.

We called him Chief Moser. He dressed in full black police uniform with shiny black boots up to his mid-calf. He wore his black uniform with gold buttons and buckles and a big gold pin stuck right over his heart on his black shirt that said,

POLICE CHIEF
Point Marion.

He had a cloth hat with a shiny rim and a gold belt around the band of the hat. He tipped his hat to people when they passed.

"Morning Chief Moser."

"Morning Miss Francie."

Wasted drunks were a common sight for George and me. If, after a few hours they were still laying on the sidewalk after staggering out of one of the bars, Chief Moser would grab the slobbering, kicking fellow and lock him up overnight in the four-cell Point Marion Jail. Bill Moser's matronly, sweet wife would give Bill a plate of eggs to take to the jail for breakfast. Then off the criminal would go, toward home, with a sheepish grin.

If the drunk had caused someone to bleed to the point that Doc Hungar had to sew them up with more than ten stitches, or if the drunk had broken a bone besides his own, then Bill would have Lazier Black put the perpetrator in the back of the Point Marion police car for a drive to the county jail in Uniontown. That was serious.

"Bill Moser had Lazier take Leroy Fields to the county pokey for breaking Jim Bob Larson's arm last night."

"Hmmmm..."

In addition to the returned servicemen, we had the people that Mama referred to as the

> Bad Genes.
>
> "Look kids, everyone in that family has a screw loose. Just walk on the other side of the street. They are harmless. They only seem to hurt their own people."

This Bad Gene category was usually the group of men who were the "peeping Toms," the "follow someone around town and stare at them," the "sit on the curb and stare at the stones in the road," and the "walk down to the Brass Rail and sit all day until Jimmy, (the owner of the Brass Rail), said it was time to go," type.

Of course, this group included several ladies who fell into the Bad Gene category. The "dress up like Eva Gabor with a crinoline skirt and big splotches of rouge, big bright red rosebud painted lips, and sashay up to Augie's for a slobbering cry over a few beers" type.

Harmless mostly.

Police Chief Bill Moser pretty much handled this group.

Once in a while, there was the kind who was a mama who would cry all day and stay locked inside her house. She would have to go to Mayview State Mental Hospital and stay for a while till she had enough shock treatments to set her straight. Then she could come home until it started up again.

Dad would say,

> "Oh Charlotte, Elizabeth Jones went off to Mayview yesterday. She should be back in about ten days, after they give her another round of electric zaps."

Interesting that everyone in town knew about these shock treatment people, but no one would acknowledge the problem or help the family, or even talk about it. Elizabeth Jones had a girl in Charlen's class, a girl in Eileen's class, and a boy in my class. She would disappear for weeks at a time and then reappear. A frail, thin, pale woman who wore fancy dresses, nylon stockings, and high heels all the time, even in the boiling, sopping, wet, heat of summer. Her husband had a mysterious big job, and she had a housekeeper. We were in awe of the lifestyle the family had. Of course, the children never spoke to me. I was an invisible crud.

> "Mama, what could make Mrs. Jones have to have electric shock treatments? She has everything."
>
> "She is just crazy. A screw loose."

We also had our share of perverts.

Mr. Bowland lived with Mrs. Bowland across the street in the Titus Building. He ran the Point Marion Pool Hall that was in the basement of Barney's Theatre. Mr. Bowland always wanted Eileen and me to come to the pool hall and see him. He said that if we would, he would give us a bag of candy. He had his pockets full of candy for "good little girls." Tootsie Roll Pops, Mary Jane's, black and pink licorice, Good and Plenty.

The only time we would get candy is when we went Halloweening. So, getting Mr. Bowland to give us a sample of the candy in his pockets was fun. Mr. Bowland was following us around.

> "Now Francie, I'll give you this box of Good and Plenty now, and then you come down to the pool hall later and I will show you how to play pool."

We could never go to the pool hall because there was a big sign at the top of the stairs leading down to the pool hall that said:

NO ONE UNDER 18 PERMITTED
IN THE POINT MARION POOL HALL
By order of the Point Marion Police
William Moser, Chief

I figured Chief Moser had this one covered too.

Mr. Bowland's granddaughter, Cherry, lived in Pittsburgh and, for a week every summer, would come to Point Marion with her mama and daddy and her little brother. Cherry was Eileen's age and the two of them were great friends for one week every summer. During this one week, Mr. Bowland was on especially good behavior.

When I walked up the street and he was on the other side of the street, the hair on the back of my neck would frizz and I would get the willies. George was always with me, and I could hear him

GRRRRRR. GRRRRRRR.

Then there was Junior Davis in a "crazy" category all his own.

Over the years, I have witnessed that so many insane people are hidden away in the underbelly of small towns. The townspeople seem to protect them, and they become part of the scenery everyone is accustomed to.

People of the hills, in general, are so busy with the business of survival that indifference is a way of life. We hide from, rather than treat, the mentally ill. Every so often, there is a catastrophe.

35

BUDDY AND GEORGE

Junior Davis was one of the many crazy people who inhabited Appalachia. Junior lived down the street from us with his old mama. He chain-smoked. Junior was in the "wander around town staring at and following people" category of crazies. He usually stuck to his street, Water Street, and the street that ran uptown, Penn Street. He was out every day staring and smoking. Daddy said he was harmless, but I was plain stark afraid of him.

He was a grown man.

In the summer before fourth grade, he began following me around town more than he had in the past. He always stayed 25 or so feet from me and looked away when I looked at him. He pretended to stare toward the traffic moving through town, light a cigarette with his zippo lighter, flip it "click" shut, and draw on the cigarette for five minutes, blowing the smoke toward the cinders in the sidewalk. Then five minutes into each cigarette, he would take the little bit of a stub between his thumb and forefinger and take a long draw on the end, flick it down into the shale pebbles, and stomp on it with a fury, jumping on the stub with his right foot and squirming the pad of his foot into the dirty sidewalk. He would look at me when the final stomp was made with a squinting stare.

Mrs. Davis dressed him in ironed shirts and pressed pants. I wondered what his life must be like, living with his mean, mean mama, and her drooling boxer dog. That dog's drool would lace down over his lips in a snarky, sticky, glue-like, cloudy string that sometimes trailed after him. Junior never spoke to anyone, not even his mama. He marched around town staring and smoking.

> "Dad, Junior Davis followed me and George over to Harvey Town yesterday when I went over to the glass chip dump to look for specimens. He walked real fast past me and just stood looking at the weeds and smoking. George growled at him."
>
> "I told you he is harmless, Francie. You and George just stay away from him."
>
> "Dad, I think he is following me."

It was a sweltering, sultry August day. The clouds hung close to the valley floor and followed the river south to crowd down on the town waiting to open and drop their built-up water in big, stinging, splattering, end-of-summer drizzles. The clouds this time of year would not release their pent-up moisture until they were nearly bursting from the water they encased. The ground-hugging, stiff, opaque billows covered the hot blazing fireball of a sun above them, soaked up its heat, and held all of us in a sandwich of misty sweltering fog during the day and in oppressive breath-catching closeness at night.

This was the time of year the old miners with Black Lung and the chain smokers would have the worst hacking attacks. George and I could hear them inside Augie's, the American Legion, the VFW, the Brass Rail, and on the street.

> WHEEZE. WHEEZE.
> CAHACK. CAHACK.
> HOCK. SPUTTER. SPIT.

The sputtering would line the sidewalks with thick green and yellow gobs of spit. The rest of the year, the spit on the sidewalk and gutters was foamy white. Mama and Daddy would sit on the porch swing outside until late at night trying to catch a breeze off the river, coughing and wheezing and smoking their cigarettes. The cicadas even had a higher pitched warning for the close breathlessness.

> CHECHE TAK TAK TAK. CHECHE TAK TAK TAK.
> CHECHE TAK TAK TAK.
> CHECHE TAK TAK TAK. CHECHE TAK TAK TAK.
> CHECHE TAK TAK TAK.

The Italians living in Little Italy, the two streets on the southside of the hill above the nearly deserted glass factory, called this time of year "the dog days." I'm not sure why it was dog days. Maybe because this time of year, not even the dogs could find anything to howl about. In fact, the clouds were so close to the ground they would cover up the moon, and the hunting hound dogs would not even have that to howl at.

About midday on the dog days, George made sure I was not needing him to tag along for a bike ride or a last-minute exploration before sneaking down to the river, all alone, to wade through the sewer mud until he reached the cool muddy water. I would see him gently push off from the muck on the river bottom when he got up to his neck. He would scratch at the brown water with his head showing, making wide circles in the cool wet. This gave his fleas a chance to scurry up to his head so they wouldn't drown. Before he made the last turn for shore, he would trick those old fleas and dip completely underwater. Then he would head to the bank of the river. The mud during dog days was warm and soft and slick. George returned from his afternoon swims muddy, smelly, and flealess.

> "Hey, Georgie. You got those ol' fleas this time!"

George returned from his afternoon cool down and skipped to town to find me. Junior Davis and his mother lived on one side of an unpainted two-story duplex on the east side of Water Street, so I walked down the west side. I was staying away from him, like Daddy said.

Water Street ran parallel to the river and the west side had no houses halfway down because the river would come up every spring to the edge of the road and float anything in its way up the river north to Spruce Town. The DeGardyn's place was the first house on the west side of Water Street. I was in the DeGardyn's garden checking out the last of their tomato plants. Mr. DeGardyn had some mighty fine Beef Steak tomatoes that year.

George came right up to me – muddy, smelling like the sewer, and sopping wet. Since George was not slick like the hounds, he had a much harder time. His fur was thick and bushy and became matted when he went swimming in the river. He tried to bay like the coon hounds, but instead of making the beautiful howling sounds like the hounds, he ended up with

BARK-A-BARK-A-BARK-A.

He was half the size of a coon hound, but George thought he was a beautiful hound and he acted like one. Coon hounds are one-person dogs. George knew he was my only dog, and I was his only person.

By August, the staked tomato plants were way over my head, so George found me behind the second row hidden from the street. As he approached me, he started to growl.

> "Hey George, what are you growling about? C'mon and see these huge tomatoes. Maybe we'll just chunk one."

Then I saw him. Junior Davis was standing right behind the next tomato plant, staring at me. He did not have a cigarette. I froze. George kept growling.

Now George was showing his stubby teeth and the mushy hair on the back of his neck and above his shoulders was starting to raise up. George believed he was a big protecting dog.

The growling continued.

All of a sudden, I looked toward the street and there was Mrs. Davis and her bulldog, Buddy. She had Buddy on a slip collar and a tightly held chain. The dog was ferocious with long, sharp teeth that were exposed, with thick, yellow drool dripping from his mouth, down onto his neck. A muscular lumbering dog, he was usually growling under his breath when Mrs. Davis had him out. George and I routinely walked on the other side of the street. George was half the size of Buddy.

Now George and I were trapped. Junior Davis was on one side, and the bulldog and Mrs. Davis were between us and the street. The tomato stakes were blocking us in. Without any warning, Mrs. Davis unhooked the leash from the growling monster dog's slip collar and hissed,

"Sssssic 'em."

The dog lunged at me. I started to run around the tomato plant. George attacked the bulldog!

"Oh no, George, run!"

George kept on attacking. The fur was flying, the dirt of the garden was being kicked up and the dogs kept on. Mrs. Davis kept saying,

"Sssssic 'em. Sssssic 'em. Sssssic 'em."

I was screaming.

Then Buddy grabbed George by the under throat with his locking jaws and shook, and shook, and shook until George lay silent in the dirt. Mrs. Davis said,

"C' mon."

Buddy backed off from George and returned to Mrs. Davis' side. She snapped the leash back on Buddy, turned around, and strutted home. Junior slinked after her.

I picked up George and carried him home. He was alive and breathing out of a gaping bleeding hole in his neck. I put him in the goat shed and gathered some hay from the goats for him to lay on. I could hear him breathing, in and out, in and out, through that big hole in his neck.

EEEEEEEE. AWWWWWWW.
EEEEEE. AWWWWWWW.

I asked Mama what I could do for George.

"Mama, I think George might die."

"You just pet him. Stay with him and give him lots of water."

It never occurred to me to ask that we take George to a doctor. The four of us kids only saw the doctor if we were bleeding bad and Mama could not stop the blood.

When I started fourth grade, I was still taking care of George. Before Thanksgiving he was up and walking around well enough to follow me most places. His open wound eventually closed, but he had a scar on his windpipe that caused his breathing to be labored for the rest of his life.

I would hear,

> eeeee awwwww.
> Eeeeee awwwwww.

And I knew George was nearby.

Throughout my growing up, George stood by me. He was there for me and seemed to inherently understand my aching heart. He protected me and loved me without reserve. I tried to do the same for him.

George completed me.

36

FAMILIES SURVIVED

I had a friend, Nancy Thorn, whose family had no real home of their own. Her family was her, her mama, her older sister, Helen, a brother Steven, and some younger sisters. Nancy's mama was on relief, and it was important to keep the babies coming in order to keep the Aid to Dependent Children coming in. Nancy told me that her mama was a nurse long ago, but she wanted to stay home with her children.

Because of the ADC money, Nancy and the other kids had food to eat. Nancy's mama could find an abandoned company house or empty building to make into a home for her family. They would move from place to place, but the family stayed near Point Marion so all the kids could go to school there.

Nancy's mama was not like some of the other mamas who lived with their children in the hollows or the empty houses. There was no daddy that was drunk and screaming at her or expected to come staggering home from the various beer gardens that lined each side of the streets in Point Marion. No one got a beating there. Their family was a mama and her many children. They were a happy family. I spent a lot of time with them.

Mrs. Thorn would settle into a shack where she would set up housekeeping with her children. If a rent man came around and wanted money too often, or if the roof started to leak more than she could handle with a piece of tin, she would move to another abandoned shack. There were plenty of abandoned ramshackle structures around the townships. There were empty coal company houses in many of the patches.

Nancy's mama drank a bit, but not so much that she slept all the time. Her mama had some other activities to keep their pocket money coming in. Mrs. Thorn was pretty. In the late afternoon, she would put bright red lipstick around her lips like a bow and pull one of those fancy tops with sparkles like movie stars wear over her ample bosom and walk to Augie's Beer Garden in town. Sometimes in the late afternoons when I would walk by Augie's, I could hear Mrs. Thorn's laughter through the swinging door. She was always happy.

Ella was the Thorn family's beautiful blue tick hound. She had a litter of pups once a year. Mrs. Thorn would mate Ella with her big blue tick coon hound, Joe Lester, and sell the puppies for extra beer money, letting her kids keep the pick of the litter. The Thorn's had lots of dogs to warn them when the rent man was near or when any of Mrs. Thorn's gentlemen callers might come around.

For a year or two, when Nancy and I were in third and fourth grade, the Thorn's lived in a shack in an area we called "Shoestring."

I am sure the name "Shoestring" was derived from the description some drunk gave the winding dirt road/rocky walkway when he staggered home from Augie's Beer Garden or the Brass Rail one moonless night.

> *"Just follow the shoestring along the riverbank. If you step into the river, you ain't on the path. Jest keep walking till you hear the hounds on yer porch."*

When walking south from Point Marion on Sadler Street up Shoestring, we never knew whether this road that meandered along the riverbank and slapped up against the hill would be flooded by the rushing Cheat waters or if the lapping waters would be a slide down the riverbanks on the east side of Shoestring.

There was a collection of shacks backed up to the hillside along Shoestring with various groups of people scraping by. If these folks had an old jalopy, they would be sure to park it high in the weeds toward the hillside, in case the waters of the Cheat would be flowing high that day. Of course, the big male hunting coon hounds were chained high near the hillside. The puppies and bitches would hang out under and on the porches. They were smart enough to stay away from the rising water. No one would ever lose a hound to the river.

Nobody seemed to care that, at any time, without warning, the water tumbling over the dam at Lake Lynn could abruptly go from a trickle to the flow of a power washer, and that something, anything, could be washed away. I often saw the water lapping up to the broken steps of the wooden porches. Year-round, the wood of the steps leading to the porches was swollen and moldy from being soaked year after year with the muddy water.

Shoestring ended in the weeds, half a mile south of town, at the 20-foot by 20-foot concrete block building owned by Mr. Gladstone. The rusting metal sign read,

POINT MARION WATER COMPANY
NO TRESPASSING

There were big red letters with the words,

Trespassers will be Prosecuted
By order of the
POINT MARION POLICE DEPARTMENT

We had only seen the Point Marion police car once on Shoestring. That was the time LeRoy Flamer was beating Rosemary so bad she ran screeching to the Borough Building in her underwear to get officer Lazier Black to come and arrest LeRoy and throw him in the town jail. By the time officer Black arrived, LeRoy had fallen sound asleep in their shack. Nancy and I were sitting on her porch swing, we heard the fracas in the end shack where LeRoy and Rosie lived. We saw Rosie run through the weeds with her baby in her arms. Her nose was bleeding, and her legs were all scratched up. Her other little children were standing in silence on their porch.

Rosie screamed as she raced by,

> "I am gonna have Officer Black throw you in the pokey. You hain't gonna do that to me no more."

Pretty soon Officer Black came in the Borough police car. Lights flashing and siren whirring. That sure got everyone's attention.

> "Come on out LeRoy. You cain't be beatin' on Rosie like that."

Officer Black brought LeRoy out in handcuffs, tossed him in the back of the police car, and blazed off to the police station. Nancy and I got the other children off the Flamer's porch, gave them each an apple, and played with them. There were three of them. I could tell they were scared. We all knew LeRoy Flamer had a reputation for being mean, and he had done this before. Rosie came back a little while later and took her children home.

I asked,

> "Miss Rosie, why do you put up with this? Can you go to your mama?"
>
> "Francie, my mama won't have me and all these kids. Besides, when LeRoy's not drinkin', he ain't so bad."

LeRoy slept it off in the town jail and came home the next morning. Nancy and I were sitting on her porch swing when we heard him wading through the weeds on the path leading up to the shack he shared with Rosie and the kids. He was slobbering something about being sorry and never ever doing that again. I knew he would not change. Nancy looked at me and said,

"That's one reason why my mama will never have a husband here."

Violence is part of the Appalachian landscape.

37

EXPLORING FREE SPIRITS

Nancy and I explored the town and tried to discover how everything worked. We were free spirits. Skipping along together, barefooted in the summer and booted up with old black miner's galoshes we found in the winter. Lanky and skinny/tall me in my ever-present pigtails and short Nancy with her hair in brown ringlets. Of course, our dogs were trotting at our side.

We walked along the riverbanks testing for sewer gas flames, and we checked out how all the abandoned coal tipples along the river were put together with intricate wood planks and creaky pieces of rusty iron.

We were curious to uncover how a loaded coal truck could:
- pull up to a perpendicular tipple that was wearily creaking over the river with a coal barge below,
- back up to the edge of the precipice,
- lift its back end up to 90 degrees, and
- dump its rocky black tonnage into the waiting barge.

All this without toppling itself into the murky river below or dropping one dollop of the precious rock into the dirty sweeping water.

If we got bored watching the workings of the town, we could head into Walnut Hill and dig into the old Indian mounds. We often found arrowheads made by the Indians before our ancestors settled the land and drove them out.

George and Ella were good rat-chasing buddies. They'd keep all the garbage and slag heap rats back in the woods and away from the houses. Ella would put her beautiful wet nose up in the wind and bay,

WOOOOO. WOOOO. WOOOO.

George would ease over to her and put his nose in the breeze,

AAAARRRFFF.

George was half the size of Ella. With his perked-up ears and her long hound drooping ears, they made quite a hunting couple. His coat was all mutt-like in a fluffy gray white/black sort of way. Ella had sleek smooth hair close to her skin with big black spots on the white of her coat. The color was mottled in and out. The sprinkling of black peppering on the white patches of her beautiful fur brought out the "blue tick" look that was so prized for a coon hound in our river valley. Ella was dragging her teats in the weeds due to so many past litters. She was usually nursing a litter or getting ready to birth and nurse a litter.

Nancy and I would check both dogs for ticks every day or so. Ella and George would hold still while we'd check around their ears and in all the crevices of their fur with our fingers. They hated the itchiness of the ticks.

Sometimes, if Nancy and I had gotten too busy exploring and forgot to do our routine tick check, Ella or George would come up to us and rub their ears on our legs. Uh oh, we need to check for ticks. We would take our fingers and search through their hair while each of them would nuzzle our toes. When we would feel that tell-tale bean filled with blood, one of us would push all the hair back in a big circle and expose the tick with its head buried in the dog's flesh. The other of us would light a match, let it flare up, blow out the flame and, while the match was red white-hot, touch the butt of the tick. The fat old tick would back right out. The one with the match would smash the tick on the ground and we'd start again.

One day in early June, Nancy and I were sitting on the swing on her porch in the afternoon breeze, trying to decide where we would go exploring for the afternoon. Mrs. Thorn said,

> "You know Francie, your George thinks he's a coon hound. Deed he does. I reckon he's about as good a huntin' dog as I've seen."

George was so happy with that. Everyone liked Mrs. Thorn.

It was a musty day in June along the riverbank. Nancy and I decided that we needed to understand how the water system in Point Marion worked. We had already spent time discovering how the coal went from mine carts to tipples to train cars or trucks to river barges. It was time to figure out how we were getting water into our houses when other people in the townships had wells.

The POINT MARION WATER COMPANY building at the end of Shoestring was a mystery. The glass on one window of the cinder block building was so dirty we could not see inside. We suspected there was a big motor in there, as it ground and groaned loud night and day. When the river would come up, it would switch off.

We watched Junior John, Mr. Gladstone's only worker for the Point Marion Water Company, drive up the dirt road/path of Shoestring in his white Ford truck. He stopped in the dust outside the cinder block hut, unlocked the chain-bolted door, and went inside. Nancy and I could hear him stirring around. We pressed up against the window and rubbed a spot on the glass to get a cloudy look. He was pouring white dust-like material into a bin next to the motor. Then he left and drove down the dirt lane back to town. We started watching Mr. John's visits to the cinder block building, keeping a log of his trips and the time. He came every other day after he had driven home for lunch. He did the same dust pouring routine. What was he doing in the building with that dust? We had to figure out this mystery.

The first piece of the puzzle was to see what that big old whirring machine was and what went on with the dust. Nancy's brother had shown us how to open a lock with a bobbie pin. We worked on perfecting this skill for a few days and then, early one morning, we tried our luck on the lock of the building.

CLICK.

We were in. The bags of white dust were haphazardly scattered around the cement floor. One was open. It smelled like bleach. Mr. John had been adding bleach to the whirring machine.

We located a big iron pipe that jutted out the side of the cinder block building toward the edge of the Cheat River and then down into the side of the riverbank that ended up in the river. The opening had a screen over it, and another big pipe went out the other side of the building with a vertical angle that took this pipe up the hill behind the row of shacks. Nancy and I, with the dogs, followed the pipe up the hill through the brambles, mud, and weeds. It was a hot and sticky day, and the dogs were panting.

Finally, we reached the top of the hill. The big pipe was spilling water into a rectangular water pond that resembled a swimming pool! The pool water was dark and surrounded by a chain-link fence. The water was not moving. The pool was open to the sky with lots of leaves in it. Near the edge on one side, there was a dirt road with another cinder block building with another whirring sound coming from it. There was a big iron pipe coming out of the building and then buried underground.

Nancy and I made a pencil drawing of our discovery from the river to the first building at Shoestring, to the hill, to the swimming pool, and we took it to my dad.

"Dad, look what we found."

Dad said the concrete building was a pump station for the town water supply. The water was pumped out of the Cheat River by the whirring motor in the building, pushed up the hill to the open-air reservoir on the top of Walnut Street. Then a pump sent the water into the ancient lead and clay underground pipes that, by gravity, distributed the water to the faucets of Point Marion's houses.

"But, Dad, that's why our water tastes and smells so bad. That swimming pool on top of Walnut Street is open to the sky; there are all kinds of bugs and animals crawling around."

Dad didn't seem to care about the water smelling and tasting so bad.

"Yup. Probably so."

Dad told me that in the 1900s there was a typhoid fever epidemic in Point Marion traced back to the wells and raw Cheat River water from this same reservoir. Dad knew where the town water came from, and other people must have known too. But no one ever questioned. No one seemed to care whether the water was a problem. These were the days before you could buy bottled water. We drank the water that circulated from the river to the pump station to the open reservoir through the lead pipes under the streets to our water faucets.

Like the constant current of the Cheat River, there was a never-ending awareness of the power of the river. The river may rise and flood one day, but it may not. Either way, there seemed to be a breeze along Shoestring and the people there had their ADC and their coon hounds to keep them wrapped in the gentle arms of Mother Appalachia.

Another Baby for ADC

That summer, Nancy's sister, Helen, had a baby. She was 17 years old.

> "Why did your sister have a baby?"
>
> "Well, she couldn't be on ADC after age 18, so now she will get relief payments for her and her baby. We love babies at our house anyway."

At the beginning of the next school year, Mrs. Thorn moved with her children and hounds to another shack on Freeling Street. Nancy and I grew apart, but I still heard Mrs. Thorn's wonderful laughter when I passed Augie's Beer Garden.

Was Nancy's family another small unit of the spiral toward the drain in Appalachia? Is this how the system plays out when there is no hope or lifeline?

It has resonated with me that this family was happy.

38

CRAZY PEOPLE

The core violent group was the one that was so difficult to anticipate. And there were plenty of them. They were unpredictable.

What jobs there were in the mountains required hard muscle work. Using one's muscles and strong bones every minute of the day resulted in a pain that was not always relieved by moonshine and drugs. Lifting a mine shovel, coaxing a mine pony to pull a cart on rusty wet tracks deep into a tunnel, and checking the roof braces every few minutes was relentless labor.

Joe Bob Musker and his family rented our next-door duplex for a year. Joe Bob was a coal miner and lucky to have work. His daddy, old Mr. Musker, and his mama lived on Main Street. They were respectable folks who had owned the mineral rights to a coal mine in Springhill township for a couple of generations. It was a small mine operation with six big coal trucks and a day crew at each of the three openings.

Old Mr. Musker supervised the work of the opening at Musker One. Joe Bob, a young buck who had dropped out of Point Marion High School five years earlier when Razzie Mae first got pregnant, was the mine foreman at Musker Two. John Butler, a longtime employee of Mr. Musker, was the mine supervisor at Musker Three. Joe Bob's wife, Razzie Mae, was a Cawley girl with three little children, each a year apart. Just crawlers.

Joe Bob would come home in his rusted-out Ford at four o'clock every day, pull up to the curb and throw the door open. Dirty, coal-smeared, sweat-covered face and arms, he was a huge man with shoulders as wide as the door. Razzie Mae would call to the kids,

"Now you all jus' sit riate sher till we sees how Daddy's feelin'."

Some days he would come home from his shift with a smile on his face and they could see his pretty white teeth shining through the coal dust. Other days he would come swinging onto the porch with his mine belt off, snapping it hard like a whip on the porch floor. (A mine belt is a piece of leather four inches wide with big buckles and two pins to hold the strap in place. It had metal hooks to hold an extra carbide light, a pickaxe, and maybe a canteen.) He would throw his mine bucket and metal hat at the screen door,

"Now, Razzie Mae! What you been doin' all day?"

Then the family would scurry. The baby would start crying.

Razzie Mae was a beautiful girl, not quite full into her twenties She was the fifth sister in the Cawley family of ten children. Despite the age difference, she and I were friends. I would go next door and sing songs with her during the day, and she taught me how to make biscuits. I was nine or ten, but she would let me help her pick and sort the beans and tomatoes in her garden for canning. I would watch the babies for her when her mama would visit. If Razzie Mae had been born a boy, she would not have to put up with the fear of that mine belt.

In the soft breezes of the evening, I could hear her singing to her babies,

> "Bringing in the sheaves; bringing in the sheaves,
> We will go a marching bringing in the sheaves."
> "Swing lo, sweet chariot; swing low. . ."

> "Francie, I love Joe Bob so much, but I am so scared of him when he starts a shout'n'. I think he might hurt us."

She had been raised in the God-fearing Cawley family. They were so poor that their main food was often lard-fried corn pone. But her daddy, the Reverend Mister Cawley, never raised a voice (unless it was in a heated-moment sermon about Jesus) or a hand to anyone, let alone a woman and her children.

When Joe Bob got that devil in him, he was mean and frightening. I was terrified of him. I used to wish he never had those days when he snapped his mine belt. Life could have been so happy for them. It never got any better.

> "Mama, why do these men rant and stomp and thrash out at the women?"

> "That's the way their daddy's always got their way; it's in their genes."

Many of the people lived so close to day-to-day survival that the natural meanness of the surroundings, and the unforgiving nature of the environment, seemed to fester to the surface in their lifeblood. It must have been easy to abuse another when they felt abused by life. The women accepted the brunt of the abuse. The options were not apparent when the women could not control their own reproduction. So many young girls became mothers before they were out of their teens, and then they kept reproducing to the point of exhaustion.

Certainly, there was no discussion of where babies came from or how to control ones' birthing system, or the dangers of sexually transmitted diseases in Appalachia. Girls were expected to be beautiful and desirable, and encourage men to touch them, but the consequences of too much touching were life-changing to a female.

Point Marion's Walking Legend

"Fat Mary" was a walking legend in Point Marion. She usually lived up on Railroad Street in a shack with Junior Ware. She usually had one or more small children with runny noses and slobber all over their faces following her and Junior around town. There was always a new baby in her belly. It seemed that once one of the little ones got to walking without falling down every few steps, the ADC people would take him or her into foster care, and the child would be gone forever.

Mary was a wide, tall woman, the size of four fire hydrants stacked up on one another. She was loud and tended to scream at her kids and Junior, anytime, anywhere. I would see her following six steps behind Junior along the railroad tracks toward Augie's Beer Garden from Railroad Street with one or two of her children toddling and falling behind her in the soot of the coal that dropped along the tracks. Their faces were red and noses dripping, crying after Mary, who would be yelling and whining after Junior.

Junior was one of the few men in Point Marion who was certified disabled with the black lung. He got a check every month. Mama said Mary had many men she had

> "shacked up with."

But she usually stayed with Junior. Junior was so skinny the only way he could hold his pants up was with an old, knotted rope. He had a dirty plaid shirt that he never took off and a red tobacco splotched Pittsburgh Pirates baseball cap that he wore crocked on his brow. He must have shaved once every few weeks because his beard was uneven, but two inches long in most spots. Junior and Mary both suffered the toothlessness that seems to characterize the people of Appalachia. Although Fat Mary, being twenty years younger than Junior, had a few front tooth snags left that may have helped her some.

Junior carried a red and white pouch of Union Workman chewing tobacco in his roped-up pants pocket and had a wad of it drizzling down his cheek. He smelled like tobacco and beer. Fat Mary and her children would spend their days in Augie's waiting for Junior. Sometimes I would see and hear her coming out of Augie's with a split bloody lip, screaming. Fat Mary would bleed all over the sidewalk. Junior, normally a quiet man, would haul off and smack Fat Mary in the face if he decided he had enough of the screeching. Riled up, he had the strength of a mountain man.

One Saturday, Chief Moser had to arrest Junior and put him in the Point Marion Jail overnight. He had hauled off and whacked Fat Mary so hard that she passed out stone cold unconscious on the sidewalk in front of Augie's. Her little children watched the foray and then sat down on the sidewalk beside her. She had a big bleeding gash on her head. The men from the Point Marion Volunteer Fire Department came by and took her to Doc Hungar's office to be sewn up.

After that, Fat Mary moved in with another man on Sadler Street for a few weeks. But, before the first of the next month's Black Lung check day, she moved back in with Junior.

>"Mama, why doesn't someone help Fat Mary?"

>>"Who would do that? She won't change. She is a BIG FAT STUPID WOMAN."

>"What about the Church Ladies?"

> *"They have their own problems."*
>
> *"Why does she keep having babies?"*
>
> *"She does not know how to stop the babies."*

The abuse of women by their partners in our town seemed to be a natural and accepted way of life. Unless there was outright murder, the population apparently compartmentalized it as one more example of life in a volatile environment.

Even in my own family, the male was the unquestionable authority. What I still question, as I look back on this undercurrent of volatile brutality and neglect is,

> *Why didn't anyone do anything?*

39

FOURTH GRADE

Miss Bendenton, our fourth-grade teacher, started her teaching career with our class of 48 students. A young woman in her early twenties, she finished her own schooling at California State Teachers College Normal School and moved, alone, to Point Marion to teach.

She was the size of one of Miss Evelyn Thompson's most prized Holstein milk cows. She had small ankles that bloomed into legs the size of the legs on our piano. She wore brightly printed dresses with huge colorful flowers that reminded me of the fancy wallpaper sold at Sadler's Variety Store. She smelled like honeysuckle in the springtime as she would sidestep between the aisles of the rows of our seats. She was too wide to face the front or back of the room and walk straight. Her double chin would quiver as she said,

> *"Now, fourth graders, just put your heads down on your desks for a few minutes. If you don't make a sound, you will get a nice treat."*

Sure enough, nearly every afternoon, Miss Bendenton would place a big sugarcoated, colored marshmallow, or some equally sweet and sticky lump, on our desks next to our hair. I figured this was her way of getting us to be kinder to her, it being her first experience teaching and all. We liked her fine.

She did not smack us and never made anyone cry. Of course, once after we were told to put our heads down, I did sneak a peak of what she was doing, and she was stuffing handfuls of candy into her own mouth.

Before school was out for the summer, all of us were sitting quietly in our fourth-grade classroom listening to Miss Bendenton drone on about some nonsensical imaginary dog that could fly. Suddenly, Mrs. Ratchet, the fifth-grade teacher, came swinging into our room, interrupting Miss Bendenton, who stood flabbergasted with her mouth wide open.

> "You people, all of you, just because you are in the biggest class in the whole school, don't think you are going to get away with anything when you come to my room! This time next year, not one of you is going to move on to sixth grade without writing their name on this paddle. Think about it."

She spun out of the room and the door slammed behind her. Kenny Murray with his family, and most important his dad, had moved to Smithfield, so we didn't have the man who jumped on Corregidor to rescue us.

I was dumb face scared. I went home and told George about the Prophet of Doom that was awaiting me in fifth grade. George put his head on my lap.

After our class went on to fifth grade, Miss Bendenton left Point Marion and never came back. Mama told me she went home to Latrobe and married a Presbyterian.

Mama said,

> "Even with those piano legs of hers, she hit the jackpot and got out of this rat hole."

Miss Bendenton made a clean break.

There was no one to protect me. I was going to march into the gates of hellfire that the apostolic minister had raved about.

40

THE EAGLE FLEW

Finally in 1956, Lennie was going into first grade and Mama had completed her standoff with Dad. We had accepted that Dad would never work. Mama started looking for a job.

Mama kept saying there were not many jobs in Fayette County for a woman who had a degree in mathematics. All we knew was that jobs were scarce. The few women who worked had gone to a "normal school" and were schoolteachers.

Mama said,

> *"Oh my god, there is no way in hell that I am going to be locked up in a room with a bunch of brats all day."*

We all knew teaching would not be her gift. Mama decided she should get a job with the State. She said,

> *"That way, there is stability."*

Whatever that was.

To qualify for a State job, Mama had to take a test. The results were sent off to Harrisburg, the state capital. We had to wait for the results. Months. She finally got a letter saying she was accepted. I was ten years old and going into fifth grade. I was so excited, I thought to myself, "Now that Mama has a job, we can buy our own groceries and pay the water bill on time."

It took a long time for the State to call her to work. There were so many complications with getting a paying job. We were all watching the mail to see if she would be called in for an interview. Finally, as the fall leaves were beginning to drop, Mama went to work for the Pennsylvania Department of Welfare. It was sixteen miles to the north of Point Marion in Uniontown, Pennsylvania. The locals who were on public assistance called her the "Relief Woman."

The first week she began her job, she told us her first-year income would be $2,750. She sat proudly at the dining room table and wrote it on a piece of paper so we could see the numbers written out on that scrappy torn-off corner of the National GRIT newspaper. Mama said she would be paid every two weeks. We were all amazed that our family would have real money. On the weeks she was paid, she would come in the door and say,

"The eagle flew."

That was a big deal. I started to feel a warm, safe puddle in the middle of my chest for the first time since Aunt MaeMae died.

Mama was delighted. For the first time since the early days when Lennie was born, she started to smile as she drove into our driveway at the end of her workday. She opened a checking account at Smithfield State Bank in her own name. She made it clear that any money she earned was in her name only – never in Dad's. Even though there was Mama's work money coming into the family for the first time, it was never enough for everything.

After Mama got a job, I missed seeing her, but I was glad she was able to bring money home for food. She would drive our old rattling 1950 Ford station wagon back to Point Marion, arriving every evening at twenty minutes to six. Mama was too tired at night to do much. She would fall asleep on the couch after supper and get up around 10 p.m. to go to bed.

She had chain-smoked since she was a teenager. There was the ever-constant Lucky Strike cigarette in her hand transferring the smoke to her lungs. This, along with the coal dust everywhere, kept her in a continual state of wheezing, hacking, and gasping. We could hear Mama's loud breathing no matter where she was. I could hear her walking around the house and garden. I can still hear the wheezing sound of my mama when it is quiet.

I would walk little Lennie to his first-grade classroom and walk him home. Mrs. Wing was still terrorizing the first graders, but I warned Lennie to tell Mama if Mrs. Wing picked on him. Dad was not strong like Mr. Murray, but Mama would straighten anyone out who gave her little boy a bad time. Mrs. Wing gave little Lennie a wide berth. She never bothered him one time.

I was forever grateful to Mama for finally getting that job. I realize now that her working allowed our family to join the ranks of the "working poor." I understand now that going to a job every day was not part of her culture. She had expected to go to Eastern Star and DAR meetings and play bridge --- to be a housewife, whatever that was, like her own mother. Like so many women throughout the millennia who expected to gain their stature, recognition, and wealth by latching onto a successful man.

Mama had to change her outlook and put her own nose to the grindstone. She was angry every day that she had to be the breadwinner of our family, and she certainly reminded us that she had the money and none of her cash would be shared with Dad. She never allowed him access to her meager bank account.

41

MRS. RATCHET'S FIFTH GRADE CLASS

As I started fifth grade, I was going into the room of a legend in the school. Mrs. Ratchet was tall and angular. She wore long flouncy skirts with plenty of slips underneath that whistled when she would briskly jaunt up and down the hall outside the elementary classrooms. A pinched nose and wire-rimmed glasses, with a tight wide belt around her middle, finished off her daily outfit.

She cheerfully brandished the paddle she had specially made by Mr. Womack, the high school shop teacher. Up and down the halls of Point Marion School, Mrs. Ratchet would prance. Swinging. That paddle was big and heavy. The lore was that she had asked Mr. Womack to drill lots of holes in it so it would especially sting when she whacked a child. After she spanked a child with it, she would force them to write their name on her weapon. She kept it hanging on a hook at the entry door of her classroom.

(I wonder what happened to her autographed stick. Is it still hanging in her notorious classroom? Was she buried with it?)

We were all frightened. But that wasn't the only thing I had to worry about.

The Bigger Issue

Mary Joe Church was my best friend in fifth grade. She was petite, smart, and funny. We would go on long hikes into the woods around town or play tag in the streetlight glare. Mary Joe lived up on the hill near the school with her mother and three sisters. She was the number two girl in the family. Her sister, Bobbie Lee, was the oldest and the same age as my sister Eileen. There were two younger sisters, Kate and Agnes. Agnes, the youngest, was five. Mary Joe told me that her dad was in Ohio working. For men to go to Ohio to work was not unusual for us. The coal was played out in our area, and there were still some good factory jobs in Ohio.

Mary Joe was lucky because she had a grandma and grandpa living a few streets over on the other side of School House Hill. I didn't have any grandma or grandpa, (except my remote grandmother in New York and invalid grandpa who I only met one time), and Aunt Dodo, who lived with another lady and surely was never going to have any cousins for us.

Mary Joe's house was one side of a duplex. The porch had a wall that divided the two sides of the house from one another. The living room with a fireplace was in front, and behind there was a dining room, and behind that a kitchen. The back door was at the kitchen. Then there was a yard with a clothesline and the alley. Upstairs were two bedrooms and a bathroom. Lots of room to play hide and seek.

It was Monday, April 2, 1957. Mary Joe and I had played all weekend between her house up on the hill and our house down at the river. On Saturday afternoon, we ran from her front porch, through the front door, through her dining room, through the kitchen, and out the back door. Mary Joe's mom was laying on the couch reading a paperback book.

> *"Now you girls be sure to shut that back-screen door."*

> *"Yes ma'am, Mrs. Church."*

I saw a man standing in the dining room as I ran through, his eyes were bleary, and he was drinking from a glass. He was staring at the ceiling.

> *"Who is that?"*

> *"That's my dad. He came home for a while."*

> *"Oh."*

Monday after supper we were all sitting in the living room. Dad and Mama were smoking, and we were watching the news on our 19-inch black and white Motorola. The Point Marion police sirens started to whirr. Whirr. Within five minutes, the phone rang, and Dad spoke to someone for a few minutes.

> *"Bob Church is shooting a gun in his house. Bill Moser has gone up there. They called the state troopers in."*

Dad said Bob Church was Mary Joe's dad. Bobbie Lee, her sister, was named after him. I guess he knew he wasn't going to have a boy since he named his first girl after himself.

To call in the state troopers was unusual. In our eyes, Bill Moser could handle anything. Chief Moser was kind and honest and fair. And he was there when anyone in town needed him. Bill Moser was there for Mary Joe's mom that Monday night. He was 66 years old. Although the paper said that Mr. Church was working in Ohio, Mama said Mr. Church was,

> *"In the 'nut house' and they let him out"*

before he came back to Point Marion that weekend. Torrance State Mental Hospital and Mayview State Mental Hospital was where they kept all the crazy people from the Point Marion area.

We later found out that, while Mary Joe and her sisters were out playing in the street in front of her house, her dad pulled a gun and threatened to kill her mom. Her mom saved her children's lives by quickly sending the girls out the back door, through the alley, to the preacher's house on the next street. Mary Joe's dad shot her mom through the head and, when Bill Moser arrived, he shot the Chief in the gut. He also shot at Chief Moser's sidekick, officer Lazier Black, wounding him in the arm. The Pennsylvania State Police were called, and Chief Moser and Officer Black were taken to the hospital in Morgantown. Mary Joe's dad then went upstairs and continued shooting for a few hours until he put a bullet in his own head.

Mama said,

> *"Most nuts find small towns like Point Marion to hide out in. These little towns protect their own. Besides, a lot of this psycho stuff comes from in-breeding. Look at all these people in this town, kids. They are all related. Look at some of these families."*

> *"Oh Mama, there are some truly nice people in this town."*

42

RANTS AND ROUTINES

Mary Joe and her sisters ended up at Mr. and Mrs. Smith's house, her mother's parents, who lived on the other side of the hill. They were Mary Joe's grandma and grandpa.

The day after the shooting, back with fifth grade, Mrs. Ratchet, in her all-knowing wisdom, decided it would be best for the entire class, yes, all 47 of us, to walk in batches across the hill to the Smith's house to see Mary Joe and her sisters. When I saw poor Mrs. Smith, she was sitting alone, and Mr. Smith was standing in his yard.

I quietly approached Mrs. Ratchet and told her that Mary Joe and I were the best of friends and, if anyone was going to see her, it should be me. Mrs. Ratchet chose who was to go and in what order. I was in the fourth wave of arrivals, getting to Mary Joe late in the day. When I was finally selected, Mary Joe rushed to me.

"Oh Francie, I heard Daddy say to Mommie that he and she would be down at Herod's Funeral Home tomorrow, and now they are."

"Mary Joe, I am so, so sorry."

Mama went to the funeral home with me and Eileen. Mrs. Church's hair, as she lay in the open casket, was as beautiful and curly and brown as ever. She looked like she was sleeping, not like someone who had been shot in the head by a nut. There was a ribbon on her front that said "Mommie." Mary Joe and I sat together and said nothing. Eileen sat with Bobbie Lee. Dad said he couldn't go to funeral homes or to funerals. He would not do it. I wondered what he would do if someone he loved was shot in the head?

The next day, the Fayette County Evening Standard Newspaper said,

> "Motive Seen in Slaying at Point Marion
> Woman Reportedly Refused to Move to Ohio with Mate"

I could not understand this.

> "Mama, do you mean that if a woman does not want to move to Ohio with a man, it's okay to shoot her in the head?"

Mama said,

> "This is Fayette County."

At the funeral home, I overheard,

> "That Richard Herod shore does a mighty fine job."

> "Yessir ee, he does. A reel professional."

I liked Mr. Herod who ran Herod's Funeral Home. They were Baptist's.

He was sympathetic and professional. His wife, Ruth Herod, was a saint who was kind, sympathetic, and supportive of Mr. Herod. She was raising three children, younger than me, in an apartment above the funeral home, with the embalming room in the basement. She was there for anyone who was sad. I should have paid more attention to her and learned from her as I was growing up.

Mary Joe and Bobbie Lee lived with their grandma and grandpa. They stayed in the Point Marion school. Kate and Agnes went to live with their aunt in a place called New England. It sounded far away.

Fifth Grade Rants and Routines

Somehow, we all survived fifth grade. Mrs. Ratchet's rants became second nature to each of us. The one tirade that shocked me more than any of her other antics came in early December. Mrs. Ratchet started with,

> *"Now, fifth graders, Christmas is coming up and I want to be sure no one in my class is dumb enough to still believe in Santa Claus."*

Then she went prattling on into some story about how, of course, we nine-year olds were all grown up.

> *"OH NO. I had been thinking that this Santa Claus thing MIGHT be a hoax, but my parents would never pretend to give me presents from a made-up character! I tried to hide my shock by staring at the spots on my shoes."*

Among her many routines was to stand in front of our class and talk on and on about her two grown children, Dianna Mae and Kentie. They were long gone from Point Marion but were, by her elaborate accounts, the most beautiful and handsome two children that had ever emigrated away from our small town. The most intelligent, too.

Our teacher set up rituals she liked to follow. One of the most dreaded, besides making sure that everyone was paddled and signed her big stick, was every

Friday. At the end of the day, we had to line up in single file and hug her. As she sat in a chair near the only door in the room, she would grab us as we trooped by. Then she would plant a big, wet, sticky kiss on our cheek or forehead. I usually stayed on the other side of Cara Anset and right behind Lester Schmidt so I could slither through without her snatching me.

Lester got paddled at least once a week, so Mrs. Ratchet was anxious to hug him before the weekend. Cara was so large that Mrs. Ratchet had to lean forward for her hug and give her a slobbery smooch. If I timed it right, I did not get tackled by her.

Cara was bright. She said to me one day,

> "I know what you are doing, Francie. You are trying to get away from her."

> "Please don't tell."

Cara was a good friend.

Mrs. Ratchet would announce to the other teachers,

> "See, these children LOVE me!"

I could see Mrs. Evans, the third-grade teacher, roll her eyes when Mrs. Ratchet would go on one of her rants. Mrs. Evans was putting her time in until she could retire. The last thing she would ever do was disagree with Mrs. Ratchet.

Of course, I was learning that all kinds of crazy people hid out in the creaks and crevices of our town. The underbelly of our existence was lined with so many silent pathologies. Some people were able to slide through and others were not.

One thing I realized was that I could not grow old in this environment.

43

THE COLOREDS

No coloreds lived in Point Marion. Most of the colored people who wanted to live near Point Marion lived in Nilan.

The eastern side of the Cheat River was accessed by crossing the Route 119 north bridge and then taking a sharp right down Nilan Road. The road leads back into West Virginia along the backwaters of the Cheat River. It is a two-mile walk along a macadam potholed road, past broken down coal tipples and trash heaps created by locals who live back beyond the road and are too lazy, or too tired and drunk, to bury or burn their trash. Old abandoned wrecked cars and pickup trucks were scattered in the weeds, along with torn-up tires, long-forgotten hub caps, and the ever-present small animal carcass with the rotten smell of seeping innards surrounded by maggots. The road was a foot or two above the highwater mark of the river. Any good rain or snow made the road impassable due to the rising water of the Cheat River.

Even so, a few brave souls, or those too drunk or too miscalculating to know better, would plow into the overflowing river with their old rusted-out jalopies trying to navigate the path of the road beneath the muddy lapping waters. These were the people who were trying to get to or from Nilan.

Sometimes this foray would result in a frantic call to the trusty Point Marion Fire Department. To my knowledge, no one ever died.

Most of the people who lived in Nilan were walkers. The men would walk to Point Marion for a drink at Augie's or the Brass Rail, and the women would walk to Point Marion to do housework or to sit.

The patch of Nilan was a treacherous walk down this two-lane blacktop road with narrow shoulders that dropped down to ruts twelve inches off the pavement. When it rained, the water went first into the ditches on either side of the road and then started to flood toward the center of the road that had a center hump to encourage the water to drain toward the sides. The unfortunate result of this kind of road engineering was that, once the water started to collect on either side of the road, it began to eat away at the under road rocks on each side. Once the water started to swish the under road stones away, it was only a matter of time before the road would fall into the fracture and create big gaps that some enterprising traveler would cover with a piece of metal or drifting plywood to allow passing. Usually, there was a big open hole in the road that was passable with caution. Or not.

Any spring or winter car ride down Nilan Road was slippery and bumpy with the many potholes. There was always a Pennsylvania Department of Transportation (Penn DOT) king cab truck full of men in orange jackets measuring and pointing and talking along the road. The men worked by the hour for the government, so results were rare, and talk was extensive.

Nilan Road was a safe place for the Penn DOT men to earn plenty of overtime. I could regularly find an empty six-pack of Duquesne Premium beer cans rusting in the ditch where the Penn DOT trucks would be parked. Always a good spot to find a cache of cans for a game of kick the can while walking through the weeds on the sides of the road to Nilan.

Of course, only white men worked for Penn DOT. Never a colored or a woman. It was a steady paycheck.

Mama made lots of comments that were prejudicial toward any minority. She said,

> "Those jigs need to be sure and stay at least as far away as Nilan. I don't want any blue gum living near us."

> "But why, Mama. Aren't they just the same as us?"

> "Oh my god, no! They are jigs!"

On Saturdays, for a month or so every spring, there would be leaflet handers in full dress Klu Klux Klan outfits standing in the center of the road, blocking traffic, at the fork in the road of Route 119. The road north went up the hill to the Fayette County seat of Uniontown. Route 166 followed along the Monongahela River northwest to New Geneva and south to Nilan.

This group of four to more than a dozen men wore full-length white sheets covering their bodies, down to their shoes, and long white pointed top hats that covered their face, with two peepholes for their eyes. We would drive by in our old Ford station wagon. The men would park their cars at the gas station across the street. Everyone knew everyone else's cars. They were not fooling anyone with their camouflage. Dad would slowly drive by them as they would be waving and blocking traffic. They would toss a leaflet into the car about that evening's meet-up.

KLAN MAN,

> "Good afternoon, Mister Dillin'er. We's havin' us a meet up over in German Township tonight. Maybe roast us a pig. Fer shure we's gonna flame up a big ol' cross. It'll be seen all over the county. Up on that thar

hill on the Buncheck farm. Need to teach them niggahs to keep their place. We's askin' ever un t' c'mon over."

Dad would always know who the Klan people were. We all did. They didn't bother to cover up their shoes, their voices were easily recognizable, and their jalopies were parked not 20 feet away.

"Nope, Junior, I don't attend those get-togethers."

KLAN MAN,

"Aw, c'mon Mister Dillin'er, we jus' wan' to make sure them Niggah's stay in their own area."

Mama would say,

"We are pretty lucky in Point Marion. Our jigs are harmless. We just have to keep them out of town."

Mama made outright mean comments about anyone who was, what she perceived, a minority. She had her pet names for every group that was not white bread Daughter of the American Revolution (DAR) stock. I listened and assumed everyone else talked this way.

My town wanderings gave me some perspective. Point Marion and its surroundings were a potpourri of delicious and amazing cultures. Susie's mom was a DeGardyn – a Belgian, and her father was a Bruni – an Italian. Her entire family embraced me and taught me so much. Evil slander was never part of their dialog. With the kind exposure to Susie's family, Mama's words began to sting me. I never could get her to moderate her tongue.

"Please, please, Mama, these are my friends, and they are good people…"

Dad had the same prejudices, but he was less verbal about it.

These preconceived notions were part of their DNA. Or maybe it was their way of underpinning a sense of superiority in their own defeat.

I am forever grateful I missed that particular genome.

MAMA, THE RELIEF WOMAN

As the Relief Woman, Mama was assigned to German Township and parts of Georges Township. Her job included the coal patches in those townships, which had big pockets of angry coloreds living in the coaled-out company towns of Edenborn, Ralph, Adah, Martin, Grays Landing, Lambert, Collier, Coal Center, Centerville, Allison, and many others. The abject poverty of the patches added to the necessity that coloreds and whites live side by side. This created a cesspool of resentment and animosity between the two groups with all the preconceived notions of discrimination that runs through the blood of the Appalachians.

The masses of people on welfare were those who were assigned to Mama's caseload. She was responsible to visit the people on relief in her geographic area and ensure they remained eligible for what everyone called the "relief benefits," which included ADC. She also processed all the new applicants in her assigned area.

On some occasions in the summer, Mama would have me accompany her in our family car when she had a field day, meaning she would go directly to the patches and see her recipients.

We would load up in the car with her papers and drive into the woods on narrow rutted roads until we came to the patch she was planning to visit. The patch was usually far down a bumpy isolated road. The roads would pass by a huge, putrid, sulfur-smelling slag heap with small glowing areas of orange burning smoke trailing toward the sky. Always there was an elaborate wood and metal coal tipple hovering over an abandoned dog leg of a once busy railroad track used to load coal cars, or over a ravine where coal trucks could back up to receive the dumped coal from a coal car being pulled out of the mine.

All the tipples were abandoned, rotting into the mountains that had been scraped away and rusting into the stagnant water that had been exposed by the deserted mine. Large, deep ponds of still, dark water that was runoff from the mine would sit stagnant behind the slag heaps, slowly creating a chemical combination of its own.

The patches were similar, unpainted lookalike one or two-story homes, some backed up to abandoned railroad tracks, usually duplexes, with two outhouses in the back. One for each family. Each duplex had a water pump from the town well at a kitchen sink, or there was a pump for water on the shared back porch. Each house had a coal burning stove in the living room and a coal burning cookstove in the kitchen. The duplexes shared a partitioned front porch. There were at least four streets of close together houses, separated by dirt roads.

One day, Mama said we were going to Ralph; most of the residents living in Ralph were on welfare. The mine of this isolated patch had long been worked out.

It was a sweltering July day. I could touch the water in the air and the sweat building up. I could feel the plastic seat covers of our old 1950 Ford sticking like paste to the back of my legs where my shorts ended and my long pony legs started. Our tires were bald, and the road was riddled with deep potholes. We were bouncing along the rutted road as Mama was driving and chain-smoking. We kept the windows open, and the breezes were tossing my pigtails back.

We came to the first row of houses. Mama pulled up to one of the unpainted houses along the red dog road and turned off the car. The street was full of women and children in various stages of sitting around on the porches and road, passing the time. The hound dogs were panting on the porches and the puppies were tangled in the dirt under the overhangs yipping at nothing but the grime that had seeped through the floorboards into the dust. A group of boys were playing with a ball and stick in the dust of the road. It was even too sweaty hot for the hounds to bay and announce our arrival.

I did hear a sullen teenage boy shout to a closed screen door,

"*The relief woman is here, Mama.*"

There was a rancid smell coming from the back of the house. The familiar permeating odor of frying lard on a smoky coal grate.

My mama marched up the steps and knocked on the door.

"*Misses Gates, I came to see you and your family.*"

A round black woman with a tiny baby in her arms came to the screen door. She was dressed in a nondescript faded shift dress that might have been pink years ago, and old tennis shoes without laces. She slid her feet over the crusty, uneven wooden floor of the room and pushed open the wooden screen door that was hooked to a rusty spring. The opening sound was an ominous

SCREAK.

Mama grabbed the screen door and walked into the room. I followed behind her, trying to make myself as invisible as possible. The floor of the room was bare except for two big redbone coon hounds laying near a wooden rocking chair. They looked at us, sniffed the air we brought in from the other side of the screen, sensed no commotion, and did not perk up. They laid their heads back onto the cooler wood of the floor.

There were wood and steel frame dining chairs in various stages of disrepair scattered around the wall and an old sofa with a torn flowered blanket over the seat and back. Several children were coming in and out of the house, and two smaller ones in diapers were crawling over the legs of the chairs and tugging on the ears of the slobbering dogs.

> "Howdy do, Misses Dill-en-er,"

said the woman.

> "Y'all set down. I see you brought your 'lil girl wif you today."

Mama said,

> "I did Misses Gates. Her name is Francie, and she's just keeping me company since there is no school today."

Mama went through a list of questions from her papers, and then asked,

> "Is that new baby yours? Who is the daddy? You know if the daddy is living here with you, you lose your benefits."

>> "Now Miz Dill-en-er, you knows I do not have a man here. I just have deese babies."

Mama said,

> "Well, if I see a man, I have to report you."

Our hostess said,

> "You just add this little baby to the benefits, dat's all,"

Mama took the information on the new baby and said,

> "Just don't let me see a man around."

Mama got up to leave and I followed her out.

She went to see several other families of women and children and then we headed toward our car. As we were walking down the dusty road, almost to the car, the largest black man I had ever seen stepped in front of Mama. He had on denim pants and no shirt, a big belly. There was a scar across his right forearm. He walked right up to Mama and was less than an arm's length from her face. I could smell the sweat from his body searing the air between us. He towered over Mama.

He said,

> "Don't you go threat-en-in' my family Miz Dill-en-er."

He wasn't angry or threatening. To me, he seemed sad.

Mama's steady look into his eyes was almost evil. She just as calmly began slapping a round, thick, heavy-looking piece of leather with two dandling thick black straps the size of a hound dogs' ear across her left palm.

SMACK. SMACK. SMACK.

Under her breath she said,

> "Francie, go get in the car."

I ran to the car. A few minutes later, she followed me to the car, and away we went. I was sure glad our old car started that time.

> "Mama, what is that leather thing?"

> "Oh, it's a blackjack, I had the shoemaker sew it up for me in case I needed it to settle down one of these big jigs. It's full of bird shot and sand. I have to bring it out every once in a while."

> "But Mama, this whole system just isn't fair. Daddies can't be around or there's no money from the welfare?"

> "It's the way it is. Nothing is fair."

> "But Mama, there is no work for anyone to get money here. What are people supposed to do?"

> "That's not my problem, Francie."

It seems government programs are not set up for people who need them most and life is not fair.

It also seemed the life of coloreds in Appalachia was a spiral toward the drain.

The hopelessness of the mountains was starting to seep into my being. I had no answers. Just questions. Mama was not sympathetic. She seemed to manifest an attitude of despair herself.

I never wanted to get that attitude myself. I was afraid I might become like her.

45

PIGTAILS AND FREEDOM

Dad insisted that we girls have pigtails. We were well aware that we were of no value to him or Mama because we had the bad luck of being born without a penis. He reminded us of this over and over.

All three of us wanted to please Dad and Charlen led the way. She dutifully wore her hair in braids until she was in ninth grade. Eileen's hair was always in a poodle. I rebelled in the fifth grade and began begging Mama to take me to Cal Forman's Barber Shop to have my pigtails cut off.

Mama said,

> "Francie, I don't want anything to do with this. Your Dad will be furious."

> "Mama, I will do it myself."

I was so sick of Lester Schmidt, who sat behind me in Mrs. Ratchet's fifth grade class, pulling my pigtails, dipping them in the ink well, and tying them in knots. I needed hair that would blow in the wind and dance with the butterflies! And I hated the nightly ritual of sitting on the floor in front of

Mama while she rebraided my hair. I think, as a manifestation of the constant anger that ran through her soul, she would relentlessly pull each partition of hair as tight as she could to the point I could hardly open my eyes. Even to this day, my hair still naturally parts right down the middle where my pigtails creased a permanent row.

After a few attempts to cut off my thick pigtails myself with Mama's sewing sheers, and the mess of what remained of my thick hair blowing around the house and causing a stir with the hounds chasing the resulting hairballs, she finally caved in.

Mama scowled as she reluctantly handed me two quarters for Mr. Foreman. I tied a rubber band in my hair near my scalp before the braids started and marched up to Mr. Foreman's barbershop. He snipped them off with the greatest ease and my head felt lighter than it ever felt. I shook my head in a sassy breeze as I skipped home. Since that day, I have never had hair touching my collar. I saved the pigtails as a consolation prize for Dad.

George took one look at me and bounded into my lap. He loved me unconditionally.

Dad would not speak to me for a week after my visit to the barber. He was furious. Somehow, he found the money to take my sisters uptown and buy them each an ice cream cone after I got my hair cut.

Not me. He would not even look at me.

Eileen could run her fingers through her poodle.

Charlen tried to make things better. She was so dutiful. Dad wanted little girls with pigtails, so she kept hers until well after she graduated from eighth grade. She wanted Dad to be proud of her.

Neither Dad nor Mama ever said they were proud of any of us girls. I don't think it mattered much to me. I was happy to not have to worry about the day-to-day issues of getting my hair pulled and surviving the next day.

Besides, I was lucky to have Susie's family. And George.

Freedom

I could not believe my good fortune. Somehow, by the grace of some unspoken (it must have been Methodist) God, I finished fifth grade without being required to write my name on Mrs. Ratchet's infamous paddle. I could not believe the luck. No paddling for me. I never told a soul that I escaped Mrs. Ratchet's classroom without a beating.

Near the end of our fifth-grade school year, we watched Mrs. Ratchet grab her weapon, with all the scrawled names, off the hook at the exit to our class and heard her flounce over to the fourth-grade classroom and announce in her loud shrill voice,

> "YOU PEOPLE! Don't think you will get to slide through my fifth-grade classroom like you have here in fourth grade. Not ONE of you will get out of fifth grade without seeing this up close to your behinds."

Until I moved out of the building where she taught, I was in constant fear of her checking the names on her child beating tool and discovering mine was missing! I had nightmares of her marching into some class, pointing me out, and mercilessly whacking me with her legendary paddle.

All these years later, if I close my eyes tight, I can see Mrs. Ratchet taking long steps with swishing skirts, swinging her flat wooden stick, looking through each row of fifth grade seats for the one child, (me), who mysteriously made it unscathed through her class.

I think of her as probably sitting on some cloud up in Methodist heaven, saying to the other teachers who are each on their own fluffy while billow,

> "You know, all those children LOVED me. I was so good to them; I made sure they all knew there was never a Santa Claus. Why, every single Friday, they all lined up to give me a big hug and kiss, right here,"

as she points to the smeared candy apple red lipstick on the corner of her mouth. My mind tells me the other teachers smile at the rain clouds following the river over Point Marion.

> "Mama, why is Mrs. Ratchet so mean? Why doesn't anybody do anything about her paddling all the kids in her class every year?"

> "Francie, you are going to run into all kinds of people in your life and you are going to have to learn to deal with them and move on."

I was learning that being able to move on was an essential life skill. Resilience.

Another Summer

Moving out of fifth grade was enchanting. I had a bounce in my step as George and I started into the oppressive wet heat of summer. George had recovered from the involuntary tracheostomy that Mrs. Davis' dog, Buddy, had torn in his throat, but for the rest of his life, his breathing would be loud and labored. Mama said he probably had a

> "Big ol' keloid scar inside his windpipe."

George and I were happy we both survived. It was the beginning of another sticky, hot, messy Appalachian summer in the clefts of the mountains.

As a special treat for George, I found an old pair of scissors and trimmed all his fur down to the nub so he was not so fluffy and heavy with winter hair. I figured the haircut would give him a chance to stay cool. At first, George seemed shy about being a short-haired dog and he hid under the dining room table. But eventually, he came out from under and started sporting his new look around town with me. I thought that, for him, it was a lot like when I finally got Lester Foreman to cut off my pigtails.

Freedom!

46

WONDER OF WONDERS

A miracle happened that special summer before my sixth-grade year. One of Dad's wild-haired ideas looked like it might *take on some legs*, as he said. This was nine months after Mama started her job as a Relief Woman.

With Dad's aversion to being an employee of anyone, needing to sleep until 1 p.m., and his never-ending requirement for beer during his waking hours, everyone in the family knew his options were limited for creating some income.

Dad's latest scheme was a bit complicated. He decided he would run for an election, as a Democrat, to become a Justice of the Peace for Point Marion Borough. That year he won the election for a four-year term. He had a desk in our hallway and people would come to the house for free advice and for him to notarize signatures. He drove to Uniontown and got a certificate from the courthouse that said he was a genuine Notary Public. He framed the certificate and nailed it above his desk. This went on for several months and Dad was paid twenty-five cents or a half-dollar for verifying that people were who they signed their names to be.

I learned a lot in helping Dad do this.

He had a book he kept by date, listing every person and the activity and the verification document that was proof that people were who they said they were. Then, he used a seal that pinched the paper where people signed. Dad also signed and dated the paper.

People needed to be verified for marriage licenses, car or truck titles, wills, agreements, or any official papers they wanted to use. One of the lifelong takeaways Dad made sure I understood was,

> *"Trust no one, Francie. People are always trying to scam each other. The least we can do is make sure they are who they say they are."*

Dad started reading the requirements for legal transactions that could be handled by a Justice of the Peace. Surprisingly, he became known in the area as someone who would give straightforward advice. Meanwhile, the groups of townsfolk and stragglers from the townships began gathering on our front porch to ask Dad for his free advice.

Dad made it clear that he was absolutely NOT available before 1 p.m. (he was sleeping); he would never be available between 5:30 p.m. and 7 p.m. (his supper time); no advice between 9 p.m. and 9:30 p.m. (his evening ritual was a walk up to Augie's for a slug of beer with Augie); and after 1 a.m. (he wanted to watch and listen to Kate Smith sing God Bless America before the test pattern for Pittsburgh's Channel 2 television station came on). Then he would smoke one last Kool, drink one more beer, hook the screen door, close the front door, and head off to bed.

During these strict hours, he was "in" to all comers.

There would be a

BANG. BANG. BANG,

on the front door, or the wooden screen door, if it was summertime. Some local would ask,

> "Is the Squire in?"

If Dad was with someone, I would ask the neighbor to wait on the porch swing until Dad would have them in to sit on a wooden chair next to his desk.

> "How do, LeRoy."

>> "Thank 'ee for seein' me, Mr. Dill' ner'. I's got me a quest yun. Thouht maybe you could help me out."

> "Well, let's sort it out, LeRoy."

I could sit on a step of our staircase that was around the corner from Dad's desk and listen to these sessions without being seen. I quietly learned to appreciate how Dad would deal with so many varied problems. He was kind to everyone who came in, and he tried to help out with his free advice, no matter how silly or offbeat the issue was. There was everything from,

> "I need to leave my husband and I can't afford a divorce, and my husband will hunt me down and kill me anyway if I leave him…"

to

> "Me and Helen, well, we have been living together as man and wife for fifteen years, and we have these four kids, but we never got married, but everyone thinks we'es married."

to

> "My son Eddie stole a car…"

It was all fascinating dither, and Dad seemed to handle each person without delay and with truth. He was not overly emotional and did not hesitate to tell someone who was sitting in the chair, wringing their hands together, that what was going on in their life was a stupid-ass situation and they would have to unwind it on their own.

During that short initiation period to being the "Squire," Dad turned out to be a somewhat respected go-to-for-free-legal-advice kind of resource. The main word was FREE. This diversion made no money, as Mama would remind all of us,

> "Leonard, you have all these low life's traipsing in and out of our house and there is not a dime of income. What is the point?"

Dad would get the hangdog expression on his face that he got when Mama was giving him the third degree. He would look at the spots on his tattered shoes and peer over his smudgy glasses, while dropping ashes on the threadbare carpet from the cigarette teetering from his yellow-stained finger. And no answer. I could see Dad liked being thought of as an expert in something.

The turning point in Dad's new venture of being the town Squire was a fellow by the name of Jack Turner. Jack was a hard worker and an enterprising energetic native of Point Marion. Jack had gone off to the service right after graduating from Point Marion High School in the late 1940s. He missed World War II and was too early for Korea, so he was sent to Germany and Austria. He fell in love with a beautiful woman named Inga while in Europe and brought her back to Point Marion. Inga embraced Point Marion and made friends wherever she went. Everyone appreciated her spark and zest for life. She adored Jack.

Even as a ten-year-old, I could see that Mr. Jack Turner was different. He was driven and happy and precise. He had a military crew cut and sandy red hair.

He was detailed and present in everything he set his mind to doing. I saw Mr. and Mrs. Turner around town, and I wanted to get to know them better. They lived up on the School House Hill in the same rented house that Miss Bendenton moved from when she married the Presbyterian.

Their two daughters, Sylvia and Claudia, were a few years younger than me, so George and I would walk up the hill to their house and spend time in their kitchen with Mrs. Turner and her girls. Mrs. Turner would tell us stories of growing up in Austria and make intricate little dumpling-like pieces of food. She was always happy and laughing.

Not missing a trick in our little town, Jack noticed that Dad had a line-up of folks hanging around our porch. One day, he came to the house and presented his plan to Dad for what he called,

> "Helping Point Marion become more law abiding."

His plan involved becoming a Police Constable and working with Dad. Of course, our town had the Chief of Police, Bill Moser, and his trusty deputy, Lazier Black, who drove around in the Point Marion police car and responded to crimes and crossed children going to school and the like.

Mr. Turner said his plan would involve him being deputized by Dad, the Justice of the Peace, as a Constable who policed the area. Jack was aware that Dad got no salary for being the Justice of the Peace, and he also knew there was no salary for a Constable. The money for Dad would come from fines and hearings and revenue for performing services like weddings or a landlord issue. Jack had a better idea. Jack knew that's how other small towns and townships worked. There was another Justice of the Peace in nearby Sprucetown, but Point Marion was an outlier.

Jack set to work. And work he did. He used his own car with a whirly blue and red light he would clip to the roof and set up speed traps for those,

> "Spoiled West Virginia University students who would race through our town going way over our speed limit,"

and anyone else he could catch breaking the law.

Jack would bring each of the culprits down to Dad's office, record the infraction and fine them. He made a big dent in holding the wife beaters responsible and having them sit out their time in the local jail. Constable Turner was known all over town. He was well respected and taken seriously. His military training served him well.

Dad started doing weddings and misdemeanor hearings and, if he performed a service, Dad in fact charged people. Sometimes people would pay. But Dad and Mr. Turner ran into a few snags in the program. Early on, they discovered that Deputy Black was stopping cars around town that he assumed were speeding. He pulled the driver over and threatened,

> "Hand over a ten-dollar bill or I will take you down to the Squire."

Constable Turner used a calculated speed meter and brought the culprits down to our house to see Dad.

Chief Moser, a living saint of the town who had served Point Marion for decades with a stellar personal reputation, was so upset once he verified the allegation made of his own Deputy, he point-blank fired Deputy Black.

The other problem that Dad ran into was when one of his friends would ask him to fix a ticket or judgment. I would hear him on the phone,

> "Now, Junior, you know I can't do that. I don't 'fix' anything, ever. Don't ask me again."

The Justice of the Peace / Constable Jack Turner relationship worked fine for a while. But like the rest of Dad's designs, his own lockstep bullheadedness got in the way of making it a lasting program. Dad had his set hours of availability and he refused to waiver one bit. Jack was a go-getter and could not operate only on Dad's made-up rigid schedule.

It all came to head one winter night around 1:30 a.m. Jack banged on the front door, shining the deer tracking spotlight he kept in the trunk of his car at Dad's bedroom window and at the side of our house, yelling at him with a loudspeaker. Jack had intervened in a drunken brawl and arrested a belligerent perpetrator who, to protect the rest of the people milling around Augie's, needed to be put in jail for the night.

On the loudspeaker,

> *"Squire, you need to come deal with this!"*

The commotion was so loud that everyone in our house was awake. I went to Dad's room to try and get a response,

> *"DAD, MR. TURNER NEEDS YOU!"*

Dad whispered to me,

> *"Be quiet, I am not getting up. It's after 1 a.m. Go back to bed; pretend you don't hear him."*

> *"DAD, this is stupid – isn't this your JOB?"*

"Do what I told you!"

I finally realized that Dad did not care about doing the right thing. He wanted his own comfort. He would avoid anything uncomfortable at all costs.

Jack stopped working with Dad after that. The policing of the town returned to how it was before. I still saw Mr. Turner. He and his family moved to Smithfield and started a successful antique business. I knew that no matter what he did, Jack Turner would make a difference.

Dad continued being a Squire on his own terms. He made enough money to buy his own beer and cigarettes. He did not have any more hairbrained schemes to make money. People still sat on our front porch waiting for Dad to dole out his form of free legal advice.

I was learning that many men escape reality simply by avoidance. It seems easy to ignore a problem or an issue and pretend it never happened or wasn't there. But what are the consequences?

This pattern of behavior defined Dad. People allowed him to get away with it and so he let them down.

I resolved that I would deal with life in the here and now.

47

ARETHA AND GREENE COUNTY

Mary Joe and I remained friends through sixth grade. Her grandma and grandpa had an especially small one-story house on a dirt road off the hill. Her grandma was nice but could not smile. She put a bed for Mary Joe and Bobbie Lee in the dining room of her little house and, on the buffet table, she put a Bible that stayed open to some important words. On either side of the open Bible was a candle. It looked so special on a hand-crocheted white starched doily. Mary Joe and I would tiptoe around it when we came in from exploring. We never did figure out what the special page in her grandma's Bible said. The printing was so tiny, and we were both afraid to look.

Things changed for Mary Joe. She started having money in her pockets. Real folding money. She said that she and Bobbie Lee got some Social Security because her mama and daddy died. We would go up to Ross's Grocery Store and stand and look at the things on the shelves. The Ross's let us wander around their store because Mary Joe had money. Sometimes we would buy interesting things that we never had before.

One day, we were looking at the shelves and Mary Joe picked out a red and white can of Redi Whip. It was sitting beside the milk on the refrigerator shelf. She marched over to Miss Cora at the cash register and pulled some smashed-up dollars out of her shorts pocket and handed her one. Miss Cora smiled and handed back a paper bag with the Redi Whip. It was that easy to get such amazing stuff if you had money.

We ran up the street and rushed behind the big sign at the top of Penn Street, hidden from view. Mary Joe sat on the rocks and pulled the Redi Whip out of the bag. We both turned it over and over in our hands. It was cold and there was a red cap on the top. Mary Joe took a rock and hit the cap and it cracked off. There was this little white whistle thing on the top. Mary Joe pushed it to the side and white, creamy, fluffy whipped cream streamed out on her leg. We spent the afternoon behind that signpost squirting Redi Whip in each other's mouths. Later we both had a tummy ache but kept quiet.

Aretha and Greene County

Mary Joe and I went on lots of hikes with George running behind us. One of our favorite places to go was Greene County. We had to walk on the bridge over the Monongahela River beside my house to get to Greene County. There was a toll bridge man sitting in a toll booth in the middle of the road on the Point Marion side. He would collect twenty-five cents from cars and five cents from each walker.

Sometimes people would see us starting to walk up to the bridge and they would pick us up so we would not have to spend our five cents. It was twenty-five cents per car no matter how many people. Mary Joe had her Social Security so we could afford the five cents each way to go exploring in Greene County. Mary Joe said she would rather have her mama than that Social Security.

When we walked to Greene County, we would go to Aretha Silver's house. Aretha lived with her mama and dad and her sister, Bella, in a house next door to her grandma and grandpa's house on Walnut Hill. There weren't any other kids around for Aretha to play with and she was bone-chilling lonely.

It took a long time to get to Aretha's because we had to cross the bridge, cross the highway, cross the railroad tracks, and then walk up the side of the steep hill on a red dog road to get to her house. In the summertime, we were sweating. But Aretha was so happy to see us, it was worth the long walk. Going home was not as awful because it was downhill.

We would play in an old shed out in the weeds near Aretha's house. Aretha liked to play dolls and that was okay with Mary Joe and me. We didn't care what we played. Dolls, sticks in the dirt, chase the stick. No matter. George hung out in the weeds huffing and puffing because he had trouble catching his breath after the Junior Davis / Buddy incident.

One dripping hot afternoon, Aretha left the shed and pushed the wood bar over the door. We were locked into that small dark shanty. It was getting late, and it was hot. Mary Joe and I started yelling at the top of our lungs. Aretha's daddy finally came and let us out. Aretha was crying.

"I just don't want you two to go home. I'm so lonely here."

Aretha's daddy would not let her walk all the way to Point Marion by herself.

"Little girls should not be on the road."

We tried to visit her more often, but she went to a different school than us, being in Greene County and all.

After sixth grade, Mary Joe and I started to grow apart. She was starting to get breasts and wear frilly dresses. I wanted to go on hikes and play chase-the-stick with George.

I was beginning to understand that loneliness is a real acid test for the soul. Aretha was so lonely she locked us in a shed.

The cause and results of loneliness were an understanding that would continue to unfold over the next several years.

48

WHITE WALLS

We never had white walls on the tires of our car like Susie had on her bike. Some people in town had those iridescent silver whitewalls on their cars that reflected in the mud puddles and off a ray of sun escaping through the cloud cover. I saw them riding through town in their brand-new Chevys or Fords. They had long tail fins on their cars and no bar between the front and rear windows. The seats were shiny plastic and I saw the wind blow through their hair as they drove with the windows down. These were the rich people. The dad in that car probably had a job in the nearly played out mines.

The rich people bought brand new tires for their cars. I could tell because I would look at the tread on their tires. Mr. Gowers had a Ford Thunderbird. It was a convertible. He had a big shock of white hair, and I would watch him speeding down Main Street toward the Cheat River Bridge, sitting in that little red car with white stripes. The top was usually down. The breeze would blow through his straight, silvery hair as the sun would catch its reflection. Mr. Gowers was elected to the Pennsylvania State Assembly from our district. He knew everyone in town, and he would show a straight line of white teeth when he smiled. (Dad said he smiled at everyone and remembered their name because he wanted to be reelected.)

"Hello, Francie, good day for a bike ride."

"Yessir, Mr. Gowers, it sure is."

Once, when he had parked it at the VFW on Main Street and had gone inside to drink and play his numbers (everyone had to get their numbers in by 4 o'clock), I snuck up to the rear of his car and measured the tread. Sure enough! I could put my school pencil, eraser side in first, into the tread and the pencil was buried up beyond the eraser.

He was rich.

Once Mama started to work, every summer and every winter we would have to buy a set of retreads for our car so she could keep driving to the county seat, Uniontown, to work. Otherwise, because the tires were smooth as a baby's ass, as Dad used to say, in the winter she would slide off the road, and in the summer the potholes would bust the tires out. If Mama did not go to work every day, I was sure we would starve. When we had to have retreads, we could not have any groceries until the payday after we bought them. Mama would take the tires on our old station wagon and trade in the bald rims for a set of recapped tires that had new tread heat fused onto them. Once we even got a single white wall in the batch. Mama had it put on the right front.

On those paydays when we had to buy retreads, we had no hamburger crumblies. And sometimes no beans. I didn't like the crumblies anyway. Sometimes Dad would fry a piece of onion in the hamburger crumbly, and then the yellow of the onion would float in the grease that was left in the big black iron skillet that Mama put on the oilcloth table cover. The oilcloth was some bright color that was stained with spots from putting a hot skillet or popcorn pan on the table. Or holes burned into the oilcloth from cigarette butts.

Little pieces of grease would stick into the burned holes and emit an odd smell of caked grease mixed with ashes on a hot day. The oilcloth was left over from a camping trip that Mama had taken the Girl Scouts on long ago. Before she was so tired.

We all knew payday for Mama was every other Friday.

On payday Saturdays, and when we did not have to buy retreads, all three of us girls could walk uptown to the A&P with Mama, get a pushcart, and walk slowly down the single aisle filled with cans and sacks of amazing things. We would make the turn at the meat counter, pass the carrots and celery on the right, and walk slowly down the return aisle to Miss Twila at the cashier's station. By this time, I knew better than to get distracted and knock down her pyramid displays.

When we needed to buy retreads for the car, we sometimes had a can of baked beans and maybe a quart jar of canned peaches that Mama had canned last summer. We had a bottle of Heinz ketchup to make the food more interesting. The ketchup bottle was glass and had this big lettering,

HEINZ KETSUP
Pittsburgh, Pennsylvania.

We lived in Pennsylvania, but I had never seen Pittsburgh. Dad would sometimes talk about Pittsburgh with a kind of breathy awe in his voice.

> "Yes, kids, I worked on the Manhattan Project during the war at Westinghouse. When the war was over, they blew a whistle, and we walked out. There was no more work. I came home."

Dad worked in Pittsburgh in 1944 and 1945 at a plant owned by Westinghouse. That whistle went off after the bomb was dropped on Nagasaki, Japan, in August 1945. Dad did not work after that.

People of the mountains set the standard for paycheck to paycheck living. Just shuffling along. Walking on down the line.

Surviving.

49

POINT MARION SERVICEMEN

With so little opportunity and a total lack of encouragement to better themselves, the children of the mountains search for a path out of the encumbering wooded environment. There is a flat-out plaintive call of "what can I do with my life?"

For the young men who have come of age, the alternatives are to try to get a job in the dwindling opportunities of the coal mines, to get involved in any illicit activity such as moonshine, numbers, and theft, or to join the service.

For a rare select few who somehow were good at sports in the second-rate high school program that only provided either football or basketball, maybe by the grace of some invisible hand, and only if they had not been seriously injured in high school, they would be ushered into an obscure sports program at a small college. These poor fellows would be lauded by the townsfolk as the Great American Dream.

> "Yesseree. Did you see Bobby Jim run that football against Mapletown High?"

> "Shore nuff he's goin' to some college in Mississippi right out of here,"

only to return the following year with lifelong injuries to set up camp at the Brass Rail or Augie's to reminisce about that glorious touchdown.

> "Fer shore I could have made it. I could have been a real player ... if only that big refrigerator of a niggah from Georgia hadn't run over me on the field and broke my knees ... They sent me straight home. I cain't even work in the mine or go on to the service now ..."

Of course, this "out" was only for boys. There was no sports escape for girls.

With scant access to and rare support or information for higher education, Appalachians lean toward what they have seen their fathers and grandfathers do. They join the service and, maybe, maybe, get free of the clutch of the mountains.

Joining the service is seen as the big life event for most of the men in Point Marion. Most every boy joined up as soon as he was out of high school. Those who dropped out of school went on to the service to get out of town. During wars, the Appalachians were the body source for the rank-and-file, hardcore, marching boys. The country-grown boys were mean, sneaky, bush fighters who loved to tramp around in the woods and create havoc.

Scrambling through the woods, carrying a gun, is second nature to an Appalachian boy. In fact, the Vietnam War saw more Appalachian's per capita, fighting and dying, than any other region. During the Vietnam War, the draft was in effect, but not all areas of the United States were represented on an equal basis. Country folks, having a strong sense of God and country, often signed up for the service, while the wealthy better educated remained in college and looked for any legal loophole to the draft, or left the country. Those who did the fighting came from the poorer regions.

Point Marion is a shining example of the masses who would proudly stand up for God and country. Appalachians have historically become the fodder on the front line; the first to be shot were routinely from places along the rivers in the south and the hill country. Going into the service was a mantra for all the boys. That's how many escaped.

Of course, there were those who had a "special incentive" to join the ranks of those going off to join the fighting.

Big Jimney Aiken started dating a sixteen-year-old God-fearing Cawley girl from Stewartstown Road. They made the mistake of spending too much time in the back seat of an old Ford. When her father, the Reverend Mister Cawley, found out she was in the family way, he married his daughter off to Big Jimney.

She and Big Jimney settled near Camp Run Creek. She began to breed and had too many kids, too fast. Before she was thirty, she had eight children. Big Jimney was well-known in town as a good worker. He worked all the time, wherever and whenever he could. Running numbers for the Brass Rail or Augie's or shoveling out the barns at Friendship Hill. The family never starved, but the kids pretty much raised themselves.

Little Jimney Aiken was raised in town and was the oldest of the six Aiken boys. He was in and out of trouble from the age of 12. Little Jimney found that school was too much for him and he dropped out at 16 and began his career of making a nuisance of himself in town. When he was 18, his record was checkered with stealing cars, assault and battery, and public drunkenness. He even had a citation from Deputy Lazier Black for urinating on the Veterans Memorial at midnight one cold November.

When he was not in the Point Marion jail waiting to be transported to the Uniontown jail for one of his 30- or 60-day sentences, he was sitting on the window ledge at Sonny's Mobil Station, cooking up some mischief with the other local hard scrabble boys.

The turning event in his life was a hot, mushy night when he and the boys from the ledge at Sonny's hitchhiked over to the dance at the Sons of Italy Hall in Greensboro. Little Jimney had more than a few sips of 'shine, and he was anxious to try his luck with one of the miner's daughters across the bridge in Greene County.

> "C'mon boys –those girls are hot."

Little Jimney spotted Patty Sue Lipinski in her cancan skirt, whirling from side to side and humming to *Monster Mash*. She was smiling at all the boys, but Little Jimney believed she was looking at him and no one else.

When Patty Sue got home, all her Daddy saw was her torn skirt, her ripped blouse, and blood in a couple of places. She was sobbing. Her daddy, a giant of a man who loaded coal at the Shanopin Portal, was waiting for her on the front porch. Arms crossed. Peggy Sue was his sweet baby girl. The orange porch light was on.

All Patty Sue could say was,

> *"Little Jimney Aiken had his way with me."*

Pa Lupinsky had HIS WAY with Little Jimney Aiken.

Judge Amity Jones looked Little Jimney square in his blackened eyes and busted lip.

> "Little Jimney, you are in big trouble now, the only thing that's gonna calm that fire you got in your jeans and get you outta another beatin from Lupinsky is to get the hell outa here.

> "Now, I figure I have two choices. I can either see that you are on the next shift of busses headed to Biloxi as a new recruit for the US Army, or I can ship you off to the Big House right now in Westmoreland County.
>
> "Now, for sure, you hain't gonna get no soft seat at the regional jail.
>
> "Them boys there are mean folk from all over the valleys. You done raped that Lupinsky girl. What will it be Buddy Boy?"

Little Jimney lost a good bit of the fire in his pants that afternoon. He vomited on the wood plank floor in front of Judge Jones and choked back a tear. He needed to sign up for the Army or he was going to the Big House, and he might not come back with anything in his pants to set on fire. Either way, it would be a long time before he would see his mama or Point Marion again.

Within months, Little Jimney was in Vietnam as a ground troop in one of the many waves of recruits to hit the ground with a rifle, and in the first pair of new boots he ever had. Unlike so many of the others from the area who came home in body bags, Little Jimney, after serving two Vietnam re-ups and somehow surviving the TET Offensive, came back to town and made up part of the core group of aging men who collected a service-related disability pension.

These disenfranchised men spent their days drinking at the VFW or American Legion. Twice a year, on Memorial Day and July 4th, they tried to mash themselves into an old uniform for the Point Marion Veteran's Honor Parade. Those that didn't even want to bother trying to tuck their various parts and their growing bellies full of beer into an old uniform simply donned their service caps and proudly marched up Main Street to Little Arlington Cemetery. TAPS was played and a full gun salute was given to them and the other men from Point Marion and surrounding areas who were buried or standing there.

Once Little Jimney returned, he did odd jobs around town and spent his disability check on beer and cigarettes. If he had anything left over at the end of the month, he walked along the road in Springhill Township to one of the shacks with a red light on the porch. He never waved at passing cars and seldom hitchhiked from one place to another. He stumbled along the road, kicking rocks here and there. He didn't look up or look at others in the eye who sometimes passed by.

He became one more angry and forlorn hill country veteran who was cast aside after being used in a faraway war.

> "Mama, I just don't get it. There are all these posters around town about how wonderful it is to serve our country. We have a special section in the cemetery for those men that served. There is that fancy Veterans Memorial monument up by the police station with all these names of men who died, but most of the men who come back from the wars are sad and angry. They just stay drunk. Look at Little Jimney Aiken. Uncle Sam uses them up. Little Jimney should be glad he did not come home in a body bag."

Mama said,

> "You need to get out of here."

50

DO I NEED A BRA?

Age 13 meant moving from sixth to seventh grade. We still had forty-seven children in our class. That seemed to be the magic number for the first set of baby boomers. Even though Kenny Murray moved to Smithfield, Sooley Sours joined our group. Sooley was lots of fun. She and her younger brother and sister and mom had moved in with her grandmother in Harvey Town. Sooley's dad was in Texas. He had stayed in the service after the war and Sooley and her family followed him around wherever he was stationed. One day, Sooley said to me,

> "My dad broke mine and my mother's heart. He ran off with a woman in Texas, so we came home to my grandma."

> "But Sooley, your mom and grandma are so nice, you and your family will do fine. They love you."

> "Yes, but I miss my dad. Don't tell my mama."

> "I never will."

Point Marion grade school was attended by the white kids who lived in town. The bunch of us baby boomers were going to attend Point Marion Junior High School. At this point, the country kids would join us, and we would also be merged with the colored kids in Nilan who went to one of the country schools through sixth grade. We were an amalgam of children with only a few black faces. This meant more than double the number of students in our class.

The cruds came on the bus from all the townships and small boroughs around. They were the farmer kids and the kids from the abandoned coal patches. The country kids would tumble off the bus in packs. They all looked scared. And tattered.

From kindergarten to sixth grade, all the town kids were in one classroom together. We were a big cumbersome group who had been together for seven years. We sorted out into the popular kids, the skinny kids, the fat kids, those who picked their noses, and those who had new clothes.

The Catholic kids sat separate from the Protestant kids. And of course, the teachers learned the names of the kids whose dads had a job. There were no black or minority children in town, consequently none in the school until we reached seventh grade. If the mom or dad was a schoolteacher, the kid got to sit in the front of the class, were chosen as hall monitor, and got As. If the mom was a friend of one of the teachers, the kid was in a special group who was called on in class. The rest of the kids were a mass of faces to the teachers.

We were separated into sections:

A Section: The popular kids who lived in town, whose dad had a job, or whose mom or dad was a schoolteacher.

B Section: For those who were poor, still picked their nose, had no new clothes, tangled hair, were bussed in from the country, and were cruds.

C Section: For the cruds, black kids, and kids from the abandoned coal patches.

R Section: For the kids who were really poor and judged by their teachers as being plain stupid, or any child the teachers thought might be disabled.

I was assigned to the B Section.

Each section had different textbooks based on what some school administrator decided would be the proper level for the group. Each section had its own specific teacher. A bell would ring every 45 minutes, and we would move as a mass of humanity from one class to another. The three-story, brick school building could not accommodate all the classes, so the school district put up Quonset huts around the school grounds for the overflow classes. The Quonset huts were used by the military during the war and were boiling in the summer and freezing in the winter.

A Section students read classic books, while B Section students read second level books. C Section students had books that were for the grade behind (seventh graders got sixth-grade level books), and the R kids were mostly in a babysitting situation.

At the age of 13, when the other girls in my class were beginning to wear a bra, I was scrawny, knock-kneed, and nearly six feet tall. I was still working on Girl Scout badges when the other girls were starting to get together behind the bushes on the playground and giggle about the boys.

Dad said to me,

> *"Francie, you are flat as a barn slat. You know the bees will always find their own way to the honey, and you aren't much."*

Dad and Mama seemed to both think that if the boys liked me, it would relieve them of some burden. Mama's follow up to me was,

"*Francie, you just have to learn to lean up against the boys.*"

"*Mama, I just don't understand.*"

Mama was not good at explaining how a girl grew up. She never took us aside and explained things. I couldn't figure out the secrets the other girls had and what I was expected to do. I was an embarrassment. I was even more ashamed of being a girl.

I decided that I needed a bra to fit in. My sister Eileen was having nothing to do with me in those years, as she viewed me as a tag-a-long pest in her efforts to be popular and included. Eileen was in ninth grade. We were both in junior high school.

"*Francie don't look at me at school. Don't talk to me.*"

Sometimes I would see her in the hallways, and she would look away. She considered me a crud. I felt like a crud. I knew no one in the B Section.

I went to my sister Charlen for one of her reject bras. Charlen was a senior at the high school. Eileen didn't talk to her either.

"*Charlen, I just don't fit in, I need a bra. All the other girls have one.*"

"*Oh, yea, okay Francie, here's one I don't wear much.*"

Charlen had three bras and she gave me one. It was a 28B. It smelled like an old rubber band that had lost its elasticity. The straps were yellowed and the clasp in the back part was a little rusty. One hook in the back was missing, but one was still there. The front part where there were two out pouched cups were wrinkled over into little mashed triangles. There was circular sewing that had turned a bland yellow color going around toward the tip of the little collapsing cones. I used the clasps in front to shorten the length to the two crushed triangles. My first bra!

I started wearing it to school every day. The straps hurt and the missing hook was sharp, but I thought I was so much more acceptable. Jimmy Lester Duchunk sat behind me in home room and started snapping the back straps through my clothes and calling me "STRAP." I thought this was about right for attention from boys. I did not like it, but I figured that was what a girl had to put up with. I got one or two sharp "snaps" every class period.

"Hi ya, STRAP,"

SNAP. SNAP.

"How ya doin' today, STRAP."

SNAP. SNAP.

That same fall, Susan Binkus passed me a note:

"HAS YOUR MOTHER TOLD YOU ABOUT NAPKINS YET?"

I carefully read the note and, looking at Susan, shook my head. Napkins? No, my mother never told me anything. My sisters did not tell me.

Susan's mom had told her that weekend and she was dying to share the information with someone. She took me behind the bushes on the playground and explained that every month girls would bleed "from down there." And the girls had to wear napkins that were supported by an elastic band and a safety pin to soak up the blood. I looked at Susan with disbelief. She knowingly nodded her head up and down. I thought this was disgusting, and I hoped this would never, ever happen to me.

This was unbelievable! One more stupid thing that a girl had to put up with.

It did happen to me a year later. In eighth grade. I was so embarrassed, but I did go to my mama. She said that sometimes we could not afford to buy the napkins that were sold at Hunkers' Drug Store, so that day she showed me how to tear up old rags and pin them to my underpants to soak up the blood. It was all so strange. I was ashamed to get this bleeding and never understood how to handle the discomfort of wearing the rags.

Later, Charlen explained how a thing called a *tampon* could make things more comfortable, but she said we could rarely afford tampons. She said they are complicated anyway.

I hated that I was born a girl.

51

GROWING UP

Brenda Goods was a wealth of information. Every day at recess, she would get me and the other girls together behind the rusty benches that led to the swings and tell us jokes about things. She would tell long stories about a boy touching a girl.

"And then they would do 'tick, tick, tick, tick,'"

she would touch her belly button and then my belly button when she said "tick." And then she would roll her eyes, and everyone would laugh like crazy. I laughed too because I did not want to be left out. One day, right after the recess bell rang as we were lining up to go to class, I asked Brenda what was,

TICK, TICK, TICK, TICK,

as I motioned to our belly buttons.

Brenda said,

"I don't know"

and rushed past me.

After that, none of the other girls talked to me about the *tick, tick, tick, tick* that girls and boys did.

I had two friends who must have known what this was and even done the *tick tick tick tick* though, because the summer we were 14 years old these two girls disappeared.

Mary Joe Church, my dear friend from fifth grade, whose daddy escaped from the nuthouse, disappeared that summer. Eileen came to me and said,

> *"Mary Joe Church is pregnant. She has to get married. She did it in the back seat of a car with that boy from Jimtown."*

I wasn't exactly sure how that could work. Mary Joe was 14 years old. She was such a sweet girl. Mama talked about it like she died. Mama never told us anything about how people "do" it. Just that it was really, really bad to do.

A few weeks later Eileen came home with more news.

> *"Bobbie Lee Church is pregnant too. She has to get married."*

Mama said,

> *"Their life is over. They ruined their lives."*

Mary Joe ended up getting married and went to live with her husband and his family in Jimtown. Her husband was a junior in high school and he delivered papers around Jimtown so they could afford gas for a car. One day, she and her husband came by our house and Mary Joe showed me her baby. She named her Chrissie. The baby was beautiful – all pink and dressed in white. Mary Joe looked so happy.

The other girl who disappeared was Judy Randall. She was the smartest and the prettiest girl in our class. We all started out together in kindergarten and Judy was the one girl that every one of the boys adored. Lester and Ben had a made-up chant they used when Judy would appear on the playground.

> "Policeman, policeman do your duty,
> Here comes Judy, American Beauty."

The most amazing issue at that time was that the girls in school weren't jealous. I certainly was not. Judy was not only a beautiful little girl, but she was also kind to everyone. As we progressed from kindergarten to then starting to wear bras and jockstraps, Judy had blossomed into a well-endowed popular girl.

When ninth grade started, Judy was married to Howard Bennie, a boy who was a junior in high school. She never came back to school. She lived with her husband's family on Freeling Street. Judy's mother-in-law was the kindly Mrs. Bennie who taught Sunday school and Bible school at the Methodist Church. Always the first one to bring a covered dish of tuna casserole to the Methodist Church suppers and the last to leave after the United Methodist Church Ladies Auxiliary had served lunch to and cleaned up from the Point Marion Men's Rotary Club.

The idea that her precious only child, Howard, was going to be a daddy was almost too much for her. But she was a good Christian woman, and she did the best she could for Judy. Judy's mom and dad disowned her. Even though they lived in the Harvey Town section of Point Marion, less than a quarter of a mile away, they might as well have been in New York City.

> "Mama, if Judy had gotten pregnant to someone rich, would that have been better for her?"

Mama said,

> "She should have kept her legs closed. She should not have let Howard Bennie get in her pants."

> "But Mama, she is only fourteen years old, and her own mama and daddy are acting like she's dead!"

Clearly, I was getting mixed messages. There did not seem to be any clear answer to being a girl. Were girls worthless? Certainly, in my own family, the girl children were of little value.

Mama was clear that the way to get out of the tyranny of the hills was to hitch my future to a male who would be successful, had money, and would take care of me.

How would I ever manage this?

52

THE PROMISE

Mama would never say what happened between her and her mother, but one thing was clear. They had a strong dislike for one another. In fact, Mama hated her own mother. Mama called her "The Old Bitch" (TOB) until the day her mother died. Our whole life we heard stories about,

> "When I get TOB's money, this, and this and this will happen. We will have a better life, things will be so much easier. She is going to try and leave the money to a dog cemetery on Long Island, but I am going to make sure I get it."

Dad had a story that I think sustained the three of us girls through the leanest times of our bone poor childhood, right up to the point when Mama's father died.

> "Look kids, your grandpa promised me that he has set aside money for you to go to college. He told me himself that he set up a plan for each of you. Yes, your grandfather has made sure that you will get a good education and go to a really good university, just like your mother and I did.

> "You will each be able to study whatever you want; you will have a good life. Just think, anywhere you want to go to be educated. You will have a good time then, kids. You just wait. A really good time. It will happen."

This made sense to us. Grandpa was himself a University Professor. He held a PhD in Civil Engineering and had built bridges and tunnels.

> "Your grandfather even has an Endowed Chair at the University in New York. By golly, he knew the importance of an education."

And Dad and Mama told us over and over this was going to happen.

> "You kids are going to be able to make something of yourselves. Your grandpa has seen to it that you will go to college."

Being the least trusting sister, I would think to myself,

> "Yes, right now girls, your teeth are rotting, and we can't afford to feed you most days, but you wait…"

We had grown up with Mama and Daddy's stories of driving shiny new cars and going to dances in feathered gowns. Of learning anything they wanted to learn in big books, smelling musty libraries with vines covering the buildings and a shiny clean desk with lots of light to study by. We heard stories of going to a real cafeteria and putting anything they wanted to eat on a tray.

> "A dish of pears, please. No, I don't think I will have the roast beef today, thank you."

The three of us would talk about going to sorority parties and being accepted as one of the girls who had clothes and money. Mama was a member of the Delta Delta Delta sorority at Bucknell University, and Dad was a Phi Kappa

Psi fraternity member. Daddy pinned Mama at a fraternity party. They would delight us with their stories of laughter and fun. Some days that was all I thought about.

> "And kids, you can be anything you want to be. You can be a teacher or an engineer or even a doctor."

As children, we tried writing to our grandmother. But we only heard from her on our birthday's and at Christmas. I figured she and Mama must have shared the same angry personality.

On our birthday, we would receive a twenty-dollar bill from our grandmother. If Mama did not need to borrow it for an emergency, this was enough to go to Girl Scout camp for two weeks! How I loved to get away and run through the woods with other girls in the summer.

At Christmas, we would send Grandma a box of presents. Small gifts we would each make for her and wrap. Likewise, Grandma sent a box to our house with a gift for each of us. Dad would open the bigger box that had all the smaller presents inside and carefully place them under the tree.

> "Francie, here is your gift from Grandma. The package says BERGDOFF."

> "Eileen here is your package from Grandma. The package says SAKS FIFTH AVENUE.

Mama would mumble,

> "Why doesn't TOB just send me the money? She knows I need it."

In 1949, my grandfather's health deteriorated from diabetes and small strokes that incapacitated him. Grandma and Grandpa stayed in New York City after that and never again visited Point Marion. Although he did not die until 1958, at the age of 73, he was an invalid for nine years. He was blind, confused, and slept most of the time. Grandma kept herself busy going to the DAR and Eastern Star meetings and playing bridge with her friends. She never worked.

In the fall of 1958, Mama got the call from her mother that her father had died, and she was to go to New York right away. Grandma had Western Union wire the money to Mama for a plane ticket from Morgantown to New York and then cab fare to Grandma's apartment. Our old 1950 Ford would never make the trip and Mama was to be there right away. No one in our family ever took plane trips. Mama hocked her diamond at the pawn shop in Morgantown so she could have enough walking around money for the trip.

Mama loved her father. She was quiet about his death. She was gone for nearly a week. We drove to Morgantown to pick her up at the airport. She got in the car and said nothing until we got home. All we had ever heard was that grandpa would leave his only child enough money to live a decent life and educate her children after he died. The family was thinking,

finally.

Dad said,

"Well, Charlotte..."

Mama looked at all of us,

"There is no money. My mother needs it all for herself."

Charlen was a senior in high school. She was expecting to go to college on Grandpa's promised money the next year. There would be no college for any of us. None of us would be joining a sorority.

The fairy tale was gone.

I was so confused. How could Mama have believed all those years that her daddy would bail her out of poverty? Why did she even expect him to? Did she have an agreement with him? Why was she making up this myth and feeding it to us?

Mama sat down and continued smoking her Lucky Strikes. Dad walked up to Augie's for a beer.

Mama was somehow able to get her ring out of hock.

I was beginning to develop a list of the cardinal virtues that I would use to navigate through life. My Trust No One theory resonated with me.

Why did my parents expect the previous generation to bail them out of life's challenges?

I later learned that this entitlement theory is a thread that seems to be stitched into the fabric of my relations.

I would proceed on high alert throughout my life.

53

THE EARTH MOVES

I was 16 years old and in the 11th grade. It was a freezing cold winter's day, the first day of a blizzard. The wind was blowing off the river in gusts of cloudy, ice cutting snow and the roads were piling up with white, slushy sleet and drifting toward the center, making the roads impassable. George had his winter fur all grown in and he was patiently waiting for me out of the wind in a corner of the front porch.

I walked home from the bus stop and made it inside the house in time to wrap George and me in an old quilt. It was early winter, December 6, so I had not even thought of searching through drawers of winter clothes to find a matching set of mittens to wear that day when I left to catch the bus to school. My hands were chapped and white pink with cold from the walk home. In the early sixties, girls were not allowed to wear slacks to school, so I pulled my socks up as high as I could and suffered through the trudge home. My bare legs were ashen with caked snow by the time I pushed the door shut against the wind.

Although I was still remarkably thin and, at six feet, the tallest girl in our class, I was enjoying my early teenage years, thanks to my first true love.

Several years before, Albert Bronakoski picked me out at a wedding reception I attended with my mama in Bobtown. I saw myself as a withdrawn, uninteresting girl of the shadows. Dad called me,

> "Slat. Francie, you are so skinny that if you turn sideways, we can't see you!"

At the wedding reception, Albert came up to me and we started talking. We danced the polka and slow danced to the band playing in the Bobtown Fire Hall.

We were in love. We had a passionate first love in so many ways. He was two years older than me, and we spent high school latched on to one another in a first love two-step. Albert graduated from Mapletown High School in Greene County the previous spring. We spent his high school years going steady; exchanging class rings, going to dances, bowling, going to the movies, going for walks, and parking in the woods. We did a lot of parking in the woods. Talking, kissing, kissing, hugging, and exploring one another.

When I was 15, I was invited to a semi-formal dance by Albert. Of course, there was no money to buy a dress, but Mama had kept all the beautiful gowns, purses, and scarves she wore during the days before marrying Dad. In a chest in her bedroom was a red, silk, velvet, long, slinky dress. The original even had dyed matching red ostrich feathers around the bottom. That dress was beautiful. She disassembled the red dress and made a pattern for me. It was beautiful. I had never touched such luxurious soft silky fabric. Albert enjoyed touching it too.

We went to many school dances and Mama was helpful finding me a dress. One of my friends had a daughter who grew out of her prom dress, and she gave it to me. It was white and bouffant, and I loved it.

Albert had a driver's license and would drive the seven miles from Bobtown to Point Marion almost every day. In the summer, we would sit on our porch swing or go for a drive. In the winter we would listen to records in Mama's parlor or ride around. During the drives, we would usually end up parking somewhere and enjoying each other's private company. These were the days before the pill, and I am sure Albert's dad had concern that I would ruin his little boy's life by getting in the family way.

Except for a three-month period of separation when Albert's dad thought we were getting too serious, we were inseparable. The separation shattered my heart. I pined away for him. I was convinced we would never see one another again. Then, miraculously, he reappeared. He soothed my soul. In our clutches of embrace in his family's brand new 1960 Chev Impala, I began to discover a real understanding of what Brenda Goods said to me about the "*tick, tick,-tick,-tick,*" that happens between a boy and a girl.

Now I got it! The earth was moving.

As a matter of fact, the feeling was so strong that when I was in a passionate embrace with Albert, we would begin to uncontrollably tremble I would feel the rumble start in my stomach and take over my body. That weekend, the shaking was so strong and overpowering that I decided I was going to agree to whatever was necessary to satisfy our mutual longing for one another. We talked about using a rubber and Albert carried them in his wallet. We were both naive, but he said his friends had told him what to do.

We were both ready.

After 16 years of believing girls had no value and didn't count, I found someone who not only valued me but adored and respected me. We spent so much time together we felt we knew each other better than anyone else.

We wanted to eventually marry, but not until we were both educated and self-supporting.

Albert's father was a mining engineer and the Superintendent of the Shanopin Mine, owned by Duquesne Light, at the foot of the hill in Bobtown. Albert wanted to be a mining engineer like his dad. When he graduated from high school, he applied to become a U.S. Steel student-trainee under a five-year engineering program operated jointly with Pennsylvania State University.

Every year, US Steel would select two boys out of high school to participate in the program. One boy would attend classes in Engineering at Penn State University while the other boy would spend time in the US Steel mines. Each semester, the students would rotate.

Albert and the other selected student both wanted to start at Penn State first, in the fall semester, so they flipped a coin. Albert lost and the other boy started at the University and Albert started at the mine. Little did I know a coin toss would change our lives forever.

Albert began working at the Robena Coal Mine.

The Frosty Run shaft was 628 feet deep.

At 1 p.m. EST on December 6, 1962, in the Frosty Run shaft of the No. 3 mine, which was owned and operated by US Steel Corp, there was a blast. The face where the blast occurred was more than three miles from the bottom of the shaft. Eighty-three men were in the mine at the time. Forty-seven fled to safety. Thirty-six men were trapped near the face. This blast occurred on the 55th anniversary of the worst mine disaster on record in the United States; one which killed 361 men on December 6, 1907, at Monongah, West Virginia. Frosty Run shaft was only forty-two miles north of Monongah, West Virginia.

I was expecting Albert that evening. His sister called and said Albert was in a mine accident. I knew nothing about mine accidents or what was going on. The only television station in our area was channel 2 from Pittsburgh. There was a local radio station I began listening to.

My mind was empty. I was alone. How could this happen? This was a huge, mechanized coal mine. It had exploded with men inside.

The earth had moved.

Due to the blizzard, the roads were so bad that getting to the remote area of the Frosty Run mine entry area was nearly impossible for family members. At first, U.S. Steel Corp. asked the families of the trapped men to stay home. Eight hours after the accident, the company began calling the families to ask them to come to the site.

I waited for news. On Saturday, December 8, I begged Mama to take me to the location of the shaft. I wanted to be present when the rescued men started coming up.

We drove through the storm to a large, corrugated structure in a wooded area with cars and trucks parked helter-skelter in the slush and mud. The long metal building along one side housed the elevator leading down into the Frosty Run shaft. A hundred family members were seated inside, along the outside edge of the steel building in single lined straight chairs. The building was cold. Everyone was silent, with some muted whispers. People of all ages sat numb and wide-eyed. There was no news.

I found the Bronakoski family along the far-right side with their backs leaning against the metal wall. Just quietly sitting. Mama and I found chairs and joined them. There was nothing to say to Albert's sister, his mother, and his father.

The first victim was brought up in the early hours of Saturday, December 8, and the last was brought to the surface in the afternoon of December 11. There were no survivors.

A funeral for Albert was held at the Bobtown Catholic Church and a reception was held at the Bronakoski home. The overwhelming sadness I felt during that period stayed with me for a long time. I returned to school and graduated the next year.

I was suddenly more alone than I had ever been in my entire life. I knew my life was over. No hope. No friends. Nothing to do. I sat alone, went to high school classes, and sat alone. Lots of time alone. Once in a while, Mr. and Mrs. Bronowski would drive from Bobtown to Point Marion to see me. They were kind people. I did not know them, as I believed they were afraid I would somehow take Albert away from them or maybe trick him into an early forced marriage. They were of a different class than my family. Mr. Bronakoski was the mine foreman. The big boss. My family scratched by. We would sit in Mama's parlor and stare at one another. It was sad for them to see me. Mr. Bronakoski, looking at me with his clear blue eyes, said to me one day,

"Don't forget, Francie, I want a dance at your wedding."

There was a cloud hanging over my existence. The Bronowski's eventually stopped coming to see me, but I tried to stay in touch with them throughout my life until years later when I reached an overwhelming depression that nearly paralyzed me. During that dark period, I was unable to reach out to anyone.

And I realized that mental depression can be deadly.

The months after Albert died were dreary and sad. Somehow, while Albert and I were a couple, I must have isolated myself into a two-step of devoted romance to the exclusion of others. So, when he suddenly and tragically was gone, I was lonely. I was never close to my sisters. Both had finished high school and were not around. They each were struggling with their own education and finding their way in life.

I think Mama was dumbfounded.

As I puzzle over her treatment of me following Albert's death, I think she hoped that Albert would be the solution to her "third girl" problem. Due to our impoverished circumstances and her own prejudices regarding the value of females, she never expected that I would amount to much on my own. She may have anticipated that I would latch on to him and he would be my ticket out of the hills that she so despised.

She never talked to me about death or mentioned Albert. Certainly, there was never a discussion of an afterlife or God.

Just emptiness.

Dad was in his terminal stupor in those days, sitting on the sofa in our small dark living room, drinking a beer with the smoke of his cigarette encircling his face. Two of the hounds asleep at his feet. The dim light of the TV would flash mellow sparks of uneven flames around the dim room. He kept the TV so loud that any attempt at conversation was impossible.

It didn't matter.

I went back and forth to school and home. I sat on the sofa. No one talked about it.

Susie was going to Catholic school down the river in Masontown. She was not around to comfort or distract me from my grief and sadness She was not able to understand the depth of my pain. After all, she was not interested in boys at that stage. She was going to a strict Catholic school up the river, and she was 2 years my junior.

I stumbled through the cloudy smoke-filled days. It was a period when I numbly drew into myself.

George and I spent a lot of time together. We walked along the mucky weeds of the riverbank and kicked lumps of stray coal that had fallen off the railroad cars along the railroad tracks. The winter was cold and blustery. The wind cut into my tears like the blade of a dull hunting knife.

Albert was the first great love of my life. We always have a place in our hearts for our first love.

A gift of the heart that will forever light our way.

Slowly, ever so slowly, I began to realize that buried deep within me was the beginnings of a growing grit and resilience that would propel me.

54

OVERWHELMING SADNESS

Ever so slowly, I started to find a ray of light.

Valerie was in my high school class. She and her family lived in Masontown, which is one river town north of Point Marion. She was the one person who seemed to understand and tolerate my overwhelming sadness and the ever-present cloud that hovered over my existence. I was no joy to be with, but she brought me home with her day after day and talked with me.

Valerie's dad, John Dick, was one of the saints in my life. He had gone off to the Second World War in one of the waves of Appalachian boys marching to the drum of Uncle Sam's mesmerizing chant,

"America Needs YOU!"

He ended up in England where he met a beautiful woman and, at the close of the war, brought her home to the smoking hills of the Monongahela Valley. Mr. Dick was a coal miner who worked the night shift. I would see him walking slowly down the long road where they lived – Sterling Avenue – at the break of day in his mine clothes and big, solid, slogging boots. They lived in a small house he had built for his family when he returned from the war. It was clear that the hours of muscle shattering work sapped the strength from his body and left him bone breaking exhausted.

In her sweet English classical drawl that was nonexistent in the bowels of Appalachia, Mrs. Dick would say,

"Now John..."

So many years before that, as a young war bride, she left her beloved family and homeland and traveled thousands of miles toward the unknown. The little town in the entrails of the Appalachian coal country must have looked to her like her homeland -- another war zone of bleak, cloudy skies and blackened earth. Except for her husband, she was completely alone. Isolated. She knew no one except this strange man with whom she had fallen in love.

Never to return.

This family had a gemstone of love they were not afraid to share with my thorny soul. They always had time for me. Valerie's father and mother were devoted to one another. During this dank period of my life, these two became my own trickle of sunlight. I found myself gravitating to the two of them. I wanted to sit in the love they had for one another.

Mr. Dick, exhausted from his underground shift, searched me out and sat with me at their small kitchen table. He talked so softly that I could hear the wheeze of his coal dusted breath. His calloused hands were wringing some unknown spot on his thumb as he tried to find the words to say. He told me how he grew up in the coal fields. He shared how he never was encouraged to get educated and how he felt compelled to serve his country in war. He talked about how much he loved his family (his two girls and his beloved wife).

Valerie's mom would stand beside him with her hand on his shoulder. He talked to me about hope. About love and never giving up. As he shared his story, I began to realize that maybe I had some significance.

Through this loving couple, I learned life's lessons.

I began developing an understanding of the people of this forsaken place. The people who are the true heroes and heroines of my life.

Inspirational people who would take the time with a meaningless girl-child and hold her in the palm of their hands to inspire her to start believing that she -- maybe -- might be worthy of becoming something. Perhaps something special. Maybe something worth loving. Something that could do good or touch another life and hold value.

The saints among us.

55

THE CLOUDS PARTED

I muddled my way through the rest of my junior year in high school and went through my senior year in a trance. I am sure I was no fun to be around.

Now, I understood lonely.

By this time Mama and Dad had made it clear there was absolutely no money to go to college, and I would have to figure something out on my own. No alternatives were offered by Mrs. Bordeaux, the school guidance counselor. It seemed she was busy adjusting her too tight girdle and arranging for the boys who were athletes to get into some regional state school to play basketball or football.

It didn't matter.

I knew girls could be a nurse or a teacher. Mama said teaching was out because we had no money for the college tuition.

"Mama, I want to go to college. I want to be a teacher."

> "Francie, I just can't do it. Go be a secretary. Francie, you could go live in some big city and work in a typing pool of secretaries."

> "But Mama, I don't know how to type ... what is a secretary?"

Mama told me that Eileen was the smart one and she should go to college.

My sister Eileen was in her second year of commuting to West Virginia University in Morgantown, which was 8 miles south of Point Marion. The out-of-state tuition for Eileen was more than our family could afford. Eileen was to get a summer job while in school to pay for books and incidentals. But she was so concerned that she was not fitting in, she spent any money she earned on clothes and personal grooming. She went to the University library and read their textbooks.

She struggled with acceptance.

After finishing high school, my sister Charlen went to a nursing school in Morgantown. She received a donation from the Point Marion Business and Professional Women's club to pay her tuition. The costs for nursing school were low, as once a girl was admitted, she worked and lived at the hospital that provided the schooling. It was a way for hospitals to train their own future nurses and have relatively inexpensive workers for the three years of training it took to become a Registered Nurse. Charlen had finished her schooling at Monongalia General Hospital School of Nursing and worked as a nurse at the hospital where she trained, then she moved on to work at a larger hospital.

At home she would tell frightening stories of gory surgeries, impossible doctors, and grueling hours. Her nursing school had closed its doors the year she finished. Charlen didn't seem to like being a nurse much and she didn't offer me any encouragement, but I decided this might be an option for me to at least launch into a way to escape.

I knew nothing about nursing. I had never been in a hospital and the only exposure to medicine I had was the few brief encounters at Dr Hungar's office in Point Marion. The only nurse I knew was the school nurse, Mrs. Gumsome, and she was plain chilling. She walked around the school district with a scowling veneer in her white starched uniform dress, white seamed nylon hose, and buckle top white shoes.

CLICK. CLICK. CLICK.

She topped off her outfit with a peaked wing-like starched white cap. She never smiled. She was the epitome of remote.

I decided to take the pre-nursing exam required to qualify for application to every nursing school. The exam was given in Uniontown, Pennsylvania, the county seat, on a Saturday in October of 1963. One full day of testing given one time a year to any high school senior girl in Fayette County. I was surprised when I arrived at the testing facility, (the auditorium of Uniontown High School), to discover hundreds of 12th grade girls from all over the county lined up to take the test. Wow. I had no idea that every girl who could not afford college and had an idea of being a nurse in Fayette County was trying to ace this exam.

The other girls taking the test told me the cost of three years of nursing school was miniscule compared to tuition, books, room, and board at a college. I soon discovered that nursing school was a cheap ticket for an extensive education.

I took the exam and filled out an application to a school two counties away that sounded interesting. Washington Hospital. This was the General Hospital for Washington County, Pennsylvania. I had not been to that county, and this was the first time I heard of the place. Mama and Dad seemed ambivalent.

Much to my surprise, within six weeks, the Washington Hospital Director of Nursing, Miss Kirshbaum, wrote me a letter inviting me to come to the hospital for an interview. I was surprised to be asked for an interview. I thought it might be a mistake and I would soon be discovered as a pretender. Surely, I was a fraud.

Two weeks later, Mama and I took off on the treacherous two-and-a-half-hour drive to Washington. We arrived at a huge brick building with a sign,

> Nurses' Residence
> Washington Hospital

a few minutes ahead of my appointed time. Mama decided to stay in the car and lit up a Lucky Strike and began coughing.

I tenderly entered the building. A nicely dressed elderly woman, seated behind a counter to the left of the shining stone floor, smiled at me and directed me to what she called the lounge area down the hallway. I found a corner and sat stiffly in one of the many overstuffed classical and comfortable chairs arranged around a grand piano in a huge living room.

Other girls who looked like sixteen and seventeen-year-olds, were scattered around the room, balanced on the edge of some of the chairs. We each began quietly studying the pattern of the soft carpet under the piano. It was obvious each of us had dressed carefully in an acceptable clean, pressed dress. I could feel my heart thumping and breath catching in my throat. If I could enter this school and finish, it would be a ticket on the northbound train out of the hills.

This was the first time for me to be interviewed by anyone, and I was sure Miss Kirshbaum would find me to be the crud that I was. I was an imposter, and I knew it was a matter of time before being discovered as such. None of the young high schoolers spoke. The tension was palpable.

Before long, the kindly, smiling woman called the names, one by one, of each girl who was to enter a door across the hall. After a while, each girl who had been directed beyond the mysterious door would quietly open the door and silently slink out.

"Miss Dillinger, you can come in and see Miss Kirshbaum now."

She directed me into a stark office and pointed to a straight-back chair where I was to sit facing a large mahogany desk that was the size of our dining room table. A brass plate sat in the center of the desk facing me.

Miss Kirshbaum, RN
Director of Nursing

Miss Kirshbaum was in a stiff white uniform with her graying hair held back under a knife pleated wing-tipped cap. She stayed seated but looked at me and smiled. I was frozen.

"Please sit down, Miss Dillinger."

This tiny precise woman was the embodiment of reserve along with sincerity. I sat on the hard wooden chair and stared at the neatly lined pencils and pens arranged on her desk. She said she was impressed with my test results. She also said she noticed I had a sister who finished nursing school, and that was a good indication of my own success. I thought how I should get more information from Charlen than the blood and gore stories she tended to spend time on.

I liked Miss Kirshbaum immediately. The environment of the nurses' residence seemed to emote a kind, professional, caring formality that drew me in.

On the long drive back to Point Marion, Mama was silent. We never talked much in those days, as she seemed to be withdrawing farther into her own thoughts.

I told Mama that Miss Kirshbaum was different from our angry pinched-lipped school nurse. She seemed to be happy in a quiet way. I began the conversation on a tentative note.

> "Mama, if this place accepts me, I might want to go here ... I would be a Registered Nurse in only three years!"

> "Francie, you see all the girls that are applying. You probably won't get in. We don't have the money anyway."

I was thinking that she agreed to drive me to the interview so I could understand, and finally accept when I was rejected, that I was inadequate.

Before Christmas, a letter arrived from Washington Hospital School of Nursing signed by Miss Kirshbaum herself. The letter invited me to start school on the second Monday of June 1964. I could not believe it. Is it possible I was not a fraud? Did these people think I was worth taking a chance on?

> "Mama, I am accepted!"

> "Francie, we just can't do this..."

I needed to do something. Maybe I could do that secretary thing at one of the county seats. Either Morgantown, West Virginia, eight miles south or Uniontown, Pennsylvania, sixteen miles north. Getting back and forth to those towns to work would be a problem, but maybe I could ride with someone who went that direction every day. There was a secretarial track at my high school, but when I entered high school at the age of 14, I had not checked that box.

I enrolled in the six-week course offered at my high school and learned to type. I practiced on the Remington portable typewriter with a black and red rolling inked tape and sticky arm-like strikers that Dad had from his college days. In six weeks, I could load paper and type a letter. Typing was not my gift, but I figured when someone asked me the vital question,

Can you type?

I could answer,

Yes.

High school graduation day was approaching and, when asked what I was going to do after high school, I told everyone nursing school. They were so impressed.

"Wow, you got into nursing school?"

It wasn't a lie, I did get in. I wasn't going to go because we had no money.

It was a muggy Friday afternoon. George and I were taking a break on the back steps watching the river move north and swatting the circling gray clouds of gnats that seem to swarm in the mist around the water. My high school graduation was that evening, and I was glad we would all wear robes over our clothes. That way I didn't have to worry about what I would wear. Everyone would look the same and I could be another face in the billowing mass of white gowns for the girls and blue gowns for the boys. Our huge class of baby boomers was going to walk across the finish line.

Many of the boys were going into the service, some of the girls were going to get married, some of the class whose parents had money were going to college. A couple of the boys were going to college on the coveted sports scholarship.

I did not realize that after we graduated, so many of us would never see each other again. It was over.

The nursing school class at Washington Hospital was starting the following Monday. George and I would hang out until I got a ride into Morgantown so I could go from store to store and ask for job.

The Clouds Parted and God Smiled on Me

The phone rang. I picked it up. Dad insisted we answer the phone with,

"Dillinger's Residence."

A soft-speaking woman on the other end said,

"Hello, I am calling for Miss Mary Frances Dillinger."

"This is she."

"I am calling from the Washington Pennsylvania Quota Club. We understand that you have been accepted at the school of nursing and you indicated in your application that you were interested in financial aid. We can lend you the money for your schooling if you are still in need."

"YES, YES, YES!"

"Miss Dillinger, just arrive at the school and we will arrange for the payments to the school."

"Thank you! Thank you! Thank you!"

It has been fifty-nine years since that phone call. I still get a tear in my eye when I think of the incredible love and bare-bones kindness those women in another city far away had in their hearts to reach out to a young girl totally unknown to them.

They thought I was worthy. Whatever they had done to accumulate the $650 required for me to go to school meant the world to me. They changed my life. I am forever grateful. The mobile phone I carry around today cost more than the amount that altered the course of my life.

The following Monday, I started nursing school.

56

OH HAPPY, HAPPY DAYS

Monday after my high school graduation, Mama drove me to the nurse's residence at Washington Hospital. We were both relieved. I was still walking in sunshine and had a bounce in my step from the kindness that had so unexpectedly been extended to me by the Washington Quota Club. I could not get the stupid grin off my face. I was grateful to be a part of the Washington Hospital School of Nursing freshman class.

It was June of 1964 and our old tired 1956 Chevrolet was gasping and puffing in the hot close air as it made its way up the final hill to the hospital. The wheel wells, rusted through patches of crusty orange metal chips, echoed in the wind in a final gasp as we stopped.

The nurse's residence, a huge brick three-story building on a narrow street behind the hospital emergency room, was surrounded by the boiler room building that serviced the huge hospital. I could hear the

WHIZ, POP, BANG

of the steam pipes and see the smoke rising from the chimneys of the building. This hospital was a city within itself.

Every girl in the class was told to arrive between the same certain hours on that Monday, so the two-way dead-end street was congested with the 67 girls being dropped off. Since we had one of the furthest distances to travel, Mama and I were in the last wave of cars.

Mama kissed me goodbye, dropped me off at the front entrance with my clothes in two cardboard boxes, and I was directed to a room on the third floor.

For the first time in my life, I had a room to myself, a bed of my own, and a bathroom shared with a girl in the adjoining room. I could not believe my good fortune.

There was a cafeteria across the street in the hospital that served three meals a day, every single day, and I was welcome to walk into the cafeteria and get any food offered.

I soon learned that all the girls in my class were much like me. We had each been vetted by the strict admission standards of the school which had been training young girls since 1897. Each one was from a town surrounding Washington. Each of us was determined to study hard and become as close as we could be to the portrait of Florence Nightingale that stood in a hallowed spot in the lobby.

I was not sure what a nurse did, but I was determined to figure it out. A senior student, Carol Marsh, was assigned to me as my "big sister." Carol came into my room, and she seemed genuinely pleased to be assigned to me.

> "Francie, I never had a sister of my own, and now I have you. I will show you around, and you let me know if you have any questions."

Carol was petite with mousy brown hair and a shy smile that evoked a kind, competent composure. The training was a full 36 months and Carol had been a student for 24 months. She was beginning her senior year. After every seven days, students would get two days off, but not always two days together. She was from the town of Washington, and because her home was nearby, she could go home on her days off. After two years as a student, she was a wealth of information, and I could see she was in the process of becoming a true professional.

That evening, I entered a hospital for the first time in my life. Carol showed me how to access the building from the back entrance in front of the Nurses' Residence and wind my way through the labyrinth of hallways to the clanging, banging cafeteria.

The first three months of our time at school consisted of walking over a mile into the town of Washington to attend science classes at Washington and Jefferson (W&J) College every morning, returning for lunch at the hospital cafeteria, and walking the same distance back to the college every afternoon. The trek was exhausting. Once we entered the antebellum grounds of the exclusive male only Washington and Jefferson College (W&J) campus, we encountered the

Gauntlet.

For many years, our school had an agreement that its starting students would take the required chemistry, physiology, and microbiology classes along with the required laboratory classes at this exclusive school. The classes were taught by the W&J professors and all 67 of us made up the summer classes. Only freshman student nurses were in the classes designed specifically for beginning nurses. The curriculum was grueling. Any girl who did not pass these required classes would not be allowed to continue.

The professors were kind but formal and demanding of attention and excellence. It was their one opportunity to instruct females, as all their classes throughout the year were with the "J Boys," as we called them.

On the first day, we stepped onto the beautiful commons of the college, and I noticed the ivy growing up the walls of the huge brick and stone buildings. The stone steps to the entry of the buildings were the full length of each building. From the drawn map we were given, I recognized the huge circular white columns set on a hewn slate that reached the rooftop of the building we were to enter. It was across a tree-lined lawn with a long sidewalk with stone walls scattered here and there. I was in awe of my surroundings.

We were a mass of seventeen-year-old country girls a few days out of high school, dressed in our skirts and blouses, or calico dresses, with hairy legs, and big feet tucked into the best saddle shoes our families could afford. We were sweating like barnyard pigs from our long walk, carrying the hardback thick textbooks handed to us as we started our march out of the nurse's residence and down the winding hill toward the college and town. We must have looked like a bevy of confused refugees to the ivy league frat boys sitting on the walls waiting to scrutinize us as we lined past them on the green.

In my wide-eyed wonder, at first, I did not notice them languishing in groups along the walls.

"Hey, look at that one, she's right out of the hills ..."

"I didn't know girls could be so tall."

"There's a skinny one."

"How did that one make the walk? She's so big ..."

SMACK. SMACK. SMACK.

"Hey, what's your name?"

Phwwwwwwhht!

The boys' taunts did not matter. Of course we were aware of them, but we each had grown up in the hard scrapple life of the mountains, and dealing with misogynistic privileged males was something we took for granted. Being a piece of ridicule or invisible to endowed males was nothing new. It was our way of life. We had all been trained to see the absurdity as normal.

Most of us finished the classes at W&J and, in September, we began our nursing classes and worked at the hospital. We were measured for the student uniforms we were expected to wear every day.

Each week we reported to the hospital laundry to get our board-like starched uniforms we were to assemble. A striped cotton starched dress with tiny holes for fishing the metal-backed pearl buttons, anchored with metal clips, down the front. A white apron that looked like a two-piece pinafore with wide white straps that crisscrossed in the back. We attached these together at the waist with safety pins. The outfit was ingenious. A similar get up had been worn by the nursing students since 1897. White shoes and white nylons topped off the ensemble. We were required to wear this every day with a small pin under our chin. Mine read,

Miss M Dillinger.

The school was formal. I was called Miss Dillinger by everyone except the other girls who opted for "Dillie." I had a new name.

The school required strict adherence to its rules of conduct and grading system. If we were to work the morning shift, we were to be on the assigned hospital ward by 6:20 a.m. Afternoon shift required arrival at 2:20 p.m., and night shift arrival time was 10:20 p.m. No exceptions

On our off hours we were required to dress as ladies. We were never permitted to wear slacks. Our hair was to be off our collars and fingernails cut short, and never any fingernail polish. Our only accessory was a wristwatch with a second hand. All lights were to be out by 9 p.m. Of course, no males were allowed beyond the parlors of the nurse's residence.

I soon learned about the wonderful matronly ladies who were called house mothers. They staffed the front desk of the residence. We signed in and out with them and they kindly kept track of our back and forth to and from the hospital which was less than fifty feet away. They worked three shifts just as we did. When we were not working on the floor of the hospital, we were attending classes in the basement of the residence.

Once we passed the core science classes at W&J, the curriculum was organized so we would spend several months in each area of the hospital concentrating on each different classification of Nursing:

> Medical Surgical, which included months in orthopedics, surgery, recovery room, cardiac, endocrine, neurology, outpatient clinics, emergency room, general medicine, x ray, laboratory, central supply, the pharmacy, and others.

> Pediatrics, newborn, obstetrics, labor and delivery, physical therapy, and dietary.

> In our senior year, we were sent to spend three months living and learning at Woodville State Mental Hospital near Pittsburgh.

The same system of training had been used since 1897 when Washington Hospital had graduated three women. In the basement of the residence, there was a gallery along a long hallway of each class who had graduated since then. It was inspirational to walk from one framed photo collage to another, looking at the faces of the young women who, like me, were dressed in the same white graduation uniform staring blankly at the camera. They all made it through and so would I. In fact, most of the Registered Nurses working at the hospital wore the unique hemstitched cap that identified a graduate of our hospital.

The training program was ingenious as, while we worked on the hospital floors, we also attended classes regarding the specialty area where we were working. Many of the attending doctors from the hospital would be guest lecturers for our classes and supplement the day-to-day teaching of the nurse instructors. On the hospital floors, we worked alongside the nurses' aides and orderlies and did the same heavy lifting with them. Our hours were long and arduous.

After the first six months of school, we were some of the muscle and brawn that staffed the hospital seven days a week, twenty-four hours a day. We didn't complain. I think every one of us loved it. We felt important. And being together all hours of the day and night made us forever fast friends.

The schedule of working and learning was intense, and it was not unusual to discover that, although the school had been cautious with whom they accepted to join the class, several of the girls could not sustain the grueling hours combined with the ever-demanding tests of our comprehension of the teaching. It sometimes happened that a friend would be asked to leave or go home and never come back. Of course, getting pregnant was an automatic expulsion and no one was permitted to be married.

Living, Working, and Learning Together

Miss Jane Dearth was my dearest friend. Born and raised in another river town, Jane and I spent hours laughing about the antics in the hospital. We talked about how the doctors were sometimes pompous and callous yet seemed to reach out for the neediest patient.

Jane lived across the road from the north flowing Monongahela River in Brownsville, which is a much larger town than Point Marion. It is at lock number five and Point Marion is at lock number 8. The Monongahela River was cleaner at Brownsville. Jane would tell me about how she enjoyed swimming in the river at the makeshift muddy "beach" right across the road from her house.

Her family adored her. She lived with her devoted mother and father, Midge and George; her father's sister, Aunt Gige, who was a maiden schoolteacher, her aged grandmother, and Bebe, their beloved hunting dog. When Bebe was not out hunting grouse with George and Jane, she was sitting faithfully at George's feet in the small sitting area near a coal stove, sometimes dozing off and fitfully nipping at the caught birds in her dreams.

The Vietnam war was raging. Jane and I decided we would enlist in the Air Force after graduation. We spent time with the local recruiters and were told that once we graduated, we could be commissioned as Second Lieutenants in the US Air Force. We would be twenty years old when we graduated, so we needed to get our parents to sign off on our admittance to the US Air Force. Jane's parents were enthusiastic. My parents were not.

> "Mama, Dad, I want to join the Air Force and you need to sign off on the papers because I won't be twenty-one when I join."

> "Absolutely NO WAY. You are not going off and get shot up in that dam war! We will not sign anything. Stop this."

I dropped the discussion and decided I would join when I was twenty-one. That would be five months after I graduated anyway.

57

MY HEARTS COMPANION GEORGE M LEADER

After leaving for nursing school, I was seldom able to get home due to the convoluted back roads and no transportation. Mama used our only car for work, there was no public transportation, and I didn't mind staying in the nurses' residence, as a new world had opened to me.

In my second year of school, on one of my rare visits home, I went looking for George. It was a sweltering hot summer day, and there was the everyday dusky smell in the air of tobacco and beer. The various hounds were lying around in a heap here and there. Dad was sitting at his usual spot on the old sofa, smoking a cigarette and drinking a beer. The small TV was flashing some senseless newscast by Bill Burns on Channel 2, (the only channel available in our parts).

"Dad, where's George?"

"Gosh, Francie, we haven't seen him in a week or so. Last I saw he went swimming in the river."

I never saw George again. After an exhaustive hunt everywhere, I accepted that he had gone into the cool muddy waters of the Monongahela to cool off and drown his fleas and decided he was too tired to swim back to the surface.

He was 15 years old. He was the best of me. I have never had another dog.

58

BROKEN

Nursing School was challenging, demanding, grueling, and the nearest thing to pure joy I ever imagined. The chief nurses and the doctors did not miss an opportunity to keep us humble and remind us that we served only at the pleasure of the hospital, and any dalliance would result in expulsion.

The environment was formal and professional, but the days with friends who were going down the same rabbit hole of intense day-in-and-day-out visceral head shaving experiences laid my soul bare and lifted me up to the brightest light of being.

Hands-on, we were raising newborn wet babies from a birth mother, doing the APGAR test, and cradling it for the first time at the breast of a new mother. We were assisting in complex surgeries as scrub nurses, standing for hours holding retractors, and handing sterile instruments to surgeons. We were sitting with a dying patient in a quiet room or rushing to stop the bleeding from a miner brought into the emergency room. We were, in a split second, starting CPR or initiating the defibrillator on a frightened patient as they were turning mottled with a gasping breath.

Medicare for the elderly and Medicaid for the needy had been started, and no one knew exactly how it was supposed to work. In those days, we took care of each patient, no matter what their pay source was. Big business owning, controlling, and profiting from health care was the silent monster on the horizon. The doctors took care of the patients and their entire families without interference from outside regulators who later created havoc in what I was seeing as the sacred bond between the patient and his or her physician.

As we started our senior year, it was time for our psychiatric rotation. We were to leave Washington for three months and stay at Woodville State Mental Hospital. Everything in our school was done by the last name alphabetically, so twenty of us who had the last name starting with D, E, and F were in my group to go to Woodville. Dearth and Dillinger were among them.

Jane and I were going to Woodville in a wave of student nurses who would work and live in this Psychiatric Hospital. We looked forward to the challenge and somewhat nervously anticipated spending our days caring for the mentally ill. We had no idea what to expect.

Transportation

Staying at Woodville, which was forty miles beyond Washington over two-lane winding country roads, would present a problem for me as the state-owned psychiatric hospital would not allow the students to stay in the residence over the weekends. Washington Hospital usually had us working weekends with scattered days off, wherein the students could go home if they had transportation. I did not have a way to get to Point Marion, so I usually stayed at the residence. Woodville required that we be gone from 5 p.m. on Friday and not return any earlier than 6 p.m. on Sunday.

> *"Mama, I have to be gone from the residence every weekend for 3 months. What can I do?"*

To my surprise, Mama was able to scour the various chop shop garages that dot the countryside where she worked. She dropped me off at a hilltop unpainted shack-like garage near one of her patches, Edenborn, and told me,

> "Go on over there and ask for Junior. He said he has a car that will run and get you back and forth to Woodville. Francie, you just lean up against Junior and he will keep it running for you ..."

Standing around garage fix-it shops with a beer in hand is a favorite pastime for the men in the mountains. Talking about transmissions, engines and brakes is a common thread that holds this fraternity of disenfranchised men together. That and the half nude yellowed girlie pictures pasted up along the bare wood and tin walls of a junked car shack, pieced together with rusty nailed planks.

A rite of passage for the men folk in the patches is to have a few dilapidated cars or trucks stuck in the weeds somewhere that they are getting ready to put on the road or use for parts.

> "... as soon as I get that damned disability check, I am goin' ta pull that transmission out with that thar block and tackle I made up with them locust trees I tore down last spring. Yess indeedee, by god, I found me a good transmission from that wrecked Impala last year. It's sittin' over near the crick where that kid from Pittsburgh ran off the road."

I entered the building through the open gaping garage door, stepped around the broken circle of men who were sitting around on old tires, laughing, scratching, and spitting.

> "Hello, I am looking for Junior ...?"

I was accustomed to dealing with groups of men sitting around passing time in the afternoon sun. This group was harmless. One of their hunting dogs came up and started licking my ankles.

"That thars' him."

I found Junior draped over the hood of a rusty Ford pickup. He was shirtless under his oil-stained overalls that covered his ample belly. Above his workspace was a huge, dog-eared poster of a shiny red truck on one side and half-naked smiling blonde girl in a seductive pose on the other. Across the bottom was scrawled

JUNIOR'S GARAGE and BODY SHOP
Bring your Bodies to Us

Junior was obviously the alpha male of the group. I stared at a curly beard and a crocked Pittsburgh Pirates baseball cap perched above his watery eyes. The air in the garage was sticky with the midday melt and cigarette smoke that circled toward the rafters around the puddles of grease and oil and transmission fluid slurping in the cracks of the chipped asphalt floor from some long ago fix.

The cicadas, thinking it was going to be a muggy day, were starting their fine tuned

WHRR CHICKA CHICKA CK CHICK ZZZZZZZZ

from the weeds surrounding the shop.

Junior tightened a bolt with a firm grip of a muscled sweat grimed arm and pulled his head out from under the radiator and gave me a toothless smile. While the snuff dripped down the side crack in the corner of his lip, he said,

"Why you must be Miz Dilliners' girl ... I got that old car going for you."

Junior was the gentleman I knew he would be. The car was a wheezing, tired and smoking faded pinkish red 1950s Triumph 10 sedan. Junior had it sitting in a clearing waiting for me. It had a forty-horsepower engine, five manual forward gears, and no heater or radio. There were no locks on the doors. It was a most basic mode of transportation the size of the golf carts I now see on the golf course behind my house.

But it worked. It wasn't happy to start up, but once I parked it on at least a 40-degree vertical angle, I could start it rolling by putting my long-left leg out the door onto the road, and pushing off, turning on the ignition, and popping the clutch to get the engine spitting. There was a manual choke on the dash that allowed me to adjust to a just right fuel mix. I developed a system to park it on a hill, away from other obstacles, with its little tires rubbing toward the curb. Once in the car, I could turn the wheels toward the street and, like a porch swing, shove.

The only other problem were the many steep hills up and down on my journey. I created another system of racing in fifth gear while going down a hill and trying to get at least a quarter of the way up the incline before starting to gear down and get more grabbing power. I could usually get to the top of the next hill. If I could not, I had to coast backwards down the hill in neutral and start again. No problem. I could do this. I did not have to

"Lean up against Junior ..."

as Mama had advised, to keep that car going. Through my own sheer grit, I kept it running. That car served me well.

Woodville

Since I would be leaving from Point Marion, the plan was that I would drive the hour and a half to Brownsville where Jane lived, pick her up, and then we would drive the rest of the distance to Woodville together.

That first day, arriving at the old macabre buildings set against the twilight, we were both quiet. This place was hauntingly frightening.

Originally founded as the Allegheny Hospital for the Insane in 1854, the campus was 335 acres with 39 buildings. Woodville Hospital was one of Pennsylvania's earliest mental hospitals. The buildings on the huge campus were ancient and scary. There were over two thousand mentally ill people housed on the grounds.

Jane and I arrived on the appointed Sunday afternoon, in time for each of us to be assigned one of the small private rooms in the Nurses Residence. The staff was serious. There must have been sixty arriving nursing students all together. Twenty from my school and several groups of other students from other nearby nursing schools. Each student had a small private room with a sink. We were told we were to stay in the residence or go "off campus" when we were not on the wards.

But we were also told,

> "Be in your room and all lights out at 9 p.m."

That's when we were locked in our rooms.

I had no interest in going off campus, as the subject of psychiatry and mental health was a true puzzlement to me. I was having difficulty grasping what I initially thought were the ambiguous haywire constructs of what goes on in people's brains. I had grown up with the thought, if you had food, shelter, clothing, and you weren't bleeding, you could make yourself happy. So, what was this about? For the first time, I needed to study.

We were assigned to the New Admissions building and were instructed to be on the ward at precisely 6:30 a.m. each morning, leave the ward at precisely 3:30 p.m. each evening, and leave the campus by 5 p.m each Friday and never arrive before 6 p.m. on Sunday. These people were grim and regimented, but we figured out how to manage in spite of the tension.

Our assignment was to keep the patients and their environment safe and clean and medicate them or assist with their "therapy." Whatever that was, I had difficulty figuring out.

Each morning, we were locked onto the ward with the many patients who were either sleeping or in a day room. In those days the only treatment available for mentally ill people was the drugs Thorazine and Lithium. Those patients who had severe, almost intractable symptoms, were given electroshock therapy.

One particular young woman would sit in the day room staring at her hands. She was 27 years old and had three children; one was a baby. Her husband would sometimes come to see her on weekends. Her skin was ashen and had no elasticity. She would not eat so I had to feed her soft foods that she would refuse to swallow. She would sit all day in the dull, blue, sack-like dress that each female patient was to wear. She would not speak. We know now that she had postpartum depression, but in those days, there were no resources for her. She sat on the same hard, yellow, plastic chair with a broken leg, day after day. When I was not busy with medicating, washing the patients and changing linens in the large ward, I would sit with her and hold her cold tense hand. She was wasting away.

For hygiene purposes, the female patients' hair was chopped off above the shoulders in a bob. The men were given crew cuts. One of the jobs of the student nurses was to use a fine-toothed comb to scrape the lice nits out of the patient's hair a couple times a week. This was grueling work, but it did give us an excuse to touch the patients. Something I think helped them connect.

Three times a week, we were required to take off our pinafores and, while wearing our base striped dresses, get into the showers with the patients and scrub them. This ritual was for all the patients except those who were alert and somewhat independent. Those patients would be allowed to shower on their own under our watchful eye for the females and under the watchful eye of an orderly for the more alert men.

We experienced every type of mental illness while at Woodville. From the criminal sociopath, the schizophrenic, and the severely depressed, to the manic and catatonic. There were so many of them. And no resources. We tried to keep them safe.

The patients who were not in the New Admission Building numbered over fifteen hundred. These people who had been at the hospital over a longer period of time were involved in the operational activities of the huge campus and were housed in the massive wards in old brick buildings that circled the campus. This was their occupational therapy. It was a working farm and an operating bustling community. The patients who were somewhat stable, sewed their own wearables, mended, did laundry, kept the grounds tidy, maintained the buildings, grew their own crops, had cows, tended the honeybee hive boxes, cooked their own meals, made bread and butter, and raised chickens. The food they made was amazing. In the evenings, the kitchen would send to the nurse's residence a big jar of homemade apple butter and loaves of homemade bread for us to devour.

Of course, some of the patients were so profoundly mentally ill they could not be productive. This was a small number for whom the medication and occupational therapy could not reach. Woodville was a watershed experience for me.

Sadly, the mental hospitals throughout the country have now been abandoned, and we see these patients who were safe and productive in my student days wandering the streets, incarcerated, or lifelong addicts. A travesty and a clear marker of the nationwide cavalier blame-frame attitude toward mental health our country has evolved into.

Every Friday, Jane and I would pile into the Triumph and slide south toward our homes. I would drop Jane off in Brownsville and then head further south to Point Marion.

> "The afternoon of Saturday June 18, 1966, the Mathies, a diesel, twin-screw Western Rivers type towboat, with a crew of 13 experienced rivermen aboard and towing seven barges, was on a voyage from West Elizabeth, Allegheny County, Pennsylvania, to the Isabella Mine in Greene County, Pennsylvania. Six barges, two abreast, were ahead of the towboat, and one barge was lashed to the starboard side of the towboat.
>
> The tow, proceeding upriver in a southerly direction, reached the arrival point for Lock and Dam No. 5 Brownsville Pennsylvania at approximately 4:00 P.M. Because the lock was in use, the boat was grounded at the river's edge along the West Brownsville shore, thus holding the tow stationary, to await the signal to enter the lock. The expected signal consisted of three blasts of a whistle at the lock. The Mathies and its tow were angled from the shoreline out into the river; its engines continued to idle.

About 300 feet south of this bridge was a 50-foot-wide area, cleared of stones and debris and marked by whitewashed stones, which for many years was used as a beach by bathers. A flight of steps led to this bathing beach from a road that paralleled the river.

On the beach that afternoon were four bathers, namely, Jane L. Dearth, Alec Sabo and two others. Jane and Alec were wading with a rubber raft and innertube in the water (chest-high) near the barge.

Jane L. Dearth and Alec Sabo were drawn underneath the barge and into a rotating propeller."

The boat was owned by Consolidation Coal Company.

Jane died that Saturday.

I returned to Woodville in the Triumph. I was beginning to understand the impact of mental health, and I resigned myself to the fact that violence and tragedy is part of the Appalachian landscape.

I determined that somewhere buried deep within me I would overcome any victimhood narrative that was hanging over me.

59

MISSING JANE

Painfully Lonely

There is no telling what Jane might have accomplished had she lived. The river she loved had taken her. After she was killed, I started spending many of my days off with her family. We were all numb and dumbfounded. I would roll into Brownsville in my trusty Triumph, climb up the weathered chipped stone steps to the Dearth cottage, and sit quietly in a forlorn pile with George and Midge in their small parlor. Together we would watch Bebe dream of a long-ago bird season while she nuzzled George's boots in her fitful sleep. We would have a simple dinner, do dishes together, play pinochle, and reminisce.

A gentle and kind man, Jane's dad, George, had lived his life in Brownsville across the street from the river that would rob him of his beloved daughter. When ruffed grouse season came that October, George taught me how to shoot a rifle, then he, Bebe and I would set out before first light of dawn to trample through the woods in Greene County, listening for the unique drumming sound of the bird in the brush. As a top notch and prized bird dog, Bebe knew to hang back until George flushed the bird out of the dry leaves. Once the bird took flight, George aimed and

POW!

Bebe's job was to retrieve the fallen bird, picking it up ever so gently in her mouth, and prance proudly back to George and place it on his boot. She was the best bird dog. She soothed George's pain.

I wasn't much of a hunter; the idea of wandering around with a gun and killing things was not my passion. But I loved being in the silent sun-streaked woods among the fall trees and leaves with George and Bebe.

One cold Saturday afternoon, George, Midge, and I huddled in front of the flame of the gas heater in their sitting room. Snow was starting to cover the road in front of their door, and the ice was beginning to frost a sharp solid glaze onto the windows facing the river. We sat closely in the little circle we formed to stay warm and feel the closeness of one another's soul. Bebe was draped over George's boots, chasing birds in her sleep.

Through weepy eyes, George said,

> "Dillie, a lawyer from Consolidated Coal came here to the house last week. He just knocked on the door with his fancy suit and briefcase. He said he wanted to settle Jane's case. Dillie, he said she would never have earned much money because she was a girl. They want to put money on the value of her life. We told that man to get out of our house and never come back."

The three of us held hands and cried.

Graduation and Freedom

The year after Jane died, in June of 1967, forty-six of us graduated from nursing school. It was glorious. We were all bouncing with happiness and pride. Most of the class was planning to marry their long-time sweethearts, some were planning to take jobs at the hospital, others were planning to take jobs at hospitals nearer their own homes.

In order to be licensed registered nurses, we had one more hurdle. We had to take a three-day state board exam and pass it with a specific percent so we could apply for our state license.

The test was given in July at the state capital, Harrisburg. We met again in Harrisburg and, along with hundreds of other graduating nurses, we took the grueling exam. We were told we would be notified of the test results by mail in a few months.

Until we received our notice of passing the state board exam and obtaining our licenses, if we passed, we could work as graduate nurses. Since I could not join the service due to my age and my parents' objection, the day after I finished the exams, with the money I had been given as a graduation gift, I bought a one-way airline ticket to Los Angeles.

I was finally OUT!

60

THE END OF AN ERA

Looking back

Early on and consistently through my first quarter of life, I was lost in a spiral of overwhelming confusion. I had no value.

As a girl child, I was told that doors would be closed to me unless I could charm a person who was not a female to provide me with kindness. Mama, lost in her own world, was not communicative, and Dad was focused on his past life. Both had convinced me I was starting out in life without an anchor and several rungs down on any possible ladder.

Their unavailability, combined with the oppressive need to come up with our family's day-to-day needs of warmth, shelter, and food, was like a thick blanket of doom settled over our lives. It was always there.

What I did have was total freedom. Combining that with a tenacious curiosity about everything, I could go anywhere. I could make up my own mind about anything. I could ask questions. I could explore, and I could talk to anyone. I could do anything I wanted. I could develop my own core values and embrace my own defining moments. The only thing I had to do was to be sitting, in my place, at the supper table every night at twenty minutes to six.

The bargain was mine.

It was a struggle to figure everything out and outlast my childhood. I was not pretty or smart. I had no particular talent. Sports were nonexistent for girls. At the age of 13, I was six feet tall and clumsy. I think I have always worn size 10 shoe. I was a poor girl in a wretched environment. There was no one to encourage me. Except me.

I finally found within me an eternal drive that could be depended upon to sustain me. At long last, it came to me that no one was going to rescue me, except me. All my life I had been given the clear message that if I was comely, attractive, flirtatious, and, as Mama told me so many times,

"Leaned up against a man,"

I would be taken care of. By standing in the shadow of this man, I, too, would be successful. I would have money, I would have possessions, I would have intelligent happy children, I would be valued, I would be important. I would get a ticket out of the oppressive environment of Appalachia.

It is certainly a mystery why Mama continued with this thought of tagging onto a successful man to gain happiness. This notion was a complete failure for her, and she was forever bitter about the path she had chosen for herself. Her choices resulted in a lifetime of sadness, hatred, and being tired.

My problem was that I was not comely, cute, flirtatious, or desirable. I did not have this currency. Moreover, Prince Charming was not living in Appalachia. If he was, he certainly was not interested in me. I began to realize that life was not fair, but I could get used to it and deal with it.

And I could make my own opportunities.

61

THE ESCAPE

Los Angeles was one big smoggy freeway. I had no car, so I took a job at a hospital where I could walk back and forth to a small apartment where I lived alone. By that time, my two sisters were married and living in the Los Angeles area. Charlen was living 15 miles away, and I seldom saw her. Eileen was not around.

Within a month, I was notified that I had passed the Registered Nurse exam with a high enough score to be registered in California and my home state of Pennsylvania.

I loved being a nurse. Almost immediately, the hospital where I worked promoted me to a head nurse position on one of their busiest medical-surgical floors. Then they sent me for advanced training at Cedars Sinai Hospital to become specialized in cardiology.

Being a Registered Nurse was perfect, but I was painfully lonely. Still living alone and working in California, I made a huge mistake. Within nine months of my arrival in Los Angeles, I married a man who I discovered after two short years was suffering the same malady as some of the people from Point Marion whose reality was lost in the Appalachian Syndrome: angry, unemployed, addicted, and regularly abusive.

Even though it has been fifty-six years since I created this problem for myself, as I look back, it remains an open mystery how I fell into the depth of isolation and made the wrong choice. This action was one I regretted for the rest of my life. The situation only got worse, and I knew I was going to have to earn my way out of the mess I had gotten myself into.

My husband, although at one time by all appearances a relatively successful sound technician in Hollywood, had developed a drug and alcohol problem and deep-seated festering anger that was destroying him and anyone around him.

And back in

After a visit we made to Point Marion, my husband convinced me that if he could get out of the pressure of the entertainment industry (where he was obviously drawn to mind altering drugs), he would remake himself in the deep countryside. It was crisis time, and the hills began calling me—their native daughter—back.

We arrived back in Point Marion, and I began working. I worked full-time, took our children back and forth to daycare, looked after my then ill parents, and managed to put myself through night school at West Virginia University.

My husband never held a paying job again.

Final Escape from Appalachia

After my parents both died and after taking care of the burials and Dillinger family affairs, I managed a treacherous divorce from my children's father. Then the long-awaited day came when I loaded my two children into a used and rusted 1979 Chevrolet station wagon and drove across the country, hoping to leave Point Marion behind forever.

I escaped the oppressive mist of the town and moved to Las Vegas. This move was my own final escape from Appalachia. I was a single mom with two children, and the only support I had was myself.

For the next ten years, through hard work, I became somewhat successful. I had earned my bachelor's degree by attending night school at West Virginia University during the tenure of enduring my abusive spouse and working full time.

Once in Las Vegas, I put myself through graduate school, earning a master's degree in business administration. Through scraping and clawing my way, while being the sole support of my family, I started and owned several successful companies, including the inclusion of two of my companies in the INC Magazine 500. I drove a Jaguar, owned a home in a guard-gated country club on a golf course, put my oldest son through undergraduate, law school and a master's program, and my youngest son was enrolled in a prestigious university. I did nothing but work.

I certainly did not date or have a social life. I was all business. I was happy. I was single. I had escaped.

62

RETURN TO THE HILLS

Ten years after leaving, I returned to Point Marion for a visit. I went back to spend time with an elderly friend, Renee, who had grown up with my father. She was born on the same property where I was born. She and her newest husband, Shanky, were both about to turn 90.

On a sweaty, August Friday, after a long day of taking orders from both Shanky and Renee, I was melting in a sweat-heap on the plastic sofa in their tiny, one-bedroom apartment. No air-conditioner. The screen door was open, but nary a breeze. The phone rang and Renee said,

"It's for you."

Strange, I just came into town, and no one knew I was there. Oh well, this is a small town.

"Hello."

"This is Joseph Klink; do you remember me?"

"Uhm. Yes. You went to high school a year ahead of me, right?"

> "Yes, I'm from Point Marion. I'd like to meet with you; I think we have a relative in common."

> "Well, I am only here for a few days, can we talk about it on the phone?"

In a small town like Point Marion, everyone knows everything about everyone else. Growing up, I knew which car every family had, which house they lived in, whether the dad mowed the lawn regularly, the names of their dogs, and which church they went to. We even knew whether they tithed with an envelope or tossed some coins into the passed basket on Sunday. Of course, we knew who was at Augie's or the Brass Rail at any moment in time, and who was running numbers or writing bad checks.

I remembered Joseph. When we were in grade school, he and his family lived in a small trailer that could be pulled behind a family car. His dad did odd jobs and, when he needed to work in another town, he hooked up the little trailer to the rear of the car and the family moved on.

His dad worked. Mine did not.

When we were in high school, he lived with his family up on McKinley Hill. His dad, by that time, had a regular job and they could stay put. Joseph had a younger sister and brother. I used to see him at the Odd Fellows Roller Skating Rink when we were both in junior high school.

He played basketball in high school but was not tall enough or black enough to make a varsity player. He dropped out of the basketball team in eleventh grade to sit on the bleachers next to Beckey Christopher and watch the game.

Beckey lived in Masontown. She was the Coal Queen Princess from our school and Joseph adored her. She dumped him when he graduated from high school a year before Beckey and I graduated. Joseph was a poor kid, and the story around town was that Beckey's parents did not approve and finally convinced her to move on to a boy from German Township. Everyone knew that Joseph was devastated by the rejection.

> "No, I would rather meet with you in person."

>> "I am meeting a friend and her family at Friendship Hill tomorrow afternoon around 3 p.m., if you can come by the picnic area, I can see you then."

> "Okay, I will be there."

I did not think of the conversation again until the next afternoon when I was at Friendship Hill with my best friend, Susie, and her family who had come in from Boston to visit. We were at the picnic area catching up.

My Secret Brother

Joseph walked toward us from the parking area with a young blonde female who looked fifteen years younger than me. Even with the receding hair line and the middle-aged paunch, I recognized him right away. He and his blonde friend sat down on the bench of a picnic table, and I sat across from them. Susie and her family went for a walk on one of the paths.

After a few

> "Nice to see you again, it sure has been a long time..."

>> "Thirty years in fact – since high school,"

Joseph introduced the blonde as his wife. I allowed silence.

> "I guess you are wondering why I wanted to see you."

"You said we had a relative in common?"

His story began.

"Well, when I finished high school, I decided to join the Air Force. I had to have my birth certificate, so I got it from my mother. My birth certificate did not have my dad's name on it. It had someone's name on it that I had never heard of. So, I knew the dad I grew up with was not my real dad. My mom would never tell me about it, and she died soon after I left home. No one would ever tell me. This summer I was visiting my Aunt Bella Mae and she said,

"Gosh Joseph, I thought you knew Len Dillinger is your dad!"

"That is why I am here."

"You are telling me that you are my dad's son?"

I looked at the man sitting across the table from me for the first time. Born in May 1945, one year before me. One year after my sister. Joseph was born while my father was in Pittsburgh during one of the rare times Dad had employment. Joseph's mother, Theresa, had worked in the newspaper store that my dad and mama owned before the war started. Theresa had lived with Dad in Pittsburgh. He had the same waved black hair as my dad and my brother, the same brown almost black eyes, and he was medium height. My dad was six feet three inches, and the brother I grew up with was around six-four. Joseph's mother was short. My mother was tall.

When Dad was admonishing me for causing him to be a three-time loser, he already had the much-wanted son.

HAPPY BIRTHDAY DIEHL

The next day was Sunday, so I knew I might have a chance of talking to a somewhat lucid Happy Birthday. If anyone could tell me the truth, it would be Happy.

As long as I can remember, Pennsylvania had "Blue Laws" that forbid the sale of liquor on Sundays. All the beer gardens were shut tight for an entire 24-hour period and the only place to get a good long drink, or a meager bottle of beer, was at the VFW, the American Legion or, of course, the Fire Hall – for members only -- and only after the fire whistle blew to call all the menfolk to the imaginary Sunday afternoon fire.

I timed my visit to early afternoon, figuring that any beer Happy may have had left from Saturday would probably be about gone.

Happy was living in a small apartment above Mary Jane's Beauty Shop. I parked my rented car in the weeds in the front area of the sidewalk and found the solid paint chipped unlocked door that would lead up the dusty narrow stairs to his musty little alcove of an apartment. I called up the steps:

"Happy ... are you there? It's Francie."

"Well, Francie girl! How are you?"

Happy was sitting on an ancient, overstuffed chair with an old gray piece of rag placed here and there covering up the many torn openings where pieces of yellowed stuffing that used to be inside the chair were poking out. Beside his legs was an old rusty coffee can that he was using for his spit jug. Happy was a Beech-Nut man. He had worked some in the mines after the war and developed his addiction to chewing tobacco during that phase of his life. His addiction to alcohol and nicotine followed him for life. He was wearing a faded t-shirt and his stained jockey shorts. His ratty appearance was no matter to either of us as I had grown up checking in with Happy in all sorts of little rented nooks. I had seen him in various stages of dress all over town.

I was right about Happy being able to talk somewhat clearly as he was drinking some coffee and, it was obvious, he was out of beer. His little TV across the room was flickering some senseless prattle.

We talked a while about him playing football with dad at Point Marion High School. Happy wanted to tell me again about the time he and my mama and dad had the flopped minstrel show and how they had been chased out of a few towns in South Carolina.

> "We just made it out by the skin of our teeth. Your dad never was any good at paying his bills. Those were good days, Francie..."
>
> "YUP, Happy, I know you and Dad were so close.
>
> "Happy I need to ask you something...
>
> "This boy came to me yesterday and told me he was my dad's son; He was born in 1945 in Pittsburgh. He said his mama worked for Dad and Mama at the newspaper store they owned before the war.
>
> "This boy was a year ahead of me in school. Happy, what do you know about this?"

Happy spit into his frothy coffee can. There was an interminable silence. Happy did not look at me. While staring at the mottled spots on his feet, in a quiet voice, he finally said,

> "Charlotte never knew..."

How could she not have known?

Aunt Delores

Aunt Delores was one of Susie's aunts. She had been part of my life since she moved to Point Marion from Fairmont, West Virginia after marrying Suzie's mom's brother. She was a DeGardyn and lived for more than 45 years down the street from our family. She was a schoolteacher, and she was someone who knew everything about everything in town. Aunt Delores' husband and Susie's mother had another sister who was married to a Jeanskin from Big Cat Hollow. The high school girl who worked in the news stand owned by my mama and dad all those years ago was from that same family in Big Cat Hollow.

I went to see Aunt Delores and explained my quandary. Simply,

> "Aunt, Joseph Klink met with me yesterday and told me he is my dad's son!?"

> "Francie, I thought you knew that. Everyone knows Joseph Klink is your dad's son."

Except me.

63

THE GRIP OF APPALACHIA

The haze of my surroundings in the woods reached up from the dark earth and grabbed me,

> "YOU CAN NOT GET AWAY FROM THIS PLACE."

The spirit of the place was calling my name
    again.

I decided to do some research about the grip these mountains seemed to have on me.

The Appalachian range of America is characterized by an inaccessible and isolated area with dense pockets of people sandwiched into small bands along the river valleys or densely packed company towns miles into a woody hollow where the coal had been all worked out 10, 20 or 30 years ago. Much of the Appalachian countryside is surrounded by winding, narrow, poorly maintained roads creating an isolation that is hard to imagine when one looks at a real map. Flattening out my home region of Appalachia would create a land area near the size of Texas.

With little opportunity for any kind of a livelihood, generations of people living in the Appalachians are in despair.

Yet they stay.

Communities of people are stashed together in a town that has little access to the outside world apart from the school bus and the postman. Stratums of existence, layers of humanity all struggling to get by, to have day-to-day meaning, or live another day.

Scratching their way over the craggy mountains from the coastal waters, the original settlers of the region discovered the blue-green hills, the crystal-clear waters, and abundant wildlife to sustain them. They claimed it for their own and fought hard and long to keep what they came to believe and staked out as their entitled land. They fought the Indians who had been on that precious earth home for hundreds of years, first pretending to be their friends, and finally outright stealing their homeland. The original white settlers either marched the remnants of the Algonquin Native American Tribe off to remote areas to the south or summarily murdered them.

The mid and late 1700s found the earliest settlers as hardy, land loving scrappers, independent and isolated from the rest of the growing nation by the remoteness of their river valleys and the mountain tops that they unilaterally decided to claim as their own birthright.

The Appalachian corridor has some areas of the most beautiful country in the world. But it is more than the lush beauty that keeps the inborn people in lock step. It is an emotion that seems to embrace its native children and hold them mesmerized and drawn into the dangerous seduction of hope in the hills without a promise of prosperity. Instead, it hauntingly draws them back with a false promise of quiet solitude and simple provision.

People stay.
They cannot get away.

It's a thread that seems to reach up from the earth's core and connect people to the hills with a song of temptation like nowhere else. Caressing the soul while at the same time smothering ambition; numbing the people into complacency. The mother mountain gently wraps her arms around an inborn son or daughter's body, dancing for a while, playing for a time, but finally squeezing much of the vitality of life from her children. It is a living, breathing organism, but broken, present, and calling us by name. Delicately, it calls its offspring . . .

Some are convinced that this destroying attraction could be what remains of the legendary curse instilled on the region by the masses of Native American Indians who originally staked the abundant meadows, clean rivers, and streams as their homeland. Then they were betrayed and displaced by the deceiving white settlers who moved across the Alleghenies into the Appalachian crevasses and wiped them out, either by inflicting epidemic diseases to which these pure-bred people had no natural immunity, enslaving them into forced labor, or forcibly marching them out. There are no native American reservations or traces of Indian tribes in the area.

In later life, I have tried to explain the seduction of the mountains and the grip that must be broken if one wants or needs to escape. I merely get that "glazed over" look from my friends and colleagues who have never experienced the hard scrapple life of day-to-day hopeless survival. I describe this response as the

"Oh yeah, sure . . ."

facial stare-without-seeing look that one gets from people who have never had to regularly use an outhouse or worry about how they would put snow tire chains on a rusty 1956 Chevy. Alone. On an 80-degree hill. In a blizzard.

Yet, my glazed over associates have never sat quietly at a rivers edge, heard the rushing of the wind through a crisp fall forest covered with the fire of nature's colors, been startled by the rustle of a ruffed grouse in the weeds, or surrounded by an abundant stand of blue spruce in the gray morning mist.

The magnetic attraction of the Appalachian valley for her native kin is not unlike a seductive drug that calls their name. It latches on to the noise in the heads of her inborn sons and daughters and chants the repetitive song,

> COME BACK TO ME.

> *"Once that river valley latches on to you, you hain't goin' nowhere. Y'all will all wise be back. She is some mean Mother...*
> *Once the river valley starts flowing through your blood—you'll never get out."*

I escaped this. So many others have not.

The world is too much with us; late and soon, getting and spending, we lay waste our powers: Little we see in nature that is ours.

William Wordsworth

EPILOGUE

"Francie, you think you can do anything."

It was the first company I was creating, and my male colleague was running his fingers through his hair as we reached another stumbling block. I told him my fix and had already begun working on it. As far as I was concerned, the crisis was minor, and I would bully through. I told him I would take this raging bull by the horns and wrestle it to the ground. He was angry, dumbfounded, and I think frustrated that I refused to be held back.

I responded,

"Yes, I can do anything. I have done everything."

Starting out with zero money, no encouragement, plain looks, and stumbling social skills, I have been able to deploy whatever I could manage to scrape together to catch the northbound train and lift myself out of poverty.

Having created over twenty profitable corporate entities and employing hundreds of people, I slowly developed a hands-on gutsy approach to leaning way out of bounds -- reaching over and grabbing the brass ring.

Yes, there was the tedious task of educating myself. I felt I had to get "my ticket punched" with an undergraduate degree and then a master's degree in order to be taken seriously by my demeaning colleagues. I had to work harder, arrive earlier, and stay later than anyone. Of course, I taught myself how to analyze and deploy factual data with hands-on grit and resilience.

I made a career of looking for opportunities when none were obvious. I taught myself to create abundance through stops and starts, horrible decisions and a few good choices.

Getting and spending distracted me.

At some point, along the way, there was a discovery.

A realization that somewhere there is a light that beams down on me. In spite of my stupid decisions and tripping over calloused predeterminations of what I could be, I found a star shining on me through the others who inspired me to first understand and then gently encourage me to reach out of my cocoon of darkness.

I began to understand that I have been sent true angels who touched me throughout my life and gently led me beyond the beaten path.

These honored everyday saints who touched my life, gave me their divine gift.

I was rescued.

AFTERWORD

I have continued to put the missing pieces of the puzzle of my life together over the years.

FAMILY

Grandma Rathbun (TOB)

I never knew my grandma. Even after we were grown, with families of our own, she never seemed to want to know much about us. She knew we were impoverished. But, for some unknown reason, she never ever reached out to us. Grandma Rathbun died at the age of 87. Mama had her put in an unmarked grave. Six years before Grandma died, Mama finally got control of her money. No, it never did go to a dog cemetery.

Mama

Mama's mother died in 1974 at the age of 87. Mama died in 1977. When she was dying, Mama's right hand twitched as she was flicking the ash from an invisible cigarette.

Mama was ill for a long time. From the years of chain smoking and coal dust, she was on continuous oxygen for the last six years of her life. There was a canula piping the air from a big tank that Dad kept in a corner on a long, long green tube attached to Mama's nose. She would wander around the house on her green leash-tube of oxygen, wheezing and coughing, holding a cigarette. If she wanted to go for a drive, a smaller tank of oxygen would be lugged around, strapped to a hand cart with some bungee cords.

"Mama you might blow up with all that oxygen and that lit cigarette."

"I don't care."

It's sad that Mama died three years after getting TOB's real money. She pined for this most of her adult years. Apparently, most of it had been deployed in the long years after my grandfather became disabled and during my grandmother's life. It is a puzzlement that, throughout Mama's life, she was preoccupied with being rescued by someone else's wealth.

As the child in the family who had to settle the estate after both my parents died, I discovered that, even though Mama stayed married to Dad, when she finally retired on disability, she took a payout that would provide for her income to the end of her life and not include Dad. Upon my mother's death, Dad was left only with Social Security survivors' benefits. He had not put enough quarters into the system himself to qualify for Social Security on his own.

Even all those years later, when she predeceased Dad, any remaining cash she had accumulated in her lifetime was specifically left to her beloved son. She left nothing to Dad and, of course, zero to her girls. It was apparent in my mother's death, as in her life, she believed the "Three Time Loser" story.

After Mama died, I had to search the records of Evergreen Memorial Park in Point Marion to find Grandma's grave. I found it along a tar top road, the last grave right smack up to where the cemetery traffic pounds on. My sisters and brother and I put a marker on the site.

Dad

Dad died three months after Mama.

We found our pigtails wrapped in tissue paper in his off-limits sock drawer, along with all our letters to Santa Claus, and our teeth for the Tooth Fairy. The pigtails went into his casket.

It is a perplexity that twenty-nine years after Dad died, I learned that Dad did have a son who was born 17 months before I was born. While I was born at home, his son had been born in a Pittsburgh hospital. He had fathered a son one year older than me, who lived his life less than a mile from our home. This child grew up going to the same school my sisters and I attended. Yet dad abandoned this baby boy and his mother and returned to Point Marion.

When Dad was admonishing me for causing him to be three-time loser, he already had the much-wanted son. How did this work? Was he so angry with me for being a mere girl? Was he angry with himself for walking away from his male child and the mother of his child? Was there something more about me?

Eileen

Years after Eileen's "horse period," she and Evie Thompson, the owner of Friendship Hill Farm, became fast friends. Eileen joined the Chestnut Ridge Hunt Club of which Evie was a founder. Eileen would regularly go to the farm and groom the horses and join in the hunts. She loved to wear high leather riding boots, tight horse-woman pants and walk around the farm saying

"Talley Ho."

Sara Charlen

Sara Charlen left Point Marion when she was in her mid-twenties. She drove to California and before long married a man who was 18 years her senior. Letters were sent back and forth of her exploits in the land of milk and honey. One day a letter arrived for Mama from Sara, as she now preferred to be called. I handed Mama the letter.

She proceeded to tear it open and something from the envelope dropped, circling down into space. Mama reached down to the floor between the tangle of the oxygen cord and the hound that was mixed up at her feet, picking up what looked like a little card while staring at it as she raised it to eye level.

"OH MY GOD!!"

Mama shouted.

Holding, with shaking fingers, a small polaroid picture, black and white, hazy. Gasping for breath, she dropped her precious cigarette. I took a look at what she had retrieved. It was a line up of eight young women standing shoulder to shoulder in a wooded area in front of a line of trees. Some had narrow sashes laced around their necks. Each had a wide smile. Sara was in the middle. They were all stark naked.

Sara had written the caption,

"Look Mama, I am the second runner up to Miss Nude Southern California"

And this was before her boob job.

She had escaped.

Aunt MaeMae

In 2010, my sister Eileen found a locket given to her by Aunt Dodo that belonged to Aunt MaeMae. She carefully pried it open. Inside was a perfectly preserved handsome picture in a full Spanish American Military War uniform of our neighbor down the street, Abe DeGardyn. Abe was one of Susie's beloved Belgian uncles. He lived two doors down the street from Grandma Tipi. Mr. Abe DeGardyn married late in life and never had any children of his own. He and Emma Dillinger were in love, but she had a duty to her family. She raised her alcoholic brother's children and cared for her parents in the family home until they died.

She was a sainted member of the Point Marion United Methodist Church.

Aunt Dodo (Chapter 5)

Ten years after Mama and Dad died, Aunt Dodo died in a Florida retirement home. Although I had not seen Aunt for many years, it fell to me to enlist my sister Eileen to go with me to Florida and clear out her room. I also had to settle her estate, of which there was zero money and a few papers, some odd items of clothing, and a few chipped figurines.

Dodo lived her life with her friend, Miss Ella Travis. Both continued with their schooling and earned a PhD in education. They called themselves Doctor Dillinger and Doctor Travis. Miss Travis, "Travie," as we called her throughout our lives, was sixteen years older than Dodo and had been a schoolteacher who taught math at Point Marion School for many years. Eleanor Margaret Dillinger, (my Aunt Dodo), was one of her pupils.

My sister Sara Charlen had been the designated Estate Executer by Aunt Dodo, but when she discovered there was nothing to settle, she told me, Eileen, and brother Len, that she would not be going to Florida for any reason. It was the day after Christmas. Eileen and I met at Miami airport, rented a car, and went to the retirement home. A week before that, we had arranged for her body to be brought back to Point Marion, we had a small service for her, and buried her in the last remaining spot in the family plot at Evergreen Cemetery next to Aunt MaeMae.

It seems that her lifelong friend's relatives had purged the contents of the small unit that she had shared with her companion who died six months earlier. The family had been circling like vultures around the two maiden aunts for years and, once Dr. Travis died at nearly 100 years old, all the spoils were taken. There was nothing left.

This certainly was no surprise to me or my brother and sisters, as Dodo made it clear during her life that she was not much interested in us. We were cruds.

As I was sorting out some shoe boxes under her bed, I came across a stack of letters from the 1930s written to Dodo from her then husband, Wayman Bennett.

Slowly, I began to piece together this chapter of her life. Long ago, Dodo went for a visit to see her grandmother in Point Marion, leaving her young husband in West Virginia. They had married while still students at West Virginia Wesleyan College. They both graduated in 1931 and stayed on in Bucannon, the hometown of her husband, Doc. They were married for eight years.

Apparently, she went home and then refused to go back to her husband. She ignored him. Letter after pleading letter was tied neatly together in chronological order.

At first it was

> *"I miss you, Dear..."*

then

> *"Your grandmother is ill??"*
> *"Dodo, please come home, I need you."*
> *"Why won't you come back to me?"*
> *"Dodo, please write to me and tell me what's the matter"*

The poor fellow was begging for an explanation.

Finally, over a year later, there were letters from a mutual friend who was an attorney in their town of Bucannon, West Virginia

> *"To Mrs. Wayman Bennett..."*
> *"Dodo, what are you doing to Doc? I have no choice but to take action for him." Please sign these documents to finalize your divorce."*

It was obvious she had simply abandoned her husband without explanation. I was piecing this together and, many years later, I was sad for her long-lost young husband. No communication. Not unlike what Dad did to the girl he took to Pittsburgh during the war, and with whom he had a child.

Gone. Whoosh.

In 1940, Dodo left Point Marion with Miss Travis. She returned only for brief visits.

She had escaped.

FRIENDS

Susie (Chapter 6)

Susie is today the most amazing person. When I finally, at age 57, found the love of my life and he convinced me to marry him, Susie came from Boston to be in my wedding.

After high school, Susie's mom and dad sent her to a four-year college in Pittsburgh and she became a Registered Nurse. She fell in love with and married an architect from Cody, Wyoming, who adored her. They have the happiest Ozzie and Harriett family. Sadly, we all lost our architect cowboy to cancer a few years ago. Susie remains consistently the most open and loving person.

I know her huge Point Marion family is sitting around on a bevy of cumulous clouds, sipping some Dago Red and munching on some of Grandma Tipi's sweet Belgium galettes looking down on her and her children as she checks her tomato plants.

> "Yepper. That's our girl. We are so proud of her"

Meredith Stewart (Chapters 14, 23)

Meredith and I started kindergarten and graduated from high school together. Her dear mother was our scout leader for nearly ten years and was a true inspiration to me. A gentle ladylike refined woman who wore ironed prim dresses, I realized early on that marching an unruly group of scraggy Brownie Scouts through the tangled woods was not her preferred time spent. But she did it with aplomb as she gently guided us through the weeds and undergrowth, naming leaves and trees and rocks while we all stumbled over boulders and dirt. She gently dabbed up the scratches of briars and the bites of insects with her dainty starched handkerchief. She carried a neat purse wherever she went. Even as we scrambled and tripped through the underbrush, I was puzzled how Mrs. Stewart stayed so neat and proper looking.

Meredith and I are fast friends. Even today when I catch a certain glint in Meredith's eyes, I recognize the sweet countenance of her mother shining through.

Valerie (Chapter 54)

Our Valerie has become an accomplished watercolorist. On a recent visit to her home, I recognized in one of her paintings a familiar figure.

> *"Valerie tell me about this painting..."*

> *"I painted that of my mom walking along a street..."*

Sadly, Valerie's Mother died soon after she entered nursing school in Uniontown. Her dad, who to most may have looked like an ordinary person, was an angel in everyday things and in ordinary ways. One of the saints of my life

Miss Twila (Chapter 7)

Miss Twila was the only Cawley girl who never married. She spent her life working in one of the several stores along Penn Street in Point Marion, earning a meager, minimum wage and walking to and from the Cawley shack on Stewartstown Road.

She aged beautifully over the years; her slim figure in her homemade calico dresses served her well in her twenties and thirties. As she became more solid and then mostly stout in her forties and fifties, she began wearing mainly sensible worn tennis shoes laced up high to accommodate the long walk to and from town. Even though it became fashionable for women to wear pants, Miss Twila was never one to wear them except under a dress for the long frigid walk to and from town in the icy bone chilling cold of winter.

Miss Twila spent her prime caring for her parents, the Reverend and Mrs. Cawley, in that small shack with the coal stove spewing hot coals and dense black smoke. On the cold winter mornings, she would bank the coal fire in the center room before the long trek to town and be sure to cook some fried bacon and beans in the evening.

Her parents passed at near the same time in the mid-1980s. She retired on the minimum social security check and spent her twilight years sitting on the porch of that shack with a couple of loyal coon hounds at her feet.

Anytime one of the country women would need refuge from an angry drunk, Miss Twila had an open door. She was a good Christian woman. She was her daddy's girl.

One day she could not get out of bed to get to the porch.

Cara Anset (Chapter 8)

Although Cara and I were in Girl Scouts together until we were seventeen, we grew apart. She graduated from high school the same year I did. She married a township boy from one of the coal patches in West Virginia who was a wife-beater. One day in a rage he nearly killed her.

She somehow had the strength to leave him, put herself through a nursing school program, and marry a man who loved her. Her new husband was from the innards of central West Virginia. She had five boys and a little girl but, sadly, she died of ovarian cancer before she was 50.

Except for the period when she was married to the wife-beater and she became so emaciated and ill she could hardly walk, Cara remained overweight her entire life. It was a life sentence for her and caused much pain and grief.

In Appalachia, if a girl was not cute early on, the cards were stacked the wrong way.

Lester Schmidt (Chapter 8)

Despite the "little boy relentless teasing," Lester has become this incredible caring gentleman. Immediately after high school, he was grabbed up by the ever-present trolling for strong boys of the mountains for the draft.

After surviving a stint in Vietnam, he returned and stayed in Point Marion. With his devoted wife, Helen, who was one of the country girls that joined our huge baby boomer class in seventh grade, together they founded and ran a small successful family restaurant in Point Marion.

The two of them worked like beavers from dawn until long after dark, day in and day out, making pies, creating, and serving downhome original recipe foods to the many people who would come to their little restaurant on one of the side streets of Point Marion.

It was the kind of meeting place that was vital to the heartbeat of a small river town. People would come from far and wide to have a piece of pie, smoke a cigarette, and talk about the flooding of the river or when Penn DOT was going to fix that pothole on Penn Street.

> "Looks like the river's gonna crest long about tomorrow morning when they release that backed up water gate at lock 8. Shore hope it don't take out my tomato plants."

During one of my visits to Point Marion as I sat with Lester at the remarkable hub of a restaurant he and Helen had built, we found ourselves reminiscing about our grade school days.

I reminded him of pulling my pigtails, of his dancing around the playground taunting me and Cara, but most of all how Mrs. Ratchet would be sure to paddle poor Lester over and over with her huge whistling weapon.

Somehow it came out of my mouth:

In those days, I tried not to bring up sad memories.

> *"Lester, who was your favorite teacher?"*

I expected him to say sweet Miss Berg or stoic Mrs. Evans, or maybe Lester liked Miss Bendenton with her constant barrage of fat yellow marshmallow bunnies on our desks.

Lester looked straight at me and said:

> "Oh, I loved Mrs. Ratchet. She was the best ever! Remember how we would hug her every Friday as we went home for the weekend . . ."

> *"Lester, she beat you relentlessly."*

Nancy Thorn (Chapter 36)

Nancy Thorn married her high school sweetheart a few weeks after high school graduation and had had her first child when she was barely 17.

Nancy Thorn and I met again at our 54th high school reunion. Wearing a sleek cat suit that clung to her every curve, at 71, she looked as striking as ever. She had divorced a few husbands and was with an adoring gentleman who looked like he was 15 years younger than our crowd.

She was still using her looks as her currency in life, which seemed to serve her well.

Fat Mary (Chapter 38)

Fat Mary eventually stopped having babies. Mama said,

> "Her body just gave out."

Junior Ware died of the black lung so, of course, the checks he sometimes shared with her stopped.

During the period that Jack Turner was bringing beaten women and their abusing men down to Dad's office, I would see her. After the Jack Turner period, she was not screaming on our front porch like the old days.

Her children were all taken by the ADC.

Mary Joe Church (Chapter 41)

In 1974, Mary Joe Church's younger sister, Kate, committed suicide by jumping off a building in Waynesburg.

Ten years later, I ran into Mary Joe in Morgantown, West Virginia. I happened to go into a jewelry store to get my watch repaired. I was working as a nurse and the second hand of my watch was skipping.

> "Mary Joe!"

She looked the same; vibrant and happy. We arranged to meet another day for lunch. When I went into the jewelry store to get Mary Jo for lunch, Mr. Golden, the store owner, was a well-known wealthy merchant a few generations older than me. He was there watching her every move. By the way old Mr. Golden spoke to her and looked at her, it was clear she was more than a clerk in his store. She told me she had divorced her husband long ago and was living in Morgantown. Her daughter, little Chrissie, was attending the University.

Judy Randall (Chapter 51)

I saw Judy Randall again when we were both 21, she had two or three children, weighed nearly 200 pounds, was divorced for the second time, and lived on ADC. She was still beautiful. Black hair, freckles, deep blue aquamarine eyes. Judy and her children lived in a run-down shack behind the railroad tracks. Judy had so much potential.

Happy Birthday (Chapters 3, 63)

Several years after Happy and I met in his dusty spot above Mary Jane's Beauty Shop, I received a letter from his sister-in-law. It was a long, neatly handwritten letter with a Blosser Hill Pennsylvania postmark. She was writing to tell me that Francis Diehl had died in the West Virginia Veterans Facility near Fairmont.

"Francie, I want you to know that Francis was so very proud of you..."

I was sad. Somehow, I thought Happy would always be there. He was gone. No one had ever said they were proud of me. Happy was proud of me?

I started thinking about how Happy, that loyal Sancho Panza to my dad's stumbling Don Quixote, had always been there. Years later, I began to ponder my own self and the secret brother and how Happy had merely said to me:

"Charlotte never knew..."

I was six feet tall by the time I was 13 years old; big-boned and eventually grown buxom. My sisters were shorter, flat chested and wiry. They each, in their own way, seemed to channel some of Dad's most obvious maladies:

Suffering with the curse of addiction and, worse, a sense of entitlement, that family somehow always owed them a filial lifeline.

The brother I grew up with was the image of the dad we grew up with. Even Aunt Dodo was a mere 5 foot 2 inches. Was there something more in this complicated mist?

Now, in the quiet, as I have the time to listen to my heart, and contemplate the reverse trajectory of my family life, the conclusion is:

Of course, Charlotte knew. . .

Whether I am Dad's biological child is a mystery for another day.

Happy is buried in Little Arlington, the honored front area of Evergreen Memorial Cemetery reserved especially for veterans. It is on the hill as one descends driving north from West Virginia on Route 119 into the murky town of Point Marion.

Secret Brother (Chapter 63)

I found myself simply surprised when I realized I had what I assumed was a long-lost half-brother. None of my other siblings were interested at all in the new brother. I contacted each of them and none had any interest in a relationship with him. They would not even see him. Of course, by this time in our lives, we were scattered all over the country. The newfound brother lived in Detroit, Michigan with his second wife.

I called my dad's sister and asked her if she had any knowledge of this sibling. She simply said,

> "Look Francie, I have enough nieces and a nephew. I don't want any more."

No definitive answer. Not a surprise, given the pattern of avoidance that runs through the base line genes of our family. In fact, my two sisters kept saying the only reason this brother was contacting me, (he never made any effort to contact them), was because he perceived me as having some wealth and he wanted to be close to me.

These were the days before DNA tests.

The tale sounded so solid, what with Happy Birthday and then Aunt Delores' testimony. I was sorry for him. I was especially sad for his young mother who, if this story is true, (and seemed to be), was abandoned with a baby in her arms in 1945. She was a country girl alone in a big city.

He was from Appalachia. He wanted a hand. I ended up helping him to move to Las Vegas, lending him money to purchase a home, and then bringing him into my company as a highly paid executive. He did not last.

I have made so many mistakes in my life that I truly regret. But bringing family – even perceived family - into the companies I owned stands out as my world class biggest error. Just a bad, bad decision.

MY HEART'S COMPANION

George M Leader (Chapter 9)

He was the best of me.

ABOUT THE AUTHOR

M. FRANCES BARRON

Francie Barron is an award-winning serial entrepreneur who single handedly escaped from the throes of poverty and the diminishment of her upbringing in the bowels of Appalachia.

Starting out with zero money, no encouragement, plain looks, and stumbling social skills, she has been able to deploy whatever she could manage to scrape together to catch the northbound train and lift her and her children out of poverty.

She has created over twenty profitable corporate entities and employed hundreds of people while educating herself with an undergraduate degree and then a master's degree. Francie taught herself how to analyze and deploy factual data with hands-on grit and resilience and made a career of looking for opportunities when none were obvious. She taught herself how to create abundance through stops and starts, horrible decisions and a few good choices.

Francie currently lives in Las Vegas, Nevada with her psychiatrist husband who seems to love her in spite of herself.

MORE ABOUT THE AUTHOR

M. Frances Barron, a resident of Nevada, is currently enjoying life.

Previously, she was the Founder President and Chief Executive Officer of the AscentrA Corporate System. This system of entrepreneurial companies, headquartered in Las Vegas, included as many as twenty-three corporate entities.

A Registered Nurse for over 55 years, Ms. Barron's career encompasses numerous start-up ventures, acquisitions, and successful harvesting of corporations and partnerships.

Francie is a graduate of Washington Hospital School of Nursing in Washington, Pennsylvania. She has a bachelor's degree in business administration from West Virginia University and holds a master's degree in business administration from Pepperdine University.

A division of the companies owned by Francie and her partners was included in the "Inc 500" listing of the 500 fastest-growing privately held companies in the nation in 1996. Another company owned by Francie has been included in the "Inc 500" listing in 2003, 2004, and 2005. Home Care Magazine consistently listed the Home Care Companies owned by Ms. Barron in the Top 60 Home Care Companies in America.

Additionally, the corporate group created by Ms. Barron was listed by Working Woman Magazine as one of America's Top 500 Women-Owned Businesses. Her companies also ranked in the Top 100 Privately Held Companies in Las Vegas.

Ms. Barron was honored by In Business Las Vegas as one of the initial Forty Most Influential Women in the Southern Nevada Business Community.

She has been the Chairperson and member of the Nevada State Board of Health, a member of the Nevada State Environmental Commission, a Trustee and past Chair of the Las Vegas-Clark County Library District, a member and Chairperson of the Las Vegas Clark County Library Foundation, and a Board member of Boys Town, Nevada. She is a past board member of the Nevada Association of Medical Product Suppliers, the Las Vegas Executives Association, the Bank of Commerce, and a founding Board Chair of a local Charter School. She is a licensed Boat Captain.

She is currently on the Board of Genu Bank, formally Kirkwood Bank of Nevada.

Ms. Barron is married to Doctor Alistair O. Barron, a Board-Certified Physician specializing in adult, child, and adolescent psychiatry.

www.ingramcontent.com/pod-product-compliance
Lightning Source LLC
Chambersburg PA
CBHW050325010526
44119CB00003B/107